D1116938

3 0700 11098 8010

The Technology of the Novel

The Technology of the Novel

Writing and Narrative in British Fiction

TONY E. JACKSON

The Johns Hopkins University Press

Baltimore

© 2009 The Johns Hopkins University Press
All rights reserved. Published 2009
Printed in the United States of America on acid-free paper
9 8 7 6 5 4 3 2 1

The Johns Hopkins University Press
2715 North Charles Street
Baltimore, Maryland 21218-4363
www.press.jhu.edu

Library of Congress Cataloging-in-Publication Data

Jackson, Tony E., 1951–
    The technology of the novel : writing and narrative in British fiction /
Tony E. Jackson.
        p. cm.
    Includes bibliographical references and index.
    ISBN 978-0-8018-9244-8 (alk. paper)
    1. English fiction — History and criticism — Theory, etc.   I. Title.
PR826.J33 2009
    823.009 — dc22   2008031488

A catalog record for this book is available from the British Library.

*Special discounts are available for bulk purchases of this book. For more information,
please contact Special Sales at 410-516-6936 or specialsales@press.jhu.edu.*

The Johns Hopkins University Press uses environmentally friendly book materials,
including recycled text paper that is composed of at least 30 percent post-consumer
waste, whenever possible. All of our book papers are acid-free, and our jackets and
covers are printed on paper with recycled content.

For Ann

CONTENTS

ACKNOWLEDGMENTS

It is hard to know where to begin and end with acknowledgment of help on a project like this. My students have helped me continuously, though without knowing it, because the main stimulus for my interest in writing came, and still comes, from the curious fact that otherwise intelligent, motivated people find writing so devilish-hard to learn. My English Department colleagues have helped me as well, because of their shared involvement with writing, which is so devilish-hard to teach. More specifically, I offer my grateful acknowledgment to these friends and colleagues, from my own department and elsewhere, who helped me along in various ways: Porter Abbott, Peter Blair, Paula Connolly, Beth Gargano, Aaron Gwyn, Kirk Melnikoff, Jennifer Munroe, Malin Pereira, Lara Vetten, and Lisa Zunshine. I thank my department and my college at the University of North Carolina at Charlotte for their ongoing support of scholarly research. My work has directly benefited from a Research and Development Leave from the College of Liberal Arts and Sciences. Finally, my thanks to Michael Lonegro, Barbara Lamb, and the fine staff of the Johns Hopkins University Press.

Some of the materials in chapters 5, 6, and 9 have appeared in essay form. I am grateful for permission to use the following: "Writing and the Disembodiment of Language," *Philosophy and Literature* 27.1 (2003): 115–32; "The De-Composition of Writing in *A Passage to India*," *Journal of Modern Literature*, 29.3 (2006): 1–18; "Writing, Orality, Cinema: The 'Story' of *Citizen Kane*," *Narrative* 16.1 (2008): 29–45.

The Technology of the Novel

To Begin

Speaking, Writing, Storytelling

⁂ I

IN THE NEW TESTAMENT, John 8:1–11, the doctors of the law and the Pharisees bring an adulteress before Jesus and ask what he has to say about the Mosaic Law, which requires stoning as punishment for her transgression. The woman's guilt is not in doubt, so it is specifically Jesus' attitude about the law that is at issue. Before he responds to their question, Jesus does an odd thing. He stoops down and writes with his finger on the ground. We never know what he writes. His questioners keep at him until he charges whoever among them is faultless with casting the first stone. Then he stoops again and writes on the ground, and again we are not told what he writes. Soon, the interrogators leave without condemning the adulteress. Jesus refuses to condemn her as well, sending her away with the admonition to sin no more.

Why does Jesus silently write in the dust instead of simply responding to the question about the punishment according to the law? And why no mention of what he wrote? This action calls attention, not to the law, not to the punishment, not to any ethical or moral issues, but to the physical action of writing itself. In fact, throughout John, Jesus speaks to the issue of writing in general and especially to the idea of the letter versus the spirit of the law, an antagonism implicit in any law but one that is drastically amplified by written law (Goody 1986). The gospel of John (and much of the New Testament) is very much about this central issue. In Jesus' eyes the old Mosaic Law has become dehumanized and rigid. It is implemented only according to its written letter, not its originating spirit. The Pharisees in particular are represented as wanting the law followed absolutely to the letter, especially when it comes to Jesus' case. So Jesus appears to take the opportunity of the adulteress to make plain that writing, the technology by which the law is a "letter" in the first place, can induce a mindless and heartless obedience, such that human beings become like the disembodied, spiritless written word.

We must also notice, though, that Jesus uses writing itself in order to make the case against writing. In this way he acknowledges that there can be no simple rejection of written law or of writing in general, which would even in his day have been impossible. Writing was already important in many human affairs; in any case, his own preaching depended directly on the ancient writings that had come before him, and the creation of the present church in his name could not have happened without the written New Testament. He does, however, insist on a new awareness of the ways in which written law can operate in a mechanical, inhuman fashion. In sum, he demonstrates an essential conflict in the nature of writing. Writing enables the very existence of a religion of the book, such as Judaism or Christianity. But it also makes inevitable a certain dehumanization of the institution it has enabled.

I offer this scenario as a little paradigm for a much larger and detailed study of the technology—writing—that even in Jesus' day was understood as a blessing and a curse. However, whereas Jesus was concerned with writing and religion, I am concerned with writing and literature.

Literary studies since the 1960s have been much influenced by theories of writing. Since that decade, there have been two distinct strains of investigation: one most prominently associated with Roland Barthes, Jacques Derrida, and poststructuralist kinds of theory; the other most prominently associated with Walter Ong, Jack Goody, and theories of writing as a technology. The two approaches to writing share many ideas but disagree about many as well. There can be no argument as to which school has been the more influential, at least in literary studies. The understanding of speech, writing, and representation in general laid out by Derrida has for several decades been a rich source of theory and interpretation.[1] So far the "other" take on writing has been most useful in studying the literature of large-scale historical shifts from oral culture to literacy: especially ancient Greek literature and medieval literature.[2] This makes sense because in such eras we would expect the effects of the expanding technology to be most clearly displayed. But I want to discuss writing as a technology in relation to times of established literacy and to a literary form that has been primarily associated with the technology of print: the novel.

The nature and effects of writing considered as a technology have been well established (sometimes discussed under the term *literacy*) in recent decades by such scholars as Ong, Goody, Eric Havelock, Marshall McLuhan, Ian Watt, Elizabeth Eisenstein, David Olson, and others. But its roots go back even earlier, to the Soviet psychologists Lev Vygotsky (1962) and A. R. Luria (1976) and to the American literary scholars Milman Parry (1971) and Albert Lord (1971).[3] What kinds of claims do these nonpoststructuralist thinkers make? First, they explain writing in a concrete and historical way: it is an invented, systematized, tool-using process for representing spoken language in visual signs. In direct contrast to writing, we have the distinctly uninvented form of verbal communication: spoken language. The relationships between these two modes of communication are always the grounding upon which any further claims about writing (or orality) are made.

Human beings are genetically predisposed to acquire spoken language, and they do so with astonishing ease. But as any teacher (or student) knows, writing must be directly, consciously taught over an extended period of time. The differences between the two activities are distinct even on the neurological level. As David Morris writes, "Neuroimaging studies show that our brains process written language differently than they process oral speech. Moreover, the ability to speak is innate for humans, but reading is an acquired skill. Genetics alone assures that children learn to talk simply through exposure to spoken language, but all readers need a written alphabet or its equivalent in nonalphabetic language" (541). We may in fact reasonably claim, in the words of psychologist Wallace Chafe, that verbal speech "is natural to the human organism in ways that writing can never be" (43). Though spoken language is plainly essential to the fundamental nature of human being, we must assume that if writing had never been invented, our species would have gone along quite well, though of course quite differently, without it. Anthropologist Ellen Dissanayake reminds us that for "eight-ninths of their history, humans could not read at all" and managed to become, arguably, the most successful of all animal species (204). But it is unarguable that we have gone along quite differently with writing than we would have without it. This is because writing is in many ways a technology of technologies. Its unique nature and effects have enabled or required the appearance of a vast array of other kinds of human ideas and practices.

Writing powerfully augments features of language and memory such as storage capacity, preservation, and accuracy, and as a result it promotes all manner of change in human life. The effects of writing are of course amplified by print, but still, writing is the foundational representation after which all the other major visual representations of speech follow. Writing "is in a way the most drastic of the three technologies [writing, print, computers]. It initiated what print and computers only continue" (Ong 1982, 82; see also Martin, 282). To this point we have had convincing arguments that writing, be it in manuscript or print forms, has in a fundamental way produced or at least enabled modernity itself (Eisenstein 1979; Olson 1994). Ong has made the case that "one consequence of [writing] was modern science" (1982, 127). Historian Henri-Jean Martin has explained how, by the time of the Enlightenment, the spread of writing had led directly to "the unleashing of mechanisms that prompted a new view of self and a spirit of abstraction" that are central to modern identity (345). Anthropologist Jack Goody has argued that "the very nature of formal reasoning as [literate cultures] understand it (that is, in terms of Aristotelian 'logical' procedures) is not a general ability but a highly specific skill, critically dependent upon the existence of writing and of a written tradition" (1987, 256). Roger Chartier has argued for the intimate connection between writing and such fundamental modern concepts as individuality and privacy (1994, 2002). And strong cases have been made for the linkage of writing and the emergence of modern concepts of law (Clanchy; Green; Goody 1986).

One of the most important effects of writing is the way it changes our thinking about, and our relation to, language. In making our speech visible, writing leads us to understand language in ways that are peculiar to literacy.[4] Once we have writing, we are able to "see" language as an object, much as we see other objects. Said another way, writing disembodies language. This entails a number of important consequences. Perhaps the most fundamental consequence is that the appearance of language as a kind of object initiates the possibility of disrupting the everyday sense of language as simply the oral expression of the embodied self. A distance between the self and language appears with writing in a way that it could not otherwise appear. Since so much of our knowledge is intimately a function of our language, this entails a related distance between the self and, at least, linguistic knowledge. "Enhanced separation of the known from the knower," Ong writes, "is probably the most fundamental value of writing, from its beginnings to the present. Between knower and known writing interposes a visible and tangible object, the text. The objectivity of the text helps impose objectivity on what the text refers to" (1986, 38).[5] This kind of objectivity is indispensable for the development of many of the kinds of knowledge we take for granted in modernity. But it also entails an ongoing, generically literate conflict; literate culture is at odds with its language and its knowledge in ways that a purely nonliterate culture typically will not be.[6]

It is important to state that this kind of objectivity, like writing itself, is not somehow indispensable to human beings in general. And its appearance and evolution do not imply that nonliterate humans lack objectivity or linguistic conflict in general. The need to mention these facts brings us to a second crucial effect of writing and one that we will have to keep constantly in mind: alphabetography (alphabetic writing), the visual representation of speech sounds, is commonly perceived as simply a superior version of spoken language, with the result that things literate are automatically considered superior to things nonliterate. As a general fact this is common knowledge, but we will do well to consider it in detail. Its ramifications are many and often subtle. Let us look at two historical examples of this effect in order to establish some baseline ideas for our ongoing investigations.

In the introduction to his *Dictionary of the English Language,* Samuel Johnson makes it clear that he has been on a mission: to save writing, and therefore language in general, from speech. It is "the duty of the lexicographer," he writes, "to correct or proscribe" the "improprieties and absurdities" of spoken language (Johnson, 75). The superiority of writing to speech is so obvious that he need not argue the case.

> As language was at its beginning merely oral, all words of necessary or common use were spoken before they were written; and while they were unfixed by any visible signs, must have been spoken with great diversity, as we now observe those who cannot read to catch sounds imperfectly, and utter them negligently. When this wild and barbarous jargon was first reduced to an alphabet, every penman endeavoured to express, as he could, the sounds which he was accustomed to pronounce or to receive, and vitiated in writing such words as were already vitiated in speech. (75)

Johnson takes it for granted that fixing what is otherwise "merely" speech with visible signs is a good thing, that the unconstrained diversity of dialects is a bad thing, and that written words carry the perfect sounds by which the quality of spoken words must be judged. Speech that does not abide by writing is "wild and barbarous" (75), a "boundless chaos" (84). Alphabetography should have, from the beginning, helped to reduce this chaos to a limited and definite form, but there has existed no written standard of orthography. Writing that itself abides by no written standards simply imitates spoken pronunciation. It is, to Johnson, plainly wrong that "our written language" should "comply with the corruptions of oral utterance, or copy that which every variation of time or place makes different from itself, and imitate those changes, which will again be changed, while imitation is employed in observing them" (78).

But this presents us with a problem. Johnson favors writing over speech because, unlike writing, speech changes instant by instant, to the point that, in his lexicographer's mind, a definable meaning can hardly be said to exist. But of course this exaggerates the facts of actual speech. Spoken language varies and changes, but it certainly has its own stability, its own common and continuing meanings; otherwise it would not work as communication. Johnson must know this, and yet he still makes a rather wholesale negative value judgment about speech. Why should this be?

Ironically, Johnson evaluates speech in this way at least in large part because he fails to distinguish speech from its written representation in writing. This conflation of speech and writing is common in literate culture. Eric Havelock does not overstate the case when he writes that it "is scarcely possible to discover any linguistic discussion, popular or learned, in which the writer does not at some point slip into this confusion" (1982, 48).[7] Johnson thinks of himself as clearly distinguishing writing from speech. But in order to judge the two as he does, he must on some level be assuming that writing is simply another form of speech, instead of an entirely different kind of representation; and he also, symptomatically, takes certain qualities of writing as the obvious standards for language in general. Writing is certainly more uniform and consistent than spoken language. Since alphabetic signs are manufactured and are arbitrarily related to nonmeaningful oral sounds, the need for a universal, standard model of letters is essential, not because of some need to "fix" the chaos of speech, but in order to work as a system of communication. With an iconic or naturalistic visual representation, we understand the visual image's initial, perceptual significance simply by how closely it resembles some imaginary or real-world counterpart. But we can only assess written letters in relation to other written letters. Given the inevitable variations of the human hand using a writing tool, unless there is somehow established a governing visual model for the alphabet, the system will not work, or at least will not work according to its own potential, which is what disturbs Johnson. Its power depends on a consistency and standardization that is alien to spoken language. The advent and power of print takes this element of writing to its next level. Further, since the visual signs represent vocal sounds, and since the human vocal apparatus has a limited set of sound-possibilities for speech, the standardization of the alphabet becomes all the more powerful. With a common alphabetography, people who cannot successfully understand each other's speech can still communicate linguistically. The full significance of this in human affairs is difficult to grasp. But there are downsides to such uniformity. We will explore some of these later, especially in our discussion of *Bleak House*. For now, we remark that Dr. Johnson is much taken by the positive aspects of this standardization.

Needless to say, he is equally taken by what he sees as writing's exactitude, which is the primary reason to compile a dictionary in the first place. A dictionary precisely "fixes" word meanings in a way that cannot happen with embodied linguistic communication. But it does not follow from these qualities of standardization and exactitude that writing is somehow superior in general to speech. Speech as a kind of communication has the standardization and exactitude that it needs in order to do the work it evolved to do. More importantly, it carries a certain kind of precision that is entirely unavailable to writing: the precision of verbal communication whose meaning is a function of the vast array of immediately present sensory inputs involved in an oral exchange. In this sense no writing can ever hope to be as fully communicative as speech. Because they are different kinds of representation, in some ways and in some situations writing will be superior to speech, and in other ways speech will be superior to writing.

And yet what Johnson does here—taking certain qualities of writing as the standards for speech in general—is quite common. To judge writing as superior to speech in the way Johnson does is rather like judging a camera and its film as a superior means of seeing in comparison to the eyes. Of course the machine can "see" certain things in certain ways that are not perceptible to the eye. And of course whatever is recorded on the film is permanently fixed when compared to any given instant of looking at our surrounding visual reality. But these facts do not lead us to conclude (or assume) that the eye is generally inferior by comparison. And yet Johnson's sense of the superiority of writing to speech operates just this way. The reason is because, unlike other invented means of representation, writing does seem like just another version of that which it represents: verbal language. It seems to be different only by degree from speech. And why not? After all, as we read or write, we "hear" the words in our minds. If we read a personal letter from someone we know well, we even "hear" that person's particular voice. But the fact remains that writing—a representational system in which arbitrary visual signs represent sounds—is entirely, even radically different from speech. And for the most part, this is obvious. Anyone directly questioned about the differences between the two will readily bring at least some of them forth, even though most of us will still commonly conflate them as different versions of the same thing. Usually, this conflation will not matter. I myself will be doing it as I go, when, for instance I "say" that Dickens "speaks" of this or that in *Bleak House*. But at times the conflation will have very important consequences, especially when, as also commonly happens, writing is taken to be the superior form.

Having looked at the conflation of speech and writing by one of the absolute paragons of literacy, we may now turn to a complementary case, one that gives us writing and speech from the nonliterate perspective. In one of the most famous slave narratives, James Albert Ukawsaw Gronniosaw memorably describes the experience of seeing his owner, a Dutch ship's captain, read either from the Bible or a prayer book:

> [My master] used to read prayers in public to the ship's crew every Sabbath day; and when first I saw him read, I was never so surprised in my whole life as when I saw the book talk to my master; for I thought it did, as I observed him to look upon it, and move his lips.— I wished it would do so to me.—As soon as my master had done reading I follow'd him to the place where he put the book, being mightily delighted with it, and when nobody saw me, I open'd it and put my

ear down close upon it, in great hope that it wou'd say something to me; but was very sorry and greatly disappointed when I found it would not speak, this thought immediately presented itself to me, that every body and every thing despis'd me because I was black. (quoted in Gates 1988, 136)

Henry Louis Gates (1988, 127–69) has thoroughly examined this passage as a paradigm of the specific relations between racism and literacy. I want to consider it as a paradigm of writing and literacy in general. Though it may be a challenge for someone, child or adult, in a literate culture to learn to read and write, at least that person exists in a scene in which literacy is to some extent a part of the surrounding life. But Gronniosaw presents himself to us here as a normal adult who simply has no concept of alphabetic writing. He is, to use a word we will return to, *enchanted* by what he sees and hears.

Curiously, his interpretation of what he sees is untrue to the actuality he describes. He says that the book appears to talk to his master because his master moves his lips and speaks words as he looks at the page. But why would the master's lips be moving if the book were talking to him? Why would he not just be listening or repeating after the book's voice? Why would Gronniosaw not hear some other voice besides the master's? In spite of what Gronniosaw says, he describes the book as somehow talking *through* the master, as if the master is a kind of robot or medium for the telepathic "voice" on the page. Gronniosaw has demonstrated the same common conflation we found with Johnson: he makes no essential distinction between written and spoken words. The actual material nature of the medium seems to disappear directly into that which it represents, as if writing were not a representation at all or else as if it were simply an iconic imitation of speech. Further, Gronniosaw has unwittingly given us an image of the way that writing objectifies speech. In the act of reading, a voiceless object made (in this case) of paper and ink, "speaks" through the reader's eyes and mind and inner or outer voice.

With these two examples, it begins to seem as if the conflation of speech and writing is at least a regularly occurring, if not somehow a necessary, outcome of the particular representational relationship between the two. The invented representation is confused with our built-in means of verbal communication by perhaps the most literate man in England,

and the same mistake is made by a yet-to-be literate slave. But if the two men are similar about writing in this way, they are starkly different in others. Johnson's sense of writing induces an accompanying sense of despair and frustration, of himself beset by chaos because no dictionary can enforce upon speech the "steadiness and uniformity" (79) of script. His sense of writing would also necessarily entail a certain generic sense of the inferiority of nonliterate, or even less literate, people and cultures. It follows from this that, as Gates points out, someone like Gronniosaw must learn to read and write simply in order to be accepted by literate culture as a member of the human race. But without prior knowledge of writing, Gronniosaw makes a quite reasonable assessment of what he sees: oral verbalization is the only means by which actual words exist outside the mind, therefore the book must be talking. He is not being ignorant or superstitious or foolish or backward, though these are the ways literate culture will see him. To the contrary, as with another famous such case recorded by anthropologist Claude Levi-Strauss (chap. 28), he immediately recognizes just how powerful this kind of verbal communication can be, and he wants to learn it and use it. And yet, given Johnson's example, we may wonder what Gronniosaw will have to give up in order to become literate—to become, we might say, *disenchanted* by this primal scene. In any event, both cases show a peculiarly literate conflict at work. In positively valuing writing as he does, each man also, in one way or another, negates the common linguistic ability with which humans are born.

Another potent effect of writing arises directly from the way we process this particular kind of representation. Of the various ways of representing speech visibly, most scholars agree that "the most radical of all scripts, the alphabet," has had the largest consequences (Ong 1982, 77).[8] The invention of alphabetic writing was a "stupefying leap of the imagination" (Goody 1968, 38) that began an epochal turn in human history. Rather than using visible signs to represent meaning, as other writing systems (e.g., hieroglyphics) had done, alphabetography uses visible signs to represent individual sound-units, most importantly of speech, but in any case of sounds the ear can hear. One established effect of this kind of representation involves our sensory systems. Without writing, the voice and the ear together form the sensory nexus of the definitively human body-mind because spoken language is so essential to human being (Ong 1982;

Havelock 1986; McLuhan 1962). Writing changes "the way words are perceived by the senses, because it shifts the emphasis in communicating language from hearing to seeing. . . . In nonliterate cultures the skills of eye and hand are associated primarily with craftsmanship and the visual arts, while the skills of language which depend on the transmission of sound are identified with mouth and ear" (Clanchy, 278). Voice and ear, then, together form the primary interface between interior and exterior, between input from and output to the specifically human world. The other senses and systems, though necessary, do not carry quite the defining weight of the voice-ear. But with the emergence of alphabetography the eye necessarily becomes indispensable to language—and therefore to human existence—in a way that it had not been before.[9] Further, the more important writing becomes in human life, the more the eye is augmented and the voice-ear diminished as elements of our body-mind systems (Ong 1967).

II

Having laid out these most general effects of writing—the objectification of speech, the conflation of speech and writing, the tendency to take writing as superior to speech, and the changed weighting of sensory domains—the question arises: What can all this mean for written story? I turn to story rather than literature in general because story provides a more solid basis from which to consider the effects of writing. In recent decades story has been, like language, well established as a definable element of our human cognitive apparatus. As psychologist Ronald Kellogg writes, the "evolutionary development of a rudimentary narrative system must be seen as fundamental in the biological and psychological history of our species" (43), for narrative in this sense "constructs the contents of conscious thought" (42). Said another way, narrative in its most basic form is a built-in "instrument for sense-making, a semiotic and communicative resource that enables humans to make their way in a sometimes confusing, often difficult world . . . a basic resource for intelligent activity across a variety of settings" (Herman, 12–13).[10] Taken on this level, story is as important to human life as is speech itself. It follows from this understanding (and intuitively as well) that the paradigm of storytelling is oral story: the corporeal communication of a narrative by one or more flesh-and-blood human beings directly to one or more other flesh-and-blood human beings, none of whom need ever have had any idea whatsoever of writing. If oral story holds this most significant place in human affairs and if writing has the general effects and consequences outlined above, we may now ask: What will be the effects of writing on and in story? We can set out to answer this question by examining specific genres of written story in order to understand how a particular genre can be related to the oral paradigm. Then, within a particular genre, we can examine specific cases in order to understand the writing/orality interface in greater detail. In this case we will focus on the novel.

But why study just the novel in these terms? The novel is "clearly a print genre" (Ong 1982, 158), but the effects that most determine its nature are functions of the larger category: writing. In fact, as I will demonstrate, the novel is the most alphabetized written story. Before developing detailed support for this claim, let me offer an analogy that may help illuminate what I am doing. A scholar could offer an explanation of the general nature of the modern American city based on automotive technology. Though many other elements will have contributed to the nature of the modern city, and though of course cities in general long predated the appearance of the horseless carriage; nonetheless, all American (and, really, any modern city anywhere in the world) cities have clearly been determined to a large degree by the automobile. Indeed, it is plain that over time some very basic cultural ideas—"the city," "shopping," "visiting," for instance—have conformed themselves to the nature and qualities of this extremely important technology. (For much of modern America, "shopping" has become nearly synonymous with "the mall." The mall is the ancient city or town center recreated in response to the automobile.) The explanation based on automotive technology need not claim that the automobile is the sole determiner of the shape of the city, but it would be hard for anyone to deny its fundamental importance. The appearance of the automobile will not necessarily have caused a revolutionary change in all cities at the same time. Some more or less entirely new cities (or very large communities) will appear that would not have appeared without the automobile, while some established cities will have changed at one rate, some at another. Further, it is clear that, given the project, some cities will be more readily illustrative than others as exemplars, Los Angeles perhaps being the paradigmatic case.

Like any analogy, this one will not be an exact parallel; besides, because writing is a technology for representing spoken words, it can have no parallel. There is literally nothing else like it. In explaining the novel in terms of writing, I do not hold that writing has been inconsequential for other kinds of story. Nor do I claim that writing is by any means the sole determiner of the novel as a literary kind. But if we look for the genre of story that seems most distinctly determined by the technology of writing and that is also the most important of such genres in the history of story (Los Angeles would certainly have both of these qualities in the hypothetical study of cars and cities), then the novel readily stands forth as the defining storytelling form (at least before film) of literate cultures.

To explain in more detail how the novel is the most alphabetic kind of written story we need first to establish the relevant qualities of the default human kind of narrative: oral story. I intend to show that what Ian Watt called an "inherent contradiction between the ancient and abiding literary values and the distinctive narrative technique of the novel" (Watt, 31) is in fact an ongoing tension between orality and literacy in general, as well as more specifically between oral and written literature. To get us into this topic, let us foreground an everyday distinction. We tend to use the same word—*story*—to cover both fiction and nonfiction. We can have a news story or we can tell the story of our day at work when we get home in the evening. This usage involves a meaningfully connected sequence of elements, but it does not entail fictionality. Synonyms for this usage would be *history* or *report*, and for the most part this *story* hardly stands apart from ordinary language as a separate category. The other primary usage involves a meaningfully connected sequence of elements that is in one way or another fictional. This modest but fundamental difference plays an important part in the discussions to come.

As folklorists and anthropologists since the late nineteenth century have shown, all oral cultures prize certain oral stories, the distinctly special stories that are told over and over again by certain proficient tellers on certain occasions. Across time and across cultures these stories and their telling carry certain similar characteristics. Most conspicuously, although oral story deals thematically with crucial issues of everyday cultural life, nonetheless it nearly always does so by including some element of the fantastic and heroic, which is to say, by excluding the everyday. Folklorist David Bynum has written that "conflation (or sunderance) of real facts into fantastic combinations is fundamental in fable-making" of oral cultures (41). This means that oral story does not gain its authority through a commitment to verisimilitude. The "sanction of fable is a tradition of telling stories, not reality or anyone's actual experience" (53).[11] Conversely, the opposite kind of content—everyday reality, we might call it—simply does not count as story in the fictional sense. Stories of everyday life as experienced by everyday people who lack the "spectacle of personal importance, status, power" would typically be gossip, and gossip, "dealing as it does with the current, and familiar, also deals with the insignificant and the ephemeral, and is not for the record" (Havelock 1982, 138). We will return often to this defining quality of oral story content as we look at specific examples of written story.[12]

In other respects the nature of oral story, both form and content, is determined by the technologically unaugmented nature of human physical and cognitive capacities. Walter Ong explains it this way:

> The heroic tradition of primary oral cultures and early literate culture, with its massive oral residue . . . is best and most radically explained in terms of the needs of oral noetic [mental, cognitive, intellectual] processes. Oral memory works effectively with "heavy" characters, persons whose deeds are monumental, memorable and commonly public. Thus the noetic economy of its nature generates outsize figures, that is, heroic figures, not for romantic reasons or reflectively didactic reasons, but for much more basic reasons: to organize experience in some sort of permanently memorable form. Colorless personalities cannot survive oral mnemonics. (1982, 69–70)

Similarly, Eric Havelock writes that because of the nature of memory, a built-in "psychological principle" favors "gods, demigods and heroes, [and] persons of some exotic status" in oral story (1982, 138). Clearly, the more fantastic the story or the characters, the more memorable they will be, simply because of their difference from ordinary life.[13] Oral story also tends to be relatively short, having what Walter Benjamin calls a "chaste compactness" (91); and longer versions of oral story are episodic for at least two reasons. First, the memory can only retain a limited amount of information before being overloaded. This determines the nature of oral story as well as story written to be delivered orally. As H. J. Chaytor observed in his pioneering work, *From Script to Print* (1950), medieval writers "wrote for recitation, and recitation at intervals of time; it was thus possible and even necessary to satisfy popular taste by the introduction of episodes and descriptions which contribute but little to the action of the plot or to the characterization of the actors. It was not possible for a twelfth-century audience to view a roman d'aventure as a whole, unless they possessed extraordinary patience and unless the reciter or reader were of extraordinary stamina; they received the story in installments" (4).

Second, as Jack Goody has argued, narrative is a kind of monologue. It "seeks to impose itself on conversation in a hegemonic way," and since conversational interchange is the human norm, long narratives are antisocial (2000, 67–68). With respect to the form of telling, the obvious fundamental quality of oral story is the communal nature of the event: the "visible, audible, olfactory, and sometimes tactile connection between performers and their audiences" (Niles, 53; also Lord, 14–17). The spoken word cannot occur without the immediate inflections of the speaker's unique body, and the audience's response—often enough itself a verbal echoing or encouragement—determines the speaker's ongoing sense of the telling (Bynum, 52). So, much as with drama, no matter how well known a given tale, "[each] act is a separate act of creation" (Scholes, 22).

This quality of the uniqueness of each performance brings us to oral story's notion of originality. The teller does not have to worry about (actually does not have the option of) making up character or plot from scratch. This can be in part because particular tales in their own cultural setting may not necessarily be taken as fiction by the members of that culture. Even the wildest (from the literate perspective) stories may be taken as true, and so a teller is not at liberty to change what is taken as history. But we should not conclude that oral story in oral culture never changes. Like other kinds of oral "history," story content can be "automatically adjusted to existing social relations" if some external need arises. Over time, gods and "supernatural agencies which have served their purpose can be quietly dropped from the contemporary pantheon; and as the society changes, myths too are forgotten, attributed to other personages, or transformed in their meaning" (Goody 1968, 33). By "automatically," Goody and Watt mean that this kind of change emerges as a function of people living and speaking together, rather than as the willful choice of a specific individual. But in the oral-cultural context a willfully created new tale (as opposed to a report) of any substance would be unlikely in any case, because an audience has distinctly limited capacities of attention and cannot be expected to readily comprehend more than fairly short completely new content. As a consequence, oral story—"well known for its conservative qualities" (Niles 1999, 57)—tends to consist of either already-told tales or new but already-known content installed into well-established forms.[14] And often enough, especially in oral epic, the tale begins with a prophecy, which automatically aids the audience's memory by laying out the basic plot to come right at the beginning (Havelock 1982, 142). This does not mean that oral story lacks originality or creativity or variety (though from an unthoughtfully literate perspective it can seem to), but only that these qualities are determined on each occasion by the immediate situation and in ways quite different from written story (Niles 1999, 58). What Mark Amodio says of bardic oral poets holds for oral storytellers in general: "Oral poets are responsible for the unique shape they give to their traditional, inherited materials, but they stake no claim to any sort of originary status" (14).

In a nonliterate setting, without writing to record, preserve, and comment upon the elements by which culture is constituted, oral story takes on a singularly important role in maintaining cultural identity over time. Traditional stories (in fact, "traditional" is redundant here), like traditions more generally (and ignoring for the moment the hyperliterate tradition of being untraditional), in a sense are the culture.[15] Therefore any storyteller who would alter them in any substantial way is, at the least, willfully violating cultural identity and, at worst, assuming a dictatorial attitude toward the common being. Hearing the already-known tale, then, is a kind of cultural nourishment, like the ritual sharing of traditional food or drink. Familiarity does not in this case breed contempt, nor does it induce boredom. David Bynum records an anthropological report by Clement Doke of storytelling in a nonliterate African community: "A good story-teller," Doke writes, "will tell over again a story, well-known to all, in such a way that [the audience] will leave their pipes and crowd nearer to him around his fire, so as not to miss a single detail" (qtd. in Bynum, 52). Repetition occurs on the level of the form of telling as well, even on the level of the plot; for tellers "of oral fable commonly emphasize important parts of their tales by repetition" (49). Beyond this roughly verbatim repetition, typically there is also "thematic rhythm," the arrangement of "sequences of episodes which seem to resemble each other thematically" (Havelock 1982, 141). But more famously, oral story, like poetry, always consists of " 'marked' language that differs noticeably from everyday speech," making much formulaic use of epithets, standard kinds of rhetorical devices, and oratorical rhythms, all of which serve to aid the normal capacities of human memory and attention.[16]

Some of these oral-story qualities, especially, but not only, of content, can naturally enough be found in written story throughout the history of prose fiction (Ong 1967). The emergence of written story could hardly somehow simply eliminate the appeal of these kinds of story (Niles 1999, 28). To take an obvious example, the superheroic and the supernatural that are essential to oral story find their regularly occurring modern forms in all manner of science fiction. Nonetheless, if we can establish the elements of the oral story paradigm, then we can explain the nature of written story by its closeness to, or distance from, those elements. But taking oral story as a baseline form in this way does not entail a value judgment. Though oral story is our default human storytelling, this does not mean that oral story is somehow generally superior (or inferior) to written story. In themselves, the two kinds are simply different, though of course a given cultural and historical setting can possibly provide standards by which to rank the two kinds hierarchically. It is important to remember in a study such as this, that, as has been regularly noted (Stock 1983, 4; Ong 1982, 80; Havelock 1986, 65; Goody 2000, chap. 1), it is not entirely possible to think oneself out of literacy once writing has been learned. But still, we can do our best. A project such as this one must constantly beware of making blanket value judgments about the superiority or inferiority of either oral or written story. More importantly, it must be kept in mind that, for whatever positive effects we may define for either, there are always correlative negative effects as well. In any case, the analysis of the intermingling of oral and written story has so far been done primarily with respect to obviously "oral-derived" written works such as the Bible, Homer's epics, *Beowulf,* and *Sir Gawain and the Green Knight.* But the relationships between oral story and the novel as written story have not yet been explored in this way.

To help us go forward, let me establish two more key terms: *oralistic* and *alphabetic.* There will be, even in written texts, some kinds of story and some specifiable story elements that can be reasonably defined as oral in nature, in the sense that the stories or elements are of the same kinds that are common to oral story in oral cultures. These I call *oralistic*. Egbert Bakker establishes something similar to what I mean in his study of Homeric epic. He discusses texts that are "conceptionally oral." Such discourse "has been written down and is 'graphic' as to its medium, but it may be called 'oral' as to its conception." It "does not display the features that are normal and expected in a writing culture" (8). My term, *oralistic*, refers to those forms or contents in written story that do display features that are definable as characteristic of oral story. These are elements of story that can be reasonably seen as, at least, what Ong calls the "residue" of originally oral story. For example, I call most elements of the supernatural or the impossibly perfect oralistic, even if they appear in written story. In this sense nearly all traditionally romantic tales or romantic elements of tales are oralistic. Again, as with all my terms, this distinction does not in and of itself imply a value judgment about the oralistic. Rather, it is descriptive and analytical. And the fact that the oralistic seems in some ways to have lost its cultural prominence in modern literatures does not signal some slow and inexorable decline. Rather, it signals the rise of certain (hyper)literate reading practices and expectations that tend to look down upon oralistic kinds of story as lowbrow. But a quick survey of movie titles immediately reveals that the story elements that are common to oral literature still constitute the most popular stories. Because of the foundational nature of oralistic story, it seems inconceivable that the oralistic will ever vanish from the human storytelling scene. This would be akin to, for instance, the material inflections of oral speech vanishing from the world because of the success of print. The oralistic will always have an audience.

By *alphabetic* I designate those types of story or elements of story that can be reasonably explained as a function of the technological nature of alphabetography. *Alphabetic* is a shorthand version of the more accurate, but awkward, *alphabetographic*. Often enough, *alphabetic* will be roughly the same as *realistic;* but *realism* as we usually use the term tends to obscure the technological cause (writing) that has so much to do with the effect (realism). As I am defining concepts here, realism in the novel is a subset of *alphabetic*. The term *alphabetic* is itself a bit clumsy, but I have to avoid the most obvious term—*literate*—because of all the excess meaning it automatically tends to carry. In any case, for much of the history of the novel, we find a mix of both oralistic and alphabetic in a given text. Some otherwise alphabetic novels may contain oralistic elements; some may not. Conversely, an otherwise oralistic fiction such as a gothic novel—in which "fantasy predominates over reality, the strange over the commonplace, and the supernatural over the natural" (Moers, 90)—will almost certainly contain distinctly alphabetic elements. Oralistic and alphabetic together operate as "end points on a continuum: as properties that come in degrees, they need not exclude each other" (Bakker, 9).[17]

III

The original successful English novelists clearly had a sense that their form of narrative sorely missed the immediacy of the oral story model, and this even though it was still fairly common in the eighteenth century to read novels aloud. Arguments have been made for some time now about the means by which those early novelists worked to overcome this definitive disadvantage (Bronson; Watt 1966; Cook). One way to consider the genre in relation to oral and other kinds of written story is in terms of showing and telling, or mimesis and diegesis. Though these concepts are a dialectical pair, and so are only distinguishable provisionally, they remain quite useful. Walter Scott described the novelist's basic dilemma in these terms long ago:

> Action, and tone, and gesture, the smile of the lover, the frown of the tyrant, the grimace of the buffoon,—all must be told [in the novel], for nothing can be shown. Thus, the very dialogue becomes mixed with the narration; for [the novelist] must not only tell what the characters actually said, in which his task is the same as that of the dramatic author, but must also describe the tone, the look, the gesture, with which their speech was accompanied,—telling in short all which, in the drama, it becomes the province of the actor to express. (qtd. in Booth, 2)

Since Plato's discussions of Homer, it has been common to limit showing and telling when we speak of written story, such that showing means, primarily, representing another's actual spoken words whereas telling means "speaking" in the narrator's own voice. But if we consider these key concepts in relation to the human body—as we have done above with writing and story—then we need to establish some significantly different baseline definitions. *Showing*, on the most basic level, means making visible to the eye. *Telling* means communicating in words. *Telling* used this way does not mean something like information, or that a reader apprehends just the words read and nothing else. As with every use of speech, the reader draws all manner of inferences from what is directly given. But drawing inferences is not the same as the experience of seeing the story with the eye. Given this distinction, we can reasonably make the case that oral story is the paradigmatic narrative in which showing and telling are most fully united. With oral story, when we speak of telling, we are always automatically speaking equally of showing, and vice versa. Although we can imagine objections to this baseline model—a blind teller before a blind audience or, in the other direction, a signing teller before a deaf audience—the very fact that these are both exceptions to the everyday norm tends to validate that norm as the default case.

A comparison of oral story to the novel and to drama or film makes this clear. In the novel, as Scott says, "all must be told" because the words on the page are all we actually see. Enacted drama and, in modern times, film are the maximum cases of showing a story because typically (there are exceptions) there is no evident storyteller as such at all. We see just the story without any apparent teller to guide us. As Raymond Williams has written, there is a "world of difference between the writing of Shakespeare for an oral public performance by a number of voices and actions, and the writing of George Eliot for silent print-reading by a temporarily separated individual" (Williams, 3). In this sense the written text of a play or film is a description of how to show a story, rather than a story itself. The novel is, relatively, all telling and no showing; film and drama are, relatively, all showing and no telling. In the normative oral story setting we see and hear the eyes, the voice, the hands, and so on, of the teller in the act of telling. This establishes the baseline degree to which a story may be constantly shown as it is told. If we pump up the showing, the storyteller must become a thespian; must more and more act out the parts, thereby gradually deindividualizing herself as the teller and moving toward drama. If we downgrade the showing in favor of only telling, then we move more and more toward the disembodiment that is characteristic of written story. To move toward this latter end of the spectrum is slowly to disembody story, in the same way that writing disembodies speech.

As we shall see, much of what drives the novel as a genre will be this enabling disability. Its fundamental disability—it cannot perform a central element of human story: showing—is what enables it as a distinctive genre at all, because it must constantly work to perform telling that can somehow make up for the lack of showing. Not surprisingly, when the novel first appears on the historical scene it comes with all manner of graphic display. But then as the novel "grows more confident . . . [it] begins a slow striptease of its graphic attire" until it is just the "bare narrative form of the novel . . . that enters the [nineteenth] century" (Barchas, 18). In short, the importance of showing for human story in general cannot be overstated. It explains in a fundamental way why so many, many people prefer television and film to reading. It explains why it is so much easier to get kids to read comic books than to read novels or stories. Given this fact about humans and showing in story, we must conclude that the novel's success seems most unlikely.

And yet the novel is one of the most successful forms of story in history. One crucial reason for this success is a paradoxical, positive effect of the disembodiment of speech into writing. Because we commonly take writing as simply another version of speech, and because we hear written words in our minds as we look over them and yet have no materially present producer of aural sounds, writing acts as a kind of telepathy. One of the thrills of a good experience of reading fiction is the sense of verbal communication that is more direct than speech. Speech can only come from other humans, and since there is no human present as we "hear" the words, we seem to receive another's thoughts without their having passed through even the intervening medium of speech. We seem to "hear" another's thoughts just as we "hear" our own. This can establish a unique sense of intimacy. Further, the telepathic effect means we have only what we experience as the voice of another to deal with. Key to what Patricia Meyer Spacks calls the "cocooned pleasure of reading novels" (304) is that we have none of the innumerable contingent, always bodily effects that can possibly disturb a story that involves showing: no worry about not being able to see or hear well enough; no worry about anyone around us interfering with our reception; no worry about interrupting the performance by having to go to the bathroom; no worry about ourselves or someone else coughing or about a stomach growling or about falling asleep. The list is infinite. None of this is to deny that we can be interrupted as we read a story. But we can always go back and begin again where the interruption happened, so we do not lose the story in the way we do at a performance. If the content of the reading strikes us in some especially moving way, this, in combination with the telepathic effect, means we have an experience of communication that has few equals; the feeling is such that *communion* might be the better word. Though there is no showing, we do not miss it because we have been consumed by a telling that seems as immediate as our own inner speech. This effect is of course an illusion, but it is nonetheless quite powerful.

With these ideas in mind, we can see in a new light the beginnings of the novel as a collection of letters. As Janet Altman has argued, "epistolary discourse is obsessed with its oral model" (135); which is to say, with the common event of an oral exchange. In some ways all written story is obsessed with oral story, but the epistolary novel makes this unusually clear. With the epistolary novel we have a unique extra element of showing, not common to other forms of novel narration. Apart from the "editor" who has assembled the collection, there is no narrator of the work as a whole. In fact, the story as a whole is not "told." The reader is shown, not a story, but copies of letters. The epistolary novel in this important way sidestepped the major disadvantage—the limitation to telling—of written story. As has long been noticed, a novel of letters operates much like drama: "Making characters work out a story by exchanging letters [is] technically similar to making them do it by exchanging speeches" (Day, 194). The reader works to infer the story in roughly the same way as a theatergoer does, though without the bodily and contextual cues provided by actors, sets, lighting, etc.

In addition, if we consider a continuum from spoken words, at one end, to writing, at the other, we find that the personal letter is a case of writing that is most like speech. Each letter is as close as writing can come to imitating an individual speaking to another individual. Since, strictly speaking (and apart from illustrations), all any written story can show is writing, the showing of samples of writing from within the fictional world (e.g., letters) is always a special case: "A letter that has been typeset . . . signifies quasi-iconically, visually reproducing, by what readers understand to be an exact transcription or transliteration, the shape of an absent originary document" (Cook, 3). This creates a singular jointure between reader and fictional world because the reader gets as close as possible to literally seeing what the characters within the story see. Although this is true with any representation of a letter, it achieves maximum effect in the epistolary novel. The reader of such a work is "included" in the fiction in a way that is not otherwise possible with written story, so the reader of an epistolary novel does not experience the missing, embodied showing of an oral teller in quite the same way as the reader of a novel written in the usual first or third person. The epistolary novel may be seen, then, as a transitional mode between drama and the normative novel form that becomes most prominent in the nineteenth century.

The other primary mode of telling in the eighteenth-century novel commonly involves a first-person narrator who is written to come across as an individual, nonfictional "speaker," whether it be the everyday informality of a Robinson Crusoe or the narrators of Fielding and Sterne. As H. Porter Abbott notes, Defoe in effect gives us "the diary in its first known insertion into fiction in Robinson Crusoe" (86), the diary or memoir being another kind of writing that comes closest to speech. Indeed, any novel told in the first person is relatively more toward the realm of oral story, simply because the "I" functions on a most basic level as it does in speech. Of Fielding, Bertrand Bronson has written that he "returns in very characteristic fashion to a close semblance—in spite of prose and print—of the early oral techniques of [Chaucer]. . . . Both authors are conspicuously present on all occasions, as ironic observers and commentators, and as essential part of the scene and total effect" (316). *Tristram Shandy* "reverts in effect to the original condition of oral discourse, and becomes a conversational exchange between speaker and hearer . . . the style has all the apparent ease and inconsequentiality of the most casual, unpremeditated talk" (317).

We may pause to say a bit more about *Tristram Shandy*, because in some ways this novel takes the notion of a first-person narrator-speaker to an early extreme. Not only does the narrator in this case constantly "speak" directly to a putatively present audience; in the effort to imitate living conversation, Sterne goes so far as to insert interruptive comments by someone, known if at all only as "sir" or "madam," who speaks in the first person directly to the narrator from where "we" are, as the audience. And of course the novel's prose runs very much like oral speech: extremely conversational and digressive. *Shandy* may be the most exaggerated example of the early attempts to get an oral teller onto the written page.

In some ways, this exaggeration gets taken to a limit. Edmund Burke wrote soon after the book's publication that "the story of the hero's life is the smallest part of the author's concern" and that all we actually have is a collection of satirical opinions "introduced with little regard to any connexion, either with the principal story or with each other" (qtd. in Sterne, 481). It is as if the novelistic need to make the teller as much like a living speaker as possible has overwhelmed the story itself.

Even, or especially, when a novel gives us a first-person narrator, it will do so in a way that is fundamentally different from the manner of a first-person oral teller. The clearest sign of what I mean is that, generally speaking, any first-person narrator of a novel is automatically unreliable. The same is not at all true of an oral storyteller. In the oral-story paradigm, the teller can make mistakes or forget things or otherwise fail, but this is not the same sense of the unreliable narrator as that figure has come to be understood with the novel. The first-person oral teller is showing and telling a story to, sharing a story with, an immediately present audience. The first-person teller in a novel is always in the text, as an unavoidably separate party from both the writer and the reader. So a first-person narrator in a written story is always himself or herself essentially being told and shown as story.

In *Tristram Shandy* this is maximally true. Because the story itself is so minimal, and because the narrator himself does not seem to take his own story seriously (after all, it is in the end a cock-and-bull tale), almost all the novel's success depends on just how the audience responds to the narrator as a "speaking" person. In a real sense the story is Shandy as opposed to his biography. The narrator near the beginning speaks of the "slight acquaintance" between himself and his reader that is slowly growing "into familiarity" and that will finally "terminate in friendship" (6). This would be the implicit goal of most first-person narratives, but it is essential in Tristram's case. If for whatever reason readers do not find his thoroughly idiosyncratic digressions and modes of expression appealing, then the novel will fail. And, relatively, so it does. Samuel Johnson as early as 1776 could say that *"Tristram Shandy* did not last" (qtd. in Sterne, 484). And, despite its peculiar brilliance, it has not lasted, except of course among hyperliterate scholars of the novel or of the eighteenth century, for the simple reason that digressive chat and opinions do not typically have the automatic, universal appeal of a story. In other words, the accomplishment of a "speaking" teller is not in itself enough to ensure more than a historically local success. To see what I mean, we need only compare Sterne's novel to *Tom Jones*. Fielding's narrator is just as conversational, and he "speaks" just as regularly in oralistic, direct address to the reader, but Fielding gives us action and suspense: a story. It is characteristic of the way writing compels newness that this extreme should have occurred so early on in the history of the genre, and it is significant that this extremity should turn out to be, in a way, an early dead end.

We can see, then, how these two most prominent forms of telling in the early novel—letters and the conversational first-person narrator—work to recover or retain that which, as written story, they automatically lose: the ability to show. Other forms of written story—medieval romance, drama, epic—do not typically demonstrate, especially in a generic way, this sense of having to overcome what is lost in the act of writing. By focusing on issues of showing and telling, then, we can chart the evolution of the novel over time in direct relation to oral story.

❧IV

With oral story established as a baseline, our understanding of certain other aspects of the novel and its history tend to change. For instance, Ian Watt wrote of Defoe and Richardson that they were "the first great writers in our literature who did not take their plots from mythology, history, legend, or previous literature." They differed in this way from such luminaries as Chaucer, Spenser, Shakespeare, and Milton, who reused traditional plots "because they accepted the general premise of their times that, since Nature is essentially complete and unchanging, its records, whether scriptural, legendary, or historical, constitute a definitive repertoire of human experience" (14). On the one hand, Watt is plainly correct here. This premise was part of the historical context. But I would argue that writing itself played a constitutive role in the generation of the historically new kinds of story we find with Defoe and Richardson. The constraints of human attention and memory come into play with the reception of both oral story and written story, but with written story, the reader can always, at will, stop, think, go back and reread the exact words again immediately or after a time. Of course, no given reader is required to read this way. Nonetheless, once writing exists, then writers, simply in the act of taking advantage of the technology's possibilities, will write for just this kind of reader. With the release from purely oral-aural memory and attention constraints, the door opens for wholly new plots and characters, for innovation of an entirely different kind than is possible with oral story—in short, for an entirely new concept of originality. This door was at least theoretically open long before the novel appeared on the scene, but in the history of story the novel is the genre in which writers finally walk through the doorway.

When alphabetic originality enters the scene of storytelling, certain recurring effects come with it. We may examine a key effect as it appears paradigmatically in a novel that, at least with respect to the English tradition, appears at just about the halfway point between the beginning of the eighteenth and the beginning of the twenty-first centuries: midpoint, then, in the history of the novel. The novel is George Eliot's *Adam Bede* (1859), and in particular I want to consider chapter 17, in which the narrator steps out of her story to address an objection she feels coming from an imaginary reader. I examine this famous passage here in some detail because I return to it regularly as I explain other novels.

It has been noted that Eliot at times "conveys uneasiness about her readers" (Spacks, 313), but the uneasiness in this example is particularly revealing in terms of the novel as an alphabetic genre. The imaginary reader objects that Eliot's Rector of Broxton is not an "edifying" representation because he is not an ideal model of Christian spirituality. Since no reader could seriously believe that all real rectors are such models, the complaint cannot have to do with some failure to imitate everyday real life. In fact, the reader (whether she thinks of herself this way or not) seems naturally to assume that a given story establishes its representational authority through an appeal to certain long-established storytelling traditions, in which the everyday real is not worthy of story. This reader, who cannot understand why Eliot has refused to "put into [the Rector's] mouth" only "the most beautiful things" (150), is operating according to oralistic storytelling traditions, which continued to function in the age of the novel. In these traditions "faulty characters" will "always be on the wrong side" and "virtuous ones on the right." "That way," Eliot continues, "we shall see at a glance whom we are able to condemn, and whom we are to approve" (151). To Eliot, the storytelling norms that were originarily necessary because of the nature of human attention seem childish and retrograde in the context of the novel. Conversely, from the oralistic perspective, Eliot's alphabetic originality appears as (nastily) arbitrary. She willfully chooses to ignore the canonical, communal story traditions and to assert in their place what must appear to be her own, merely personal idea of the character. This sense of arbitrariness is an unavoidable outcome of the originality that writing calls into being, and novelists have felt it from the beginning. It is another element in the near-universal need to present the early novel as a factual history or biography, rather than simply as a freestanding fiction.

What is the nature of this arbitrariness? A turn to alphabetic originality necessarily entails a turn away from oral story. Since the writer is not bound by the constraints of what Ong calls "oral mnemonics," she has no need to present the fantastic, the supernatural, the impossibly perfect, the unforgettably ideal. Again, this hardly means that there are no novels with impossibly perfect characters but only that such novels still carry oralistic elements within them, even though they are no longer required to do so by the storytelling situation. One outcome of the turn away from oralistic story is a turn toward content, which, from the oralistic perspective, simply does not count as "story": the everyday real. If the storyteller appeals to the real as the sanction for story, it necessarily follows that the story is a function in a very key way of that individual teller. Though no individual is an island, nonetheless any individual representation of the real must necessarily be dependent on individual perceptions and understandings. From all this it follows that the more story conforms to the nature of writing as a technology, the more the writer is uniquely responsible for that story in its entirety. (We will run into the situations and consequences of alphabetic responsibility constantly as we turn to specific novels.)

Conversely, with oral story in oral culture, the teller is responsible for the performance, which is a serious responsibility; but he is not responsible for the story itself, which is always a kind of communal possession. From the essentially social perspective of oralistic story, then, an alphabetic story has two serious faults: it tells a "story" that is no different from everyday life, and it amounts to only one person's opinions. What gives this individual his or her authority, especially if that person has no relevant special standing in the social order? Accuracy of truth to the real must be the anchor of authority. But why should one person's necessarily subjective apprehension of the real deserve our attention, especially when the technology eliminates all the paralinguistic means—material context and bodily cues—by which we judge a person's statements? What more arbitrary source for story could we imagine than just this? These questions seem almost silly to us now, but this is because we have long been accustomed to alphabetic fiction.

Eliot in this famous passage makes one of the most important statements in the history of story. Turning the narrative tables on her opposition, she declares that to represent "unexceptionable," that is, perfect or ideal clergymen, is to represent an "arbitrary picture" of the world: "things as they never have been and never will be" (150). She refuses to represent such impossible perfections, she says, because to do so would be to "refashion life and character entirely after [her] own liking." This latter statement is a perfect historical crux. To Eliot, the real is the only sure authority to which universal appeal may reasonably be made, at least for fiction that is to be of significant value. In relation to the real, any fantastic or oralistic character can only be the product of some unreflective, individual wish fulfillment and therefore must be arbitrary. But of course this is only the case if we assume alphabetic story to be the right story. From the literate perspective the characters and plots of oralistic story are distinctly untrue to the real (even if taken as history rather than fiction by oral culture), but it does not follow from this that they are the product of arbitrary individual fancy. At most they could be said to be the fancies of a social-communal desire, because the oralistic teller is not at all free to fashion the story in this sense after her or his own liking. Eliot is right that realistic fiction is true to the real, but her assumption that such story eliminates individual arbitrariness is again only true from the perspective of alphabetic story.

Even though Eliot takes this narrative bull by the horns, we can see, by the way she goes on to defend herself, that she is hardly at ease about it. Evidently, stepping apart from oralistic story, even as late as 1859, automatically brought about a sense of insecurity and loss. Eliot directly confronts the outcome of the reversal she has performed. If story is to appeal to the individual's perception of the real, then truthfulness and sincerity become as important as a writer's facility with language. On some level she senses that her reader is missing the embodied cues by which we ordinarily confirm such human qualities in speech communication. Since she cannot show these cues as she tells her story, she feels the need to tell outright what the cues would show. She claims that she will do her best to avoid arbitrariness and "to give a faithful account of men and things as they have mirrored themselves in [her] mind." She acknowledges that any such individual account will be "doubtless defective," but she will nonetheless strive to tell as "precisely as [she] can" the actuality of her perceptions (150). Further, she confesses that she dreads "falsity," because falsehood "is so easy, truth so difficult" (151). She backs up this point with a most revealing and conflicted analogy: "The pencil is conscious of a delightful facility in drawing a griffin—the longer the claws, and the larger the wings, the better; but that marvelous facility which we mistook for genius is apt to forsake us when we want to draw a real unexaggerated lion" (151).

To explain the difficulty of truthfully writing stories of the everyday real, she turns to an example of pure showing: a drawing or sketch of a griffin, a mythical figure from the most ancient of human stories. The turn to showing as an example is a kind of concession to the human desire for showing in story. She invokes drawing, we must assume, because, unlike painting or sculpture, it uses the same working instrument as writing. In the analogy the pencil itself, rather than the artist (be that artist ancient or modern), is the conscious agent; and it takes delight in noticing, not just the image it creates, but the ease ("facility") of creating such an image. The more outsized and spectacular the image, the more pleasure in the creation. In other words, the pleasure, though not quite conscious to the creator, comes with seeing how easy it is to be good at drawing this kind of impossible figure. The imagined reader who protests about Eliot's rector is the present manifestation of the audience that wants griffinlike content. That reader operates unconsciously in a way as well, but as an animal rather than a writing instrument: he or she wants to enjoy story with a "true ruminant relish." In contrast, there exists a "we," who has evidently become conscious in a way "the pencil" is not, for the "we" has an awareness that can encompass the "pencil." Like the ancients, this "we" in the past created griffins. But now it realizes that it made the mistake of seeing this facility as "genius," rather than as, much like the griffin, simply a kind of showy marvel. In Eliot's mind, it takes no genius to represent the marvelous or the fantastic, because we have no means of judging their accuracy or inaccuracy, their truth or falsity. Still, just in the act of diminishing (if not outright rejecting) this ancient, marvelous facility, she also invokes it in the form of a living, judging authority. "We" do not vanquish this facility. Rather, this facility with which human storytelling began "forsakes" us, willfully and disapprovingly leaving us behind to fend for ourselves when we decide to accurately represent the real. The contradictoriness is symptomatic. From the alphabetic perspective, oralistic story is primitive, childish, unconscious, easy. At the same moment, it is the original, authoritative human story, and when we conform story to writing we violate something very basic in human life.

This ambivalence appears throughout these pages, in which Eliot steps forward as a straightforwardly first-person "speaker" in order to defend her commitment to alphabetic arbitrariness. For instance, she declares outright that she will write as if she "were in the witness-box narrating [her] experience on oath" (150). If the reader will only think of her as speaking on oath, then there should be no problem with the lack of larger-than-life characters and events. But just in the act of invoking speech, she invokes writerliness. I have already noted that in a continuum from writing on one end to speech on an opposite end, the personal letter exemplifies the writing that is most like speech. With courtroom testimony we find a case of speech that is most like writing. Court testimony depends on speech, but both the form and content of speech in that context are strictly constrained, formalized, and punishable by the written laws that sworn statements are required to serve. Not surprisingly, everything said in court is recorded in writing, for this is the only way in which a witness's speech can be assessed in the way that writing is normally assessed. So Eliot wants to secure her authority by linking herself to orality. Perhaps this is why (apart from the usual conflation of speech and writing) she speaks of narrating on oath rather than submitting an affidavit, which would be the proper comparison. Still, to make this work she must ally herself with the speech that is most like writing.

Her invocation of courtrooms, speaking on oath, and trials brings out another originality-effect that comes with alphabetic story. What would be the sense of truthfulness and precision needed for the telling of oral story in oral culture? It would have to be much the same as that of an actor performing a part. It does not have to do with creating the story or, to a large degree, the specific words, but rather with truthfulness to the already-known content and with showing the telling in a precise enough way to create anew the old pleasures of the tale. But story that works to conform itself to writing requires the creation of the story with the creation of each word. Whatever the plan or idea in a writer's mind, no matter how fully or vaguely thought out, the act of writing literally constitutes the story word by word. If alphabetic originality entails an appeal to the real and to individual perception, then it follows that a given story will only be as original as the exactness and fidelity with which it represents the unique perceptions or thoughts of the author.

A result of this is an almost automatic turn to a fairly extreme self-skepticism. "Examine your own words well," Eliot writes just after the griffin analogy, "and you will find that even when you have no motive to be false, it is a very hard thing to say the exact truth, even about your own immediate feelings—much harder than to say something fine about them which is not the exact truth" (151–52). She does not say "think" about your own words, but rather "examine" them; that is, look over them as if they were written down or, at least, as if they were spoken in court, where motives and exact truth are always in question. Further, we should examine the exact words for those most inexact elements of human being: the emotions. In everyday life there will be occasions on which a given person might have to struggle with getting the exact verbalization for an immediate feeling. But for the story-writer this is the ongoing, word-by-word state of affairs. It is a fact of alphabetic originality: the story-writer's words are always on trial in a way that cannot happen with oral story in oral culture. And the writer herself is the skeptical judge of her own words. This effect causes both a historically unprecedented, continual innovation in form and content as well as, at least at times, a debilitating sense of—well, being on trial. So when Kieran Dolin in *Fiction and the Law* asks, "How is it that the canons of legal evidence come to govern the practice of fictional storytelling?" (2), I answer that before the influence of any specific legal systems or ideologies, the nature of conforming story to writing had already installed a distinct relationship between the novel and the law. We will constantly find the effects of this as we look at other novels.

Eliot shows us, then, fairly clearly some of the consequences of storytelling that is determined by writing. Realistic, or what I am calling alphabetic, fiction resituates arbitrariness in a key way from the community to the individual. If fiction is to be distinct from nonfiction, then by definition fiction will have to involve something of arbitrariness in relation to the real. The question then becomes, how will arbitrariness be manifested? In the oralistic tradition, content that is worthy of story is entirely distinct from content that is worthy only of report. Larger-than-life and supernatural characters and events are taken for granted by all as the obvious and natural elements of story. The issue of arbitrariness on this level would not come up unless some specific teller presented a tale that violated the common elements by which the community always recognizes story. To tell a tale that is only with difficulty distinguishable from nonfiction is such a violation. In the history of story the novel takes on its particular nature in the act of committing this violation. As a consequence, the genre seems plagued by a sense of anxiety and defensiveness about its existence, even after it becomes institutionalized as a, or rather, *the* major kind of written story. Other studies of the novel have noticed these elements in the history of the novel. Often, the explanation for these effects will have to do with print capitalism and the emergence of a nonaristocratic reading public. Patrick Brantlinger, for instance, writes of the "anti-novel attitudes within novels" that arise as a result of a pervasive "anxiety about mass literacy and the huge, largely anonymous, ever-increasing readership for fiction" (3). Because the novel takes as its content everyday reality, it will, even more certainly than other forms of literature, be the carrier of all manner of cultural conflicts and worries. But as we shall see, beneath or within or along with whatever socioeconomic kinds of anxieties there continually runs a more fundamental concern about the very act of writing story at all.

We have seen that Eliot takes a very direct approach to making a place for alphabetic fiction. Other novels have taken more indirect approaches. Most noticeable in this light is the famous line of novels that have to do with characters who lose their sense of reality to their reading. *Don Quixote* has been read in terms of its paradigmatic parody of the then-current reigning form of nondramatic fiction: medieval romance. Harry Levin (1963) and George Levine (1981), to name perhaps the most famous scholars, have explained how the progress of realism in the novel was carried forward after Cervantes in much the same way—through the parody of a currently reigning romantic fiction within a text that thereby established its own realistic credentials—by writers as various as Austen, Scott, Eliot, and Flaubert. Levine argues that the story of the "disenchantment" of Austen's Catherine Morland with the gothic novel develops into the more generalized case: "the story of hero or heroine who must learn to recognize and reject youthful fantasies (normally first learned from books) in order to accept a less than romantic and more tediously quotidian reality" (71). Levine's point is true enough, and the idea of "enchantment," with its etymological ties to magical incantation and song, seems to me just right.

But our understanding of writing and orality causes us to see all this differently. To be exact, the famous paradigm specifically involves a literate character who foolishly does what we must assume that an oral audience would not do: somehow confuse the fantastic nature of oralistic story with immediate, everyday reality (*Don Quixote* conspicuously uses the illiterate Sancho to make just this point). The recurrence of this story changes significantly over time. If we take *Don Quixote*, *Northanger Abbey*, and *Madame Bovary* as a kind of historical sequence, we can see that each novel involves a steadily reduced kind of oralistic story: from the encyclopedic array of medieval romances in chapter 6 of *Don Quixote*, to the long list of gothic titles in chapter 6 of *Northanger Abbey*, to a more generally defined romantic fiction: "stories that rush you along and make you frightened," of *Madame Bovary* (Flaubert, 96). We will consider the nature of this change later. For now, we need only be aware that there are no signs that these same characters would make this mistake in response to orally delivered tales of this kind. Though each character may have different individual psychological causes for (mis)reading as they do, all necessarily go through the same thoroughly antisocial experience of reading: being alone, suppressing the body into a kind of waking stillness, giving the eyes up to the long, continuing strings of written letters, and giving the ears up to the telepathic "speaker." So the oralistic content only becomes this kind of problem when it is experienced in and as written story.

But why would there be this concern about readers of oralistic fiction as opposed to hearers of oralistic fiction? It is as if the technology of writing is producing a story that will make the kind of story produced by the technology acceptable to creatures that are fundamentally oralistic. Alphabetic story makes private that which is otherwise essentially communal and public, and makes purely an act of telling out of that which is otherwise showing and telling. It follows that with alphabetic story the reader makes judgments about the content in isolation. In normal speech communication we always have at least the showing that comes with any actual speaking. This means that we have the bodily "expressions" of another human being by which to judge our own judgment of the content. In other words, in speech communication we interpret linguistic meaning as we go, but our sense of our interpretation is strongly affected by cues from the speaker and any other people who may be present. So in the oral story scenario, we, as listeners, would necessarily have other humans by whom to judge ourselves if we somehow began to confuse fantastic fictions with everyday reality. The private reading that is essential to alphabetic story has no such social check on our response. The words of written story are experienced as being directly spoken into the mind. The possibility, perhaps the likelihood, of an individual taking those words as almost supernaturally authoritative is, if we consider *Don Quixote, Northanger Abbey, Madame Bovary,* and the like, apparently a serious worry. But if alphabetic story stakes the authority of its content on an appeal to the real, then there will be no risk of enchantment: or at least there will only be the enchantment of the real. Alphabetic story, then, seems to be clearing the way for its noncommunal nature.

The novel as a genre also evolves in part as a function of excluding not only oralistic content but also oralistic form. This is evident in the changing situation of showing and telling. When we chart the evolution of the novel, we chart, among other things, how it changes in the process of trying to do what it cannot do: show instead of only tell. We have seen that the novel begins largely with two efforts to show: the epistolary novel tries not to tell at all, but only to show samples of writing most like speech; otherwise, there is a strong inclination to present a single narrator with as much individual personality as possible, thereby simulating a verbal teller. As the novel becomes established, accepted as a popular means of storytelling, the basic human storytelling impulse can conform more and more to the nature of writing as a storytelling medium. The evolution of the genre involves a kind of synthesis of the showing modes that characterize the novel of letters and the individualized narrators of Fielding and Sterne. The maximum case of written showing, the novel of letters, is largely left behind in spite of its initial popularity. I would argue that it fades because, strictly speaking, it is written but does not tell a story. Taking off from our oral-story paradigm, we know that both showing and telling are fundamental to story in the most general sense. The epistolary novel has the advantage of a certain kind of showing, but of course it only actually shows written documents. Although it operates like drama or film in one way, it cannot possibly equal either because it does not actually show the story. By contrast, the individualized, first-person narrators tell a story, but since we cannot see those narrators the sense of showing is seriously hampered, even with a case as extreme as *Tristram Shandy*. A kind of compromise between the two forms occurs in the act of telling the story without invoking some particular, identifiable, knowable teller. In other words, given the limitation to telling, by removing any signs of a knowable teller a written story comes as close as possible to simply putting the content on display.

This effort leads to either of two extremes. At one extreme we have a neutral third-person description that remains strictly exterior to character, scene, and event, as if there is no filtering individual perceiver at all, but only a sensory apparatus registering rather than telling the story. In relation to other forms of storytelling, and especially to oral story, such a work reads like a report. It seems to present a disembodied story: "story" as such, we might say. Wayne Booth argued long ago that the goal of a story in the third person without any signs of an individual teller is to seem "to be unwritten" (52). But it is equally true that the goal is a story that seems to be purely written, not affected by the sense of a human teller at all. Joyce's *Dubliners* is a fine example of this, though Hemingway's novels may be the most famous of the type. At the other extreme we have the attempt, in either the first or the third person, to remain aligned as strictly as possible with the interiority of the private self. All perceptions can only occur within some individual mind. Such interiority cannot be shown as such, except in its exterior manifestations. Alphabetic story that is working to distinguish itself from oral story not only can tell about such interiority, which an oral teller could do. It can, more than any other kind of story, put that interiority on display from within, so to speak. The from-within perspective, taken to its maximum with what has traditionally been called stream of consciousness, is like the neutral third-person describer in that it goes as far as possible to do away with any sense of an identifiable teller who is apart from the tale. But of course this is maximally interior as opposed to maximally exterior. And we have plenty of mixed cases of both. In sum, these two kinds of story tell the story in as showing a way as possible, given the nature of writing.

❧ V

Having considered some of the large-scale implications of writing for the novel—the general issues of showing and telling, and of form and content—we have a basis for practical interpretations of specific novels. It is reasonable to expect of a theory that it will provide insights into even the most thoroughly studied texts or will enable us to find significance in previously unstudied texts. I have chosen the former route in order to set up what I hope will be an interpretive paradigm. In subsequent chapters, I explore a series of canonical novels in order to show both what more we can learn about the novel as a genre from this theory of writing and what more we can learn about the theory by studying these novels. I stay tightly focused on the issues of writing and orality. All along, I make linkages between the general effects of the communications technology and specific textual elements that may or may not have an overt, direct connection to these effects. In every case, there is a profound, not quite conscious ambivalence about writing in human affairs, literary and otherwise.

All the examples will also necessarily be bound up with the unavoidable contradiction of using written story to question, if not outright condemn, writing. It is perhaps here that my own understanding of writing seems most similar to, but is in fact most separate from, poststructuralist understandings; for unlike poststructuralist-derived theorists, I do not extrapolate from this necessary contradiction to make claims about language and representation in general. The empirical and historical fact is that, once writing becomes a serious influence in human affairs, the nature and success of the technology require using that technology in order to consider the nature of the technology. We can of course talk about writing, but if our thoughts about writing are to have an effect beyond the immediate range of our spoken words, we must put our thoughts into writing. Walter Ong realized and stated this quite clearly: "Once the word is technologized, there is no effective way to criticize what technology has done without the aid of the highest technology available. Moreover, the new technology is not merely used to convey the critique: in fact it brought the critique into existence" (1982, 80). The scene in John 8 reveals just this realization as well. All our novelists experience this necessary contradiction.

I examine a series of novels spanning the eighteenth to the twenty-first centuries in which I show the unfolding of a process of change. But unlike the work of, say, Ian Watt, Lennard Davis, or Michael McKeon, I make a historical argument only in the limited sense that the nature of the technology induces changes in certain directions. To return to our earlier analogy: a history of urban development could be written as an explanation of the ongoing conformation of city spaces to the automobile, though the automobile would not be the only cause involved. In a similar way, I have written a history of the novel in terms of the technology without which it could not have come into existence. I am not concerned here with why the novel should have emerged at the particular time it did, nor with the existence of other possible examples of the novel before the eighteenth century. I explain its nature only once it becomes sufficiently established as a distinctive genre in the history of story. Neither am I directly concerned with ideological or other related issues of, for instance, race, class, or gender, though I hope such possibilities should be fairly evident. And yet, as with ideological readings, my claims depend importantly on a notion of unconscious causality. By this I mean that writing, like other communications technologies, affects the way knowledge happens. So, although a user of the technology will always have specific, identifiable conscious intentions in mind, there will also always be some evidence of how the technology is unconsciously determining or affecting the actuality of the writing, apart from the content of the intentions. This will necessarily be true of my own writing as well. I leave the examination of the effects of writing on my own project to another scholar.

CHAPTER TWO

Writing, Reading, and Disembodiment in *Pride and Prejudice*

≋I

AS A FIRST EXAMPLE of what my theory of writing can reveal about actual novels, and of what novels can reveal about the nature of writing, I turn to a key scene in Jane Austen's *Pride and Prejudice*. The scene, spread over chapters 11 through 13 of the second volume, is one of Austen's most famous. It involves Fitzwilliam Darcy's proposal to Elizabeth Bennet, her rejection of him, and her reading of his letter of self-explanation. Because the scene ends with Elizabeth's moment of self-recognition, most discussions of this novel spend time on this scene. In terms of the acts of reading and writing in themselves, Felicia Bonaparte, Katherine Newey, Gary Kelly, Jodi Devine, and Patricia Meyer Spacks have all discussed the letter and the general notion of reading as "both a fact and a metaphor" in the novel (Bonaparte, 141), typically stressing the analogy between reading written texts and "reading" human beings as if they were texts. But none of these scholars takes into account the technological effects of writing.

Chapter 11, in which Darcy proposes, begins with Elizabeth close-reading her sister, Jane's, letters. As an entry into the novel's most dramatic scene, then, Austen directly invokes writing and what I call alphabetic, or close, reading. Because writing is relatively permanent, it can be reread long after its initial inscription and long after a given first reading. This basic fact carries many consequences. Since the words that we read in the past remain exactly the same, and since human beings and material reality constantly change, a rereading will always, to one degree or another, reveal some change in the reader. If a text is read one way at one point in time, and the same words read another way at a later time, then something about the reader must have changed. But within this general property we have the special case of rereading with a consciously different sense of receptivity, of directly thinking of ourselves as reading anew with a specific, previously untried aim or understanding at work. In order to reread in this manner we must in some very particular way deactivate any tendency to take the words simply as they would normally, or at least as they had previously, come into our minds.

In this instance, Elizabeth rereads letters written since Jane's suitor, Bingley, suddenly ended his attentions and went away to London. Elizabeth wants to reread because Colonel Fitzwilliam has unwittingly told her that Darcy had willfully saved Bingley from "a most imprudent marriage" (122). So Elizabeth reads with an even more negative opinion of Darcy than before. She finds that Jane's letters "contained no actual complaint, nor was there any revival of past occurrences, or any communication of present suffering" (124) over the Bingley affair. But in rereading with her new knowledge about Darcy in mind, she notices in every letter "and in almost every line of each . . . a want of that cheerfulness which had been used to characterize [Jane's] style" (124). This time, she stops to study "every sentence conveying the idea of uneasiness, with an attention which it had hardly received on the first perusal," and she comes away with "a keener sense of her sister's sufferings" (124). Originally, Elizabeth had read simply as "Jane's sister," a roughly normative, unified complex of beliefs, desires, values, memories, etc. Now she consciously steps outside of that normative addressee and discovers meanings that her usual "Jane's sister" awareness had missed. Only writing (before audio recording) enables this kind of returning to words.

Now, the more alphabetic a given story, the more that story will conform to the possibilities of its enabling technology. In this case that means the story will be constructed *for* this kind of rereading. As any one who teaches literature knows, close rereading is even more demanding than reading in general. It requires directed training in ways that reading in general does not. Gary Kelly has written of how Austen includes "tests" for her readers, so that they will "recognize the way she herself is renovating the conventions of the novel" (1982, 30). To claim that Austen is renovating the conventions of the novel is true, but inexact; these "tests" have to do with the issues of renovating story into writing. Austen seems on some level to sense that her readers will not just automatically engage with the story in a fashion that reciprocates her writing of it. She is in a way like an engineer who senses that a user of her invented product will simply enjoy that product without any awareness of its actual complexity. As if to create at least the possibility of a more reciprocal reading, she opens the novel's climactic scene with a quick model of the consciously directed rereading that will be, not required, but satisfying in a way peculiar to the kind of fiction she herself is writing.[1]

Let us follow Elizabeth's example and closely (re)read this scene in order to discover what it reveals about writing and storytelling, but especially about one of the primary consequences of the disembodiment of speech: the problematized situation of the emotions. The emotions are problematic because, as we have already established, writing is restricted almost entirely to telling, not showing. But with spoken language the emotions, which are essential to the act of communication, are very largely a function of what is shown by embodiment—the paralinguistic and other elements of a speech-act taken in by the senses along with the verbal content. As we shall see, this scene is in many ways about emotions and the technology of writing.

Soon after Elizabeth's rereading of Jane's letters, Darcy calls on her unexpectedly when she is alone. The two engage in what Kay Young calls a crux conversation (59), one toward which everything has moved to this point and from which things directly unfold going forward. Darcy tries to be casual, but in spite of his usual reserve and calm he is abruptly overcome by emotion. He first sits, then nervously walks about the room. Suddenly he comes "towards her in an agitated manner." His words, certainly the most dramatic of the novel so far, seem just to burst forth, apparently in direct violation of an earlier, well-considered decision. He has "struggled," he says, but "it will not do." His "feelings will not be repressed" by his judgment (125). Evidently, Austen herself finds the proposal too emotionally loaded to try to put into writing, for she does not tell us what Darcy says. As has before been noticed (Frantz, 168), this is Austen's usual tack at such moments, and, true to form, she will not give us the actual words later when Darcy makes his second proposal (239). Instead, we are told about the speech. We have a summary of what he says of his positive feelings about Elizabeth and his negative feelings about her family. The narrator reports that he speaks with "warmth" and is "eloquent." Naturally, even a man as stiff as Darcy expresses emotions in such a situation, and naturally he expects a reciprocally emotional response from

Elizabeth. And her emotional response is building, though not in the way that he expects.

He goes on long enough that Elizabeth has time to begin to "compose herself to answer him with patience when he should have done." Then, at the key moment when he is concluding his proposal, we are told that Elizabeth can "easily *see* that he had no doubt of a favorable answer" (italics added) even though the content of his words convey the opposite. Though "he *spoke* of apprehension and anxiety . . . his countenance expressed real security" (125, Austen's italics). We have first been given by the narrator what we must take to be an objective description of the speech; not, of course, any sort of absolute objectivity, but the relatively specific objectivity that we may expect a narrator of this sort to provide when he or she takes up the position of uninvolved observer. And then we are given a limited third-person report of Elizabeth's subjective perception of what the objective report did not (implicitly could not) register. Being on the spot, she perceives what only a flesh and blood interlocutor can see. Darcy's face and tone, his body in general, "show" something other than what his words actually "tell." Said another way, she sees an emotional expression that belies the purely informational content of his words. We have, then, an example of the way in which emotion and information or consciously intended meaning can work at cross-purposes in a speech-act.[2]

We also have a revealing display of the nature of telling in the novel. The objective telling does the general kind of work described by Walter Scott, cited in the opening chapter. We can see no actor to show us Darcy's "agitated manner" or "warmth" in speaking, so a narrator tells this as information. In straight telling this way, the novel does not really equal, much less surpass, the efficacy of oral story or drama or film, all of which can visually show the audience such qualities. But in the example of limited third-person, subjective knowledge we are given the kind of telling that has most securely established the novel's distinctive importance in the history of story.

There is no need to argue that getting unverbalized mental states into story is a fundamental challenge: we have some crucial content—thinking—that has no visible or audible manifestation to others. Such states tend to be essential to a character's unique psychology but are not dramatic in any usual sense; although these states involve emotions, the emotions do not force themselves out in any usual ways. They do not emerge directly into words or other vocalizations. If they are made visible at all, they will necessarily involve bodily signs, but not the most commonly meaningful bodily signs: public expressions such as blushing or frowning or smiling or wringing the hands, etc. The signs of emotion in this case tend to be extremely context-dependent, essentially intimate and private, and therefore fundamentally undramatic. Strictly speaking, such a state cannot be shown, but must be told. The difficulty of representing such states is not limited to only one character's thoughts. In fact, things get even more complex with the kind of interaction that Austen gives us, in which we have the interior apprehension—Elizabeth sees meanings that she does not voice or show at the moment—of another's unself-acknowledged interiority. In real-life interactions of this kind, the dense richness of bodies, minds, and context can enable us, often effortlessly, to intuit such states in someone else. But though we have in one sense an entirely typical human interaction, nonetheless, the nature of the interaction cannot be represented in forms of storytelling that depend on showing, especially not in such detail and with the kind of precision Austen achieves.[3]

Written story before the novel could possibly have represented such states but rarely did. I would argue that with respect to representation in story form, such states are intrinsically alphabetic and, therefore, in my terms, novelistic. The technology of writing enables the possibility of putting this kind of unique interiority into story: the more alphabetic the story, the more it will attend to such interiority, and the more precise will be the representation of it. One need only think of Henry James to see just how precise writing enables story to be in this respect. Indeed, it is hard to imagine any other form of story ever quite outdoing the novel in this way. We have two unshown elements: an unexpressed apprehension of another's interiority. A reader of such a scene, then, "hears" the apprehension of the other in the same silent, unvocalized way that the perceiving character experiences it internally—the same way, in essence, that the reader herself would experience it in lived life. The reading about the silent understanding is distinctly of a kind with the silent understanding itself.

To return to *Pride and Prejudice*, after this paradigmatic distinction between objective report and limited third-person subjective report, we are then cut loose, so to speak, as readers, and immersed in the written representation of actual speech-acts. We read Elizabeth's courteous but also heated and sarcastic no to Darcy's proposal. Once Darcy has managed to regain "the appearance of composure" after this response, he asks for an explanation but cannot do so without emphatically bringing in the added question of why she has made "so little *endeavour* at civility" (126, Austen's italics) in the form of her rejection. It is, to him, the insulting way she has spoken rather than just the content that most immediately draws him to take his turn in the conversation. Right away, the exchange about the most important possible decision between such a man and such a woman threatens to run off the rails onto the relatively tangential issue of courtesy. In speech, the primary informational content is constantly subject to this kind of redirection. The flow of ideas, especially at such a loaded moment, is determined by emotions—what the body shows—as much as, or more than, by rational intentionality. In such a conversation our emotions, if they are real, depend, perhaps even more than our words themselves, on reciprocation in kind. Though an emotional response seems simply to well up from within, to be most thoroughly our own authentic expression, it nonetheless wants a reciprocating emotional expression in order to validate itself. The stronger the emotion, the stronger must be the response, to the point that it can be infuriatingly dissatisfying if we do not get the kind of response our emotion calls for, and all the more so if we get no emotional response at all. It is in this way that emotions begin—along with, but also apart from rational intention —to determine this conversation.

Elizabeth retorts that, assuming (without agreeing) she "*was* uncivil," she is justified because he was the one first to offer offense and insult in the way he proposed. She goes on to say that she has "other provocations" to incivility, but the example she then gives is really a reason for refusing the proposal. She charges him with having prevented the marriage of Bingley and Jane. Elizabeth pauses, waiting for him to speak, but then is compelled to continue because Darcy looks completely "unmoved by any feeling of remorse." She is forced to demand a response, and gets one. With an air of "assumed tranquility," he defends his actions. But she is so dissatisfied with this as to disdain even "the appearance of noticing [his] civil reflection" about the thwarted marriage. Ironically, his civility is now the problem for her. We must conclude that she wants to see an emotional response rather than the civil, rational defense she has ostensibly asked for. She is no longer only somehow saying no.

Determined to draw out the missing emotional response from this man who seems so very unemotional, she turns the conversation to the story of Wickham, about which she feels confident that Darcy can have no defense. And it appears that she has intuited just the right attack. We can infer this because Darcy refuses to respond to her elaborate charges about Wickham: "And this," he cries, "is your opinion of me!" (127). He leaps right over the issue of the Wickham story in general (as well as the actual invalidity of what Elizabeth knows) to take up what he perceives to be the implied meaning: she must think him capable of such actions toward a family friend, which means she must feel that he is not honorable, not the noble gentleman that he considers himself to be. From this leap he then quickly changes the conversational direction again, and this time we have the complementary opposite of the earlier case of emotions showing something other than what words are intended to tell. Darcy sees from the "energy" with which Elizabeth has reacted (as opposed to what she has said) that what has most mattered is the offense to her pride when he spoke negatively of her family, so he turns to that rather than to Wickham. "But perhaps," he goes on, "these offenses [the thwarted marriage and Wickham] might have been overlooked, had not your pride been hurt by my honest confession of the scruples that had long prevented me from forming any serious design." He claims that it is only "natural and just" that he should take into account relations "so decidedly beneath" his own place.

In saving himself from the Wickham issue, he has charged her twice: once, with not realizing her own motives, and second, with having an unjustified sense of pride. As we will soon find when she reads Darcy's letter, Elizabeth is most acutely sensitive to his particular criticism of her family because she, on some not-quite conscious level, feels much the same way as he does. Furthermore, Elizabeth must in fact agree with both Darcy's general attitude about such things and with his forthrightness. Earlier, after reading Mr. Collins' officious letter of self-invitation and of apology about the Bennet entail's effects, she asks "what can he mean by apologizing for being next in the entail? — We cannot suppose he would help it if he could. — Can he be a sensible man?" (44). Darcy by contrast abhors "disguise of every sort" and is "not ashamed of [his] feelings" (127) about her family. By Elizabeth's own standards, he is being sensible.

Revealingly, with this, Elizabeth finds herself "growing more angry every moment." Darcy has clearly struck a very sensitive nerve with these charges because Elizabeth reacts just as he had reacted when she brought up Wickham. Rather than respond to the charges, she changes the flow of ideas again, and this time in a way that will simply end the conversation. She now flatly refuses his offer of marriage, though she does manage in the process to accuse him, overtly this time, of ungentlemanly conduct. This reciprocally strikes the most sensitive nerve in Darcy, and he likewise ends the conversation.

Given this analysis of the scene as a whole, we may generalize that, after Darcy's proposal has been stated, Elizabeth, no matter what words she actually speaks, is "talking about" the insult he has given to her family. Darcy is, no matter his actual words, constantly "talking about" the insult she has given him as a gentleman by refusing the proposal in the way that she has. These two primary emotional responses determine everything else.

We will look more at the situation of emotions shortly. For now, we must pause to consider that just in the act of explaining what is told in Austen's text, we have begun to follow the model of alphabetic close reading set by Elizabeth herself at the beginning. Interestingly, though, this last scene of emotionally conflicted dialogue is as close as the novel comes to drama. We could easily stage the verbal interchange between Elizabeth and Darcy and could well come up with a similar analysis. In other words, we have brought Elizabeth's close-reading practice to bear on a portion of the novel that is not in itself particularly alphabetic. With this, we see another example of how, once we have alphabetic standards, they tend to become normative, in this case, the obvious way to read all literature. It is possible to perform such an analysis of a tense verbal exchange in a play, but unless the analyst were to see the work many times, he or she would have to turn to the written text for this kind of detailed understanding.[4] Otherwise, there is too much for a viewer's mind to have to keep track of. Our capacities of attention and memory just are not up to such a task.

We see this in the history of Shakespearean criticism. It is hard to imagine how any of the scholarly understandings of Shakespeare's plays could possibly take place without the written text to study. And this has long been acknowledged. Contemporaneously with Austen's career and the emergence of the novel as the primary form of written story, Coleridge, Lamb, A. W. Schlegel, and William Hazlitt were all claiming that "the full richness of Shakespeare . . . cannot be obtained from the stage and that we must read the plays to penetrate their depths" (Patterson, 654). "Full richness" must mean reading the play, and not only for the story as it might be viewed on stage in its oralistic manifestation, the manifestation in which literacy is not even required for comprehension and appreciation. Rather, this means reading the play as a *written* text entirely apart from its staged storytelling form, which entails going back and forth many times, constantly stopping and starting, paying attention at the level of the individual word: reading, then, according to the nature of the communications technology. The same is true with "depths," which, also like "full richness," tends to be an alphabetic value judgment. Alphabetic reading reveals full richness and depths only if we assume that an oralistic encounter with the story is at best partially full and shallow. There exists no absolute perspective from which to establish that either kind of encounter is the better. The oralistic encounter is truer to the actual experience of a story that both shows and tells, while the alphabetic encounter is truer to the nature of writing. In any case, even though Aristotle first noticed this quality of good drama centuries earlier, I would argue that the full-blown emergence of this kind of reading is not simply coincidental with the emergence of the most alphabetic of written story. The more story conforms to the possibilities of the technology, the more reading conforms as well. Then, once alphabetic reading exists, it can be fruitfully applied to any story (or other literature) whatsoever.

II

In the past decades there has been a notable scholarly interest in the ways in which the human body is represented, or otherwise functions, in literature, perhaps culminating in Austen's case with John Wiltshire's *Jane Austen and the Body*. But nowhere do we find a discussion that takes off from what I would argue is a, if not *the,* foundational level: the novel as a historically unprecedented disembodiment of spoken language and of story into writing. We have examined Austen's representation of spoken language through this lens. Now we turn to the situation in which the missing body becomes most significant: Darcy's letter to Elizabeth.

Darcy gives Elizabeth a letter the morning after the failed proposal. The unusual situation of this letter reveals much. In the typical novelistic epistolary situation, as in real life, letters are written because of physical distance or some kind of coercion. Most of the letters of Richardson's Pamela are to her parents, who are far away. She is more or less a prisoner and so is forced to communicate by letter. Clarissa Harlow must often communicate by letter to her family and, later, even to Lovelace and his minions, who are right downstairs, because she is only safe in her room. Otherwise the usual epistolary situation has someone reporting from some distance because of travel, as in *Evelina* or *The Expedition of Humphrey Clinker*. But in Darcy's case he writes, not because of distance but because of nearness. He cannot speak directly to Elizabeth about these personally important issues because he cannot trust his judgment to prevail over his emotions in the act of speaking. And yet the very thing —writing—that enables him to overcome, so to speak, nearness, also automatically causes him to be anxious about the distancing that is an essential quality of writing.

On the one hand, the message Darcy needs to communicate is so loaded with emotions that he must disembody it into writing rather than speak it. He has, we may say, written his emotions out *in* the letter as well as out *of* the letter. Written out *in* the letter is the information about, the rational explanation of, the emotionally charged sense of himself as a gentleman. And in order to explain his emotions he has had to write them out *of*, leave them out of, the language by which he would communicate. Said another way, writing gives him the ability to do what as a living human being he cannot do in an actual speech-act: restrict himself to telling, with as little showing as possible. On the other hand, he evidently feels it absolutely necessary to put the letter directly into Elizabeth's hand, and to do so when she is alone, and even some distance from any domestic space. Why should this be? After all, Darcy could easily enough have had the letter taken to Elizabeth, instead of wandering in the grove on the expectation that she would happen by. He could hardly suspect that she would dismiss its authenticity if it were delivered in the usual way. Neither would he expect her to read so private a message aloud if she received it in the presence of others. So hand delivery by him alone to her alone is an integral part of the letter itself. Though Darcy can only communicate this information by disembodying it into writing, everything about the actual transmission of the letter works to embody it again. Since his written signature will validate the letter and the contents themselves are unmistakably of the highest consequence, the hand delivery by the writer is an altogether extra kind of authentication. Darcy is, paradoxically, "signing" the disembodied language with his whole, embodied self.

Before reading, Elizabeth examines the letter as an object, noting its distinct physical nature: "two sheets of letter paper, written quite through, in a very close hand—The envelope itself was likewise full" (129), this even though Darcy could hardly have been short of letter paper. With this, Austen makes plain that writing can carry signs of emotion, just in the specific nature of its material manifestation. Before and apart from typing, there is necessarily a fundamental physical "relatedness between the body and letter writing," simply because "without the hand and the eye, one [cannot] effectually write a letter" (Schneider, 113). The individual quality of a sample of handwriting will be especially significant in this respect, though Austen does not specifically mention Darcy's actual script. Still, the materiality of this letter becomes a figure for its writer: silent but overfull, packed with written words to the limits of its material substance. Darcy, overfull with unvocalized speech, is much the same.

Like the letter, Darcy manages to communicate but exempts himself from the contingencies that always beset a verbal *exchange*. In writing, he can do his best to offset offense before it happens and to mollify it when it is unavoidable; he can qualify; he can be exact. And he can go on at length of his own choosing. Since the letter is "dated from Rosings, at eight o'clock in the morning," since it is so very long and meticulously worded, and since Darcy himself has earlier said that he writes "rather slowly" (32), we must assume that he has likely spent all of the previous night composing it. Like the letter, Darcy is verbally folded in upon himself. We have seen all along that he is unsure of himself as a verbal, and therefore as a social, person. He is awkward and stiff in public settings, scarcely able to carry on a conversation in the dance (62). He says outright that unless he knows someone well he "cannot catch their tone of conversation, or appear interested in their concerns" in order to make the most basic social talk (116). In other words, he can always understand the informational content of speech, but without intimate knowledge of an interlocutor, he is at a loss either to understand or to express the showing elements, the emotional elements that are an integral part of speech-acts.

We have, in contrast to his speaking abilities, seen that he regularly writes "generally long" letters (33). And yet apparently even in his letters he lacks a certain everyday sense of linguistic comfort. Bingley says that Darcy "does *not* write with ease. He studies too much for words of four syllables" (33, Austen's italics). Though this may imply that Darcy is ostentatiously intellectual, it also suggests one reason he fails at conversation. The alphabetic sense of precision, which requires him to be so studious about choosing his words, spills over into his sense of spoken language. Though speech has its own exactitude, it is not, in general, of a kind with writing. Anyone who (consciously or unconsciously) judges casual speech by alphabetic standards of precision will not likely be at ease in most conversational settings, and certainly not in emotionally intense ones.

We also know that his letter to Elizabeth is not the first time he has substituted writing for emotional speech. A year before, Darcy had gone to stop his sister from eloping with Wickham. Instead of a verbal confrontation, Darcy "wrote to Mr. Wickham," who was, like Elizabeth, still present on the scene (133). We may wonder how a man such as Darcy could possibly express himself about issues of emotional importance in any way other than by writing. As he himself writes in closing his explanation, he had not directly told Elizabeth everything the evening before because he "was not then master enough of [himself] to know what could or ought to be revealed" (134). This implies that he would, apart from that specific overwrought scene, be able to tell her all this verbally, but of course he does not try to do this. The technology enables him to do what he otherwise could not do.

And yet, as we have seen with the hand delivery, on some level he knows that separating his words from his body comes at a cost. Accordingly, at the end of what reads distinctly as an affidavit—with mentions of offenses laid to his charge (129), weighty accusations (131), witnesses (132), motives (132), need for acquittal (133)—he invokes the "testimony" (134) of his cousin Fitzwilliam as a further means of giving some form of flesh and blood back to his words; and unlike Darcy's own communication, Fitzwilliam's must be spoken. Darcy even goes so far as to send Fitzwilliam to be present when Elizabeth returns from the lane after reading the letter (though she wanders by herself for so long that he must leave [138]), as if to provide a kind of embodied witness's "signature" to follow up his own embodied "signature" in the hand delivery.

If in the opening of this sequence of events we had a sort of quick view of the method of alphabetic reading, we now get a detailed anatomy of the process, and once again the situation of the emotions becomes important. Because writing removes our words from our bodies, the activity of writing automatically diminishes, if not outright eliminates, the affect of emotion that is part of any speech-act. We can of course compose emotional passages of writing, but any one who has ever written understands that we cannot do so with anything like the immediate emotionalism of our spoken words. Writing is never simply, as it is so often imagined to be, the spontaneous overflow of powerful feelings (Wordsworth himself did not think this). In fact, the more emotional we actually are, the less able we will be to operate the technology effectively. To conform feelings, powerful or otherwise, to alphabetography, we must recollect them as rationally manipulable concepts after the body is no longer directly involved. And because the technology is so difficult to operate, most of us need some removed, emotionally tranquil place in which to perform this recollection. This is why it takes Darcy all night to write the letter.

The same would not seem to hold for the reader, however. The reader can take up the finished words and more or less spontaneously experience very strong emotions. People love written story for just this reason. But to read in conformity with the technology by which the alphabetic text is communicated means to perform an alphabetic reading. Understanding and appreciating writing *as* writing (rather than simply as content) requires a willing disembodiment, a willing divorce of our immediate emotional responses from our rational consideration of the text. Of course I intend only relative differences here. Given the embodied nature of human beings, the rational will always be entwined with the emotional (though the opposite does not seem quite so true), but still we can reasonably establish actions and states that are more distinctly in the one or the other direction. To read written story as *written* story, rather than as story that just happens to be occurring in writing, necessarily involves a relatively disembodied involvement with the text. The same would hold for any of the arts. With architecture, for instance, a building can in principle strike awe into anyone with eyes. But to look at the building *as* architecture necessarily means thinking of the building apart from that sensory appeal.

These general ideas are clearly demonstrated in the representation of Elizabeth's reading process. Interestingly, her interaction with the letter bears distinct similarities to Darcy's earlier verbal interaction with her. He had been driven by emotion to speak, and when he spoke he was blindly confident of what he expected to hear in return. Elizabeth is driven to read and is blindly confident that he will have nothing unexpected to say. Darcy had walked about anxiously during the interview. With "thoughts that could rest on nothing, she walk[s] on" continually during the readings of the letter (135).

Reading the first part of the letter, dealing mainly with the story of Bingley and Jane, Elizabeth's emotions determine her understanding. At first, she is so eager "from impatience of knowing what the next sentence might bring" that she is "incapable of attending to the sense of the one before her eyes" (134). Darcy's account of her family makes "her too angry to have any wish of doing [his explanation] justice" (134). And she cannot be "satisfied" because he expresses no regret. Once again she is most directly stung by the facts about her family and as a result wants, not his explanation, but his expression of emotional penance. And just as Darcy had been stung by what he perceived as a lack of verbal civility in Elizabeth's refusal, now Elizabeth is offended by the form of his writing: she finds that "his style [is] not penitent." He is once again civil when, in her mind, he ought to be emotional.

Once Darcy moves on past the most sensitive topic, to Wickham, she can "read with somewhat clearer attention." But of course Darcy's version of this story throws her into complete turmoil because if it is true then the implications for her sense of herself are intolerable to consider. The letter, again, reads like an affidavit, and it stages Elizabeth as a judge or prosecutor who must be convinced of Darcy's case. But now, that role suddenly reverses. She becomes the one on trial. Her automatic response to the Wickham story is so strong that she is driven to exclaim denials out loud to no one, not just once but repeatedly: "This must be false! This cannot be! This must be the grossest falsehood!" (135). She reacts to the affidavit—the unadorned, semilegalistic written statement of the facts—very much as if it has literally put her on the stand before an invisible jury. She becomes so emotional that she can only skim the rest of the letter and then declares, apparently again out loud, that she will "never look in it again." But while this vow vanishes as soon it is spoken, Darcy's letter remains materially present. The straightforward next step is to destroy the letter. This she evidently cannot do. On this first reading she finds much of it offensive, and much incredible, so why not just tear it up? She had no trouble at all bringing a decisive end to the verbal exchange with Darcy the evening before. Dismissing a material object should be a trifle in comparison.

The nature of writing, as opposed simply to the content of this particular letter, surely comes into play here. Because we so regularly see writing as superior to speech, because the written word carries a kind of materialized solidity unavailable to speech, the written expression carries more weight than the actual verbal expression of the same content by the same person. And obviously Elizabeth's emotional responses have been expressed more or less in a vacuum. Since, unlike in the conversation the night before, she cannot either elicit or demand a reciprocating emotional response from Darcy, she is left suspended, unvalidated. Returning to the letter is her only means of possibly finding any reciprocity. Darcy, whether he thinks of it in this way or not, is depending on these effects. He uses the technology *instead* of speech, rather than as a means of communicating over distance. He also depends on Elizabeth engaging with the letter as the kind of reader who would complement himself as a writer.

As we have seen, at first she fails to do this. She has so far been reading as if she were responding to speech, even to the point of exclaiming out loud over the silent page. Though it may be her unreciprocated emotional response that drives her to return to the letter, she hardly expects to somehow be reciprocated in kind by a written document. Only by reading for the informational content can she hope to relieve the emotional turmoil she feels. Otherwise the second reading will be no different from the first. So she chooses to read in the way she had close-read her sister's letters. Just as Darcy had to disembody himself into writing in order to communicate this content to Elizabeth, if she is to receive the content in conformity with its technological medium, she has to disembody herself as a reader. She has to read, relatively, with her emotion in check.

Paradoxically, given that the letter is intended to entirely end their relationship, her ability and willingness to read in this way means she is just the kind of woman that someone like Darcy most needs. We have been prepared for this much earlier in the novel, when Darcy specifically says that reading is a "more substantial" quality in a successful woman than any of the usual female abilities (27). The parallel between Elizabeth as reader and Darcy as writer is made overt in a direct echo of Darcy's words ("it will not do" [125]) as he had begun his proposal. Soon after Elizabeth puts the letter away, we read that "it would not do, in half a minute the letter was unfolded again" (135). As Darcy was compelled to speak in spite of his rational judgment, so she is compelled to reread in spite of what we may call her emotional judgment. She commands herself "to examine the meaning of every sentence . . . to read and reread with the closest attention" (135). In fact she takes on the role of perhaps the maximal close reader: a lawyer or judge in a court of law, though it turns out that she presides over a case against herself. She moves through the text in an extraordinarily detailed way, constantly stopping to compare the text's statements with her own understanding of the world in general and of the specific events in question, thereby presenting an even more elaborate model of how an alphabetic text induces an alphabetic, or close, reader.

When she has finished this time, her emotions return, as they should, more powerfully than before, because Darcy's affidavit has convinced her that she has "been blind, partial, prejudiced, absurd" (137) about Wickham. She cries out her guilt verbally to the absent jury: "how just a humiliation!" is the discovery that she has not been the kind of woman she believed herself to be. But then she considers Jane and Bingley and is not quite convinced that Darcy is innocent there. She reads "[the letter] again." With this, Austen gives a distinct and very ironic replay of the earlier scene in which Elizabeth reread Jane's letters. In that case, the second reading gave her a sense of self-validation because the letters proved that Darcy was guilty. As before: "Widely different was the effect of a second perusal" (137). But this time Darcy is innocent, which necessarily means Elizabeth is guilty. Finally, in this rereading, she comes to what has all along been most important, "that part of the letter, in which her family were mentioned, in terms of such mortifying, yet merited reproach." This last, most difficult truth must be admitted. "The justice of the charge [strikes] her too forcibly for denial" (137). Finally, after a very long session of study, she realizes the truth and exclaims in the famous words: "Till this moment, I never knew myself" (137). She speaks aloud, but this time her emotions are not expressed in a vacuum or to some invisible jury. She herself is both speaker and addressee.

If the novel has made it seem clear that Darcy could never have communicated all this without being able to disembody his words, it also has made it seem clear that Elizabeth could not have taken in this knowledge, at least in this most effective way, unless it came to her in, precisely, disembodied words. It is in one way "ironical that [Darcy's] writing, not his face-to-face proposal, should gain Elizabeth for him" (Kelly 1984, 166); but in another way it is not ironical at all. It is perfectly consistent with the kind of man he is. It does seem ironic, though, that Elizabeth should turn out to be just the partner for just such a man.

⁂III

This letter and its reading also present a paradigmatic nexus of the cognitive challenges made by an alphabetic fiction to the reader. We have seen that oralistic story is constructed so as to conform to the capacities of memory and attention of a listening audience. Written fiction need not work within these cognitive parameters. A story that conforms to the technology of writing will tap into capacities of memory and attention that are of course far beyond those of any listening audience; but in fact, the more alphabetic the fiction, the more it will tap into cognitive capacities that are beyond even a first-reading by a literate reader. Both the quality and quantity of detail far surpass what a person can be expected even to fully apprehend, much less interpret, with only one reading. This is certainly true of *Pride and Prejudice*.

In the letter-reading scene we have a quite realistic representation of a woman recalling, as she close-reads a written letter, certain events of her past that have led up to the present moment. Now, the letter itself is not a fiction, though it does consist of personal stories. Elizabeth has much more at stake "than anyone coming to terms with a work of fiction. Yet she stands as a model for novel readers" (Spacks, 310). In the novel itself it is simply realistic to have such a reading of a nonfictional text because in everyday life there is commonly no reason to attend to written story as one would want to attend to such a letter. But just this fact makes the construction of the letter all the more important. As Elizabeth steadily, with as little emotional involvement as possible, revisits her memory of the various events mentioned in the letter, we have direct mentions of many, many passages over which the reader has passed on the way to this point. Although for Elizabeth this is simply the process of comparing the letter to her memory, for the reader it is automatically a process of comparing the letter to the memory of having read this story. So Elizabeth's action readily transfers from the realm of nonfiction writing to the realm of this written novel.

If a reader chooses (or, perhaps, as a student is required) to reread after this most detailed model, that reader, like Elizabeth, is led back with a changed consciousness to precise passages on specific pages earlier in the text. I will provide only one example to show what I mean. At one point in her reading Elizabeth recalls how Wickham had "boasted of having no fear of seeing Mr. Darcy—that Mr. Darcy might leave the country, but that *he* [Wickham] should stand his ground" (136). If we reread, perhaps after finishing just this section, but in any case after finishing the novel, we will go back to find the passage to which this memory directs us. And eventually we will locate, much earlier, Wickham's spoken words: "It is not for *me* to be driven away by Mr. Darcy. If *he* wishes to avoid seeing *me*, he must go" (53–54). Any close reader of Austen's fiction will have discovered this kind of extremely detailed integration across the text: it is a definitive accomplishment of both Austen and of the novel as a genre. Conceivably, there may exist some readers with attention and memory capacity that would enable them to retain the entire novel in mind in such a way as to apprehend this kind of microlevel connection on a first reading. Such readers would be extremely rare. Any reader is likely to retain at least a handful of such fine points. But the fact is that the nature of the alphabetic text exceeds the usual cognitive capacities of, not just memory and attention in general, but even the memory and attention required for a first reading. Only an alphabetic reading, a close rereading, can possibly make all this apprehensible. We can see from this that, along with its effects on story, writing seriously affects the nature of the reader's attention.

Lastly, the novel's being the most alphabetic kind of story produces a distinctive readerly pleasure. If we reread, for instance, the passages with Wickham on pages 53–58 after having read the passages on pages 134–38, then we discover, as Elizabeth did with the letters, how the very words we read earlier have changed their significance. With the second reading, it is plain how Wickham is steering the conversation with Elizabeth in ways that she (and we) could not have known at the time. While this discovery is utterly humiliating, and for Elizabeth, transformative, it gives a distinct pleasure of discovery to the alphabetic reader. I would argue that this kind of pleasure is exclusively alphabetic and consists of two awarenesses that operate jointly.

First, the reader who expends the effort to discover this kind of textual detail, which can only happen with rereading, experiences a positive validation as a certain kind of reader. Stated more precisely, because we have performed this kind of operation on *written* story, we have, whether we realize it consciously or not, the sense of achievement that anyone may have in coming to understand the inner workings of some technology encountered in everyday life. Indeed, alphabetic reading in its most basic sense is a form of reverse engineering: working to discover the technological means by which a finished product or established system has been developed. To reverse engineer the text is consciously to put critical-reading attention ahead of the primary pleasures of story. We experience, then, a certain sense of our own technological prowess. And since we have achieved this technological prowess with written *story*, we have at the same time the sense of having gained a certain prowess with one of humanity's great forms of art. As close readers we know story in a way that other readers do not.[5]

The second, co-occurring awareness is a kind of awe at what the writer has been able to do. We have the sense of the story as a whole, a self-contained unit, like any other single story. But it seems almost impossible that anyone could hold in mind a whole constituted from such an immense complexity of parts. This is one of the enchanting illusions produced in reading story that has been fully technologized into writing because, of course, this is not what the writer has to do. Because she constantly has the already-written to go back to as she composes going forward, Austen never has to hold anything like the entire text in mind at once. At the same time, though, simply having the already-written does not automatically assure that a given writer will compose a story of such complexity. First, writing must exist to be used at all, but then some writers will, and some writers will not, exploit the possibilities of the technology. The same holds true for readers.

CHAPTER THREE

The Monstrous Writing
of *Frankenstein*

Particular human cognitive capacities determine in certain ways both the forms and contents of oral story in oral cultures. These kinds of forms and, especially, contents can still appeal when they show up as oralistic elements of written story. Of course, not all examples of written oralistic stories will succeed equally, and some will fail outright. But still, no matter how much culture changes, we regularly find that many broadly popular stories are oralistic. To take only a well-known example, although the specific technological paraphernalia of *Star Wars* (or most other epic science fiction, written or cinematic) would not be recognizable to, say, an ancient Greek audience, nonetheless the primary character types and plots would be. It hardly needs arguing that much of the "science" in science fiction is what would more rightly be called magic. Fantasy fiction as a written genre remains vastly popular, no matter how technologically advanced our culture becomes. Such stories remain so appealing because they apparently have to do with something very fundamental in the psychology of the human animal. The spectacularly memorable (be it horrible or beautiful), the heroic, the larger than everyday life do not lose their appeal simply because storytelling media change. But written story that moves away from oralistic content has been popular as well, especially since the emergence of the novel. The nature and history of the novel can be charted by examining how it does or does not structurally incorporate elements of oral story, and by how it represents orality and literacy on the levels of theme or imagery.

Some novels will offer especially rich soil for the investigation of what we might call the interfaces between the oralistic and the alphabetic. One such novel is Mary Shelley's *Frankenstein*. With our understanding of writing in mind, this novel offers us more than one possible angle of approach: its specific epistolary format for instance; or the fact of this particular young woman, with her heritage of hyperliterate parents, taking up the pen in this way at this time in the history of story; or the relationships between this writing and scientific writing of the day. We will touch on some of these aspects along the way, but our focus will be on the creature, for the creature and writing are much involved with each other.

I

Before getting to the novel and its creature, however, we must look closely at the preface and the 1831 introduction to the third edition. These two nonfictional texts lay the groundwork for certain conflicts and tensions that we will later find in the novel itself. The preface opens with a rejection of claims by Dr. Erasmus Darwin and certain German "physiological writers" that the novel's great "event"—the creation of a living being in the laboratory—could be a scientific possibility (6).[1] Nonetheless (as with nearly all science fiction), it matters that "the basis of [Shelley's] work of fancy" be putatively an invention of science. Otherwise her story will be "merely . . . a series of supernatural terrors" and therefore not "exempt from the disadvantages of a mere tale of specters or enchantment" (6). The "German stories of ghosts" in the *Fantasmagoriana* collection that led to the composition of this novel (7) are just such tales. Not surprisingly, the majority of those stories are written versions of folk tales, some of which Shelley summarizes (inaccurately) in the later introduction (224). Further, Shelley and her little group enjoyed these tales orally. At some time during the nasty weather they "crowded around a blazing wood fire" and amused themselves from the book, so they must have been reading the tales aloud. In this little scene of origins we have a perfect transitional case: an oral story scenario in most respects—the tales themselves, the close gathering of living bodies united as an audience, the living teller—except that a written text rather than a human being actually possesses the story, and of course the audience is very literate.

The event is so enjoyable that the group wants to repeat it. But the way they repeat it is revealing. They could simply share around the reading, have each member of the group read another ghost story from the already-published collection. This would most preserve and, in truly making the event into a ritual, even augment the oral-story elements of the evening.

But it is decided that everyone should become an individual originator of an equally engrossing, original tale. From a "playful desire of imitation," they decide that each should write a story "founded on some supernatural occurrence" (7). This scene and its aftermath are a tableau vivant of the transition from oral story to written story and of the way that writing tends to subsume the most ancient storytelling modes and practices. The oldest, most common kinds of story and the ancient communal scene of telling still appeal. But the alphabetic orientation to the individual and to originality comes almost automatically into play as well, and it seems entirely to override the original storytelling pleasure. It is perhaps not surprising that the scene in fact never gets repeated.

In her introduction Shelley recalls trying to write a ghost story and being confronted with "that blank incapability of invention which is the greatest misery of authorship" (226). It turns out that something that would seem so easy—creating, not any sort of complex, highbrow literature, but simple ghost stories just for "playful" fun—is not easy at all. Shelley's distress has to do with the fact that, as in the scene of reading aloud round the fire, she is mixing written and oralistic story. No folktale teller was ever confronted with the miserable inability to invent a tale, because such tellers do not invent tales. But writing that wants to be more than a transcription of spoken words always requires invention. This is true even in the attempt to imitate one of the most common, ancient, and simple kinds of story. And invention, or originality, of this kind is as universal a difficulty for writers as we are likely to find.

Our spoken words flow from us more or less unproblematically nearly all the time. But writing seldom flows in the way of speech. Obviously, any such flow would be impeded by the material requirements of the technology: special eye-hand coordination, writing implement, and display surface. But the difference is not simply a matter of speed or, more generally, of basic ability to make written signs. The difference has to do with the way we experience the written, as opposed to the spoken, word. In general all written words are experienced in the same ways that we experience only certain special cases of speech: courtroom speech being the paradigmatic example. Only in certain very special situations must we think carefully about each word we utter. Writing seems of its nature to require care with all, or certainly the great majority of, words. Said another way, writing is like speaking on trial. This is not tied strictly to context or content. Even the most casual content, even a personal letter to an intimate acquaintance, will not roll out of us with anything like the flowing ease of speech. It takes concentrated, willed work in order to sound casual.

This explains the sometimes-lamented demise of the letter writing that was such a staple of interpersonal communication before the telephone. *Of course* perfectly literate people will telephone or send preinscribed cards rather than write personal letters. Once we have these alternate means of communicating over distance, writing is, for many people, simply too much work, and not (or not only) because of laziness. In the case of a personal letter, we experience a conflict between what we want—the easy immediacy of casual or intimate communication—and what we must do: the isolated, concentrated work required in order to get even this most everyday desire into writing.[2] By "work" I mean that process of having to decide which word is needed when; of realizing, without being sure why, that a just-written phrase does not feel right; of having to decide about the order of things; of spelling and grammar; of finishing the whole and then, on rereading, discovering something altogether wrong—in short, of having to pay direct attention to so many details that either do not matter at all or can be taken for granted in the actual conversational exchange. Compared to speech, writing can rarely be casual. Why should this be?

At the level I am considering here, the issue is not simply one of rhetoric, not simply a problem of conforming to some established alphabetic norms and standards (which are, however, always present). The issue has to do with an evidently automatic *feeling* about our written words, and the feeling has to do with our sense of ourselves as linguistic beings. Needless to say, our ego, just in the sense of who we are as individuals, is directly invested in our spoken words. But spoken language, taken in its default nature, which is what all humans begin with and perform all the time, is always a communication in the truest sense—a sharing with other(s) immediately present. Linguistic and paralinguistic responses from others are always an ongoing, constitutive element of the normal speech-act, as essential to the act as the speaker's own words. As we communicate in a speech-act, we receive feedback from others, and we typically adjust our words accordingly. We can willfully or unintentionally misunderstand the feedback, of course, but it is the necessity of such input, not its accuracy, that matters here. This fact entails a kind of ongoing, unavoidable personal responsibility for the parties of a speech-act. When we speak, we have a responsibility to be aware of others as communicants and to speak accordingly, to abide by unstated rules of etiquette, politeness, turn-taking, and the like. (These rules will vary according to cultural contexts, but they are always present in some form.) Because we are social beings as well as individuals, our ego investment in our words is always dependent in large part on these not-strictly linguistic elements of spoken communication. For many of our everyday speech situations no thought whatsoever need be given directly to this. Humans are constructed cognitively with a theory of mind capacity that makes them adept at successfully registering and responding to the specificities of a wide variety of speech situations.[3] Speaking is, most of the time, just not much of a problem.

Our egos are also directly invested in our written words. We experience them, like speech, as emerging from within ourselves and becoming manifest in the exterior world. But of course we cannot color them with the showing of our bodies, and in any case we have no immediate feedback from other human beings. In writing, as Walter Ong put it, "To make yourself clear without gesture, without facial expression, without intonation, without a real hearer, you have to foresee circumspectly all possible meanings a statement may have for any possible reader in any possible situation, and you have to make your language work to come clear all by itself, with no existential context" (1982, 103). Nonetheless, the responsibility to be aware of others remains unavoidably in operation: it is an element of linguistic communication in general. The result is that the writer must take responsibility not only for his or her own words but for playing the part of the missing other communicant as well. For this reason, with writing, the responsibility for the other communicant entails a corollary quality: originality. In fact, alphabetic responsibility and originality on this level are two sides of the same coin. When we speak in the normal ways (apart from special cases of speaking aloud alone), although our words originate in ourselves, that sense of origination is always essentially inflected by the material presence of others. By contrast, the technological nature of writing (as opposed to some particular form or content) seems to require that we generate entirely privately what is otherwise social and public. Therefore, the words are much more just our own than they are in a speech-act. If being original always involves taking the risk of going it alone, then when we write we always take that risk.

Further, since we lack direct feedback as we write, we experience a generic, amplified uncertainty about the efficacy of our words as compared to a speech-act. That efficacy can ultimately only be judged by some actual other reader. Because our written words are so solidly permanent compared to speech, and because they can go out into the world at large instead of only to whom we pick and choose, we can have no guarantee that any actual reader will be in any way similar to whatever reader we have assumed in our isolated origination of the words. To return to some earlier ideas, the writer is automatically caught in a conflict between public and private. On the one hand, because the writer is responsible for both himself or herself and for the other communicant, the activity of writing is most thoroughly private, even solipsistic, by oralistic standards. On the other hand, because the words are permanent, they become public in a way that spoken words (before audio recording) never do. Whatever the nature of the actual eventual reader(s), we are always still responsible for every word—which is to say, our egos are on the line—in a way that happens only with special cases of spoken language. No wonder writing is so fundamentally difficult, compared to speech. Certainly, with training and work anyone can get to be more and more capable and comfortable with writing. Rhetoric and composition studies, for instance, focus on the issue of audience when teaching writing so that the solipsism can be lessened. But Shelley's blank incapability of invention about something so seemingly modest as a ghost story occurs, not only because in some general way it is hard to find the right word(s), but also because of the nature of the communications technology itself.

If, added to this, we set out to write a story, then other problems automatically arise as well. Earlier in the introduction Shelley recalls having gone through the miseries of authorship as a little girl. With two literary parents, it evidently seemed natural to her to write stories. "As a child I scribbled," she says, but her written stories always failed in comparison to the "castles in the air," the "waking dreams" of her imagination (222). When she tried to put into writing the "romantic woes [and] wonderful events" that as a child she simply took for granted as the stuff of story, she found that her "dreams were at once more fantastic and agreeable than [her] writings" (222–23). In line with this, her own life "appeared to

[her] too commonplace an affair" to write about, so she did not make herself "the heroine of [her] tales." As with the most ancient traditions of oral story, the everyday life of everyday people seems self-evidently unworthy to be a serious story.[4] Whatever other elements of her personality and circumstances may have come into play at that young age, it is this specific early disappointment that the mature Shelley recalls bringing an end to her writing. Even as a child she experienced a conflict between oralistic story and writing, and in a sense her childish, more or less instinctive choice to give up on forcing the two together was a perfectly good one. She had not yet become literate in such a way as to feel what she feels with the same problem (writing and oral story) as a hyperliterate adult: that the story *must* be gotten into writing.

In addition, even as a child she had experienced the peculiarly alphabetic sense of story originality. In her writings she was always only "a close imitator—rather doing as others had done, than putting down the suggestions of my own mind" and, as well, had written "in a most commonplace style" (222–23). Writing in general comes with the word-for-word originality problem explained above. Written story comes with both that general problem and a more specific one. An oral teller of oral tales is expected always to tell the same stories, but a writer of any story whatsoever, including a retelling of an already-existing story, is automatically expected to create something fundamentally new. Although this expectation—experienced both by the writer and by others—becomes institutionalized in various ways, originarily it is a function of the technology of writing. But of course oral tellers can only be seen as telling "the same" tales if we assume the alphabetic perspective as the only perspective that matters. If we step out of our alphabetic perspective, then the "concepts of repetition and reproduction are not as appropriate [to oral story] as those of reinstantiation, recreation, reiterability" (Bakker, 21).

The idea of "the same" story in oral terms differs significantly from "the same" story in alphabetic terms for a couple of reasons. Without writing, only memory can establish to what degree one story is the same as another. Unlike writing, memories are imprecise and fading, so "the same" story told repeatedly at, say, ceremonial occasions, just will not register as what would be called "the same" in alphabetic terms. And strictly speaking (ironically, by alphabetic standards of exactitude), no two tellings of the same story can possibly be "the same" because they are communications between living human beings, which means that every instant of telling is also an instant of showing; apart from film, showing can never be the same twice. To claim that certain traditional oral stories are the same is a reasonable enough generalization from a number of actual cases, but the generalization leaves out precisely that which constitutively distinguishes oral from written story: showing. Still, this helps us see the problem of originality that comes with written story. Written story lacks the showing that automatically gives a certain fundamental newness to any oral story. This means that written story must always be distinguishing itself from other stories entirely in its telling, and that telling can always be compared, word for word, to other written story. So a felt need to be new, to be original, comes along sooner or later with the technology, no matter who is doing the writing. Shelley's worry as a child about being too close an imitator is still happening as she sets out to write *Frankenstein*.

As we shall see in our discussion of Ian McEwan's *Atonement*, all these alphabetic effects have their positive corollaries. For now, we turn from Shelley as a little girl to Shelley as an adult woman writer. We leave the introduction with her eventual generation, after a dream, of the "hideous progeny" that will become her novel (229). It turns out, though, that the story is hideous precisely because it is *not* a ghost story. For we find that despite the originating scene of reading ghost stories aloud and the agreement to imitate a supernatural tale, the preface assures us that her novel will not be imitating anything of this kind. As we can see from the "merely" and "mere" of the preface ("merely . . . a series of supernatural terrors" and therefore not "exempt from the disadvantages of a mere tale of specters or enchantment" [6]), the alphabetic value system that tends to categorize oral story as inferior to "real" literature (the opposite of the values at work in the little girl) is in operation here. Incredibly, a reference further on, elevating this novel above "the enervating effects of the novels of the present day," makes it sound as if *Frankenstein* is, like *Don Quixote* and *Northanger Abbey*, doing its historical part to undo the negative effects of oralistic written story.

At the same time, we read that the very impossibility of the creature "as a physical fact" enables an imaginative "point of view" that is "more comprehensive and commanding" than a point of view deriving from "the ordinary relations of existing events" (6). This latter condescending phrase both refers to the kind of story that had become so successful with the emergence of the novel and directly links the novel as a genre to the scientific work of those "physiological writers" of science, the same linkage so well established by Ian Watt in *The Rise of the Novel*. So as a material object, this will look and feel like a novel, but it will not stoop so low as to tell a novelistic story. Rather, this text will operate more in line with certain famous predecessors: *The Iliad*, two of Shakespeare's most magical plays—*The Tempest* and *A Midsummer Night's Dream*—and *Paradise Lost* (6), which are all among "the highest specimens of poetry" (7). These particular examples, all of which overtly depend on, and even take for granted, the supernatural, are in both their form and content rather far removed from alphabetic story. They feel no need whatsoever to disguise or eliminate the fantastic and are in fact touchstones, as Matthew Arnold might say, in the system of literary value as it was established before the novel came onto the scene. Such works establish a "rule" about the use of supernatural content to communicate even the most lofty human truths. The interesting thing here is the felt need to mention all this. These concerns only become a problem with the emergence of alphabetic story. This ancient rule can justify "the most humble novelist" in trying, precisely, to exempt herself from the disadvantages of the "ordinary relations of existing events," namely, of a story that tends to be "only" a report, or what I am calling alphabetic story.

The contradictoriness of all this should be apparent. The preface insists on the scientific basis that will exempt the tale to come from oralistic story, which automatically aligns it with alphabetic story: the novel. And at the same time the tale is aligned with canonical highbrow epic and drama that are dependent on the supernatural and on poetry, thereby automatically exempting it from the novel. The resulting narrative is "hideous," I will argue, but not just in the sheer material nature and circumstances of the creature. In trying to write neither an oralistic nor a novelistic fiction, Shelley ends up producing a novel about the necessary but debilitating, even monstrous effects of writing in human life.

II

Turning to Shelley's famous creature, we find that he has been considered in terms of language (Marder, Brooks, Favret) and regularly in terms of reading and education (Lamb, McWhir, Richardson 1991, McLane, Cantor, Marshall, O'Rourke, Lipking, Brantlinger, Sharp, Bugg). Gilbert and Gubar have rightly described the novel as a "book about books" and made the case that, for the uncommonly well-read Shelley, "pages and words [stood] in for flesh and blood" (222, 223). Beth Newman has mentioned the tensions between speech and writing. Maureen McLane has come closest to considering the novel directly in our terms. She mentions the "problem of phonetics and the alphabet, posed by the monster to himself" as he learns to read and write (973). She sees that "speaking and alphabetic writing appear to him as two equally alien media which he requires in order to be recognized" (973). Still, she focuses primarily on writing's content: "The trajectory of Frankenstein's creation offers a parable of pedagogic failure—specifically a failure in the promise of the humanities, in letters as a route to humanization" (959). But as we shall see, although the content of the creature's reading certainly matters, the technology that enables reading in the first place is more fundamental to his story.

The conflicted sense of writing and orality in the preface and introduction sets the stage (though not as was perhaps intended) remarkably well for the novel itself, beginning with the characterizations of childhood. In telling his story to Walton, Frankenstein recalls that his cousin Elizabeth read the "aerial creations of the poets" (30). His special friend, Henry Clerval, read "books of chivalry and romance" and wrote fairy tales as well as romantic plays based on the characters of Orlando Furioso, Robin Hood, Amadis de Gaul, and St. George, all classical oral-story heroes (30). Both are thus aligned with oralistic literature. In contrast, Frankenstein himself read about "facts relative to the actual world" (30), which takes us directly back to "ordinary relations of existing events" (6). Further, the "mere" ghost stories dismissed in Shelley's preface did not affect him even as a boy, for he never so much as "trembled at a tale of superstition" (47).

As it turns out, Frankenstein is of a kind with those "physiological writers of Germany" (6) who had theorized that Shelley's creature could be a real possibility. He reports that he was led to his work by a serious study of "physiology" (46). He comes to his discovery by making observations of "the natural decay and corruption of the human body" (46) and by "examining and analyzing all the minutiae of causation": in other words, by employing a contemporary version of scientific method (47). But then when we come to the "event" of discovery itself, an uneasy mixture of science and the supernatural returns, presented in terms of writing. Of his final success Frankenstein says that "some miracle might have produced it," though in scientific terms, "the stages of discovery were distinct and probable" (47). But of the climactic moment, his discovery, he writes that it

> was so great and overwhelming, that all the steps by which I had been progressively led to it were obliterated, and I beheld only the result. What had been the study and desire of the wisest men since the creation of the world, was now within my grasp. Not that, like a magic scene, it all opened upon me at once: the information I had obtained was of a nature rather to direct my endeavours so soon as I should point them towards the object of my search, than to exhibit that object already accomplished. (47–48)

Here we have a crucial ambiguity or perhaps inconsistency on Shelley's part. Let me say right away that it would be untrue to Shelley's tale to hold it to consistencies and probabilities that would conform to our everyday world. Of course she is not bound by verisimilitude of this kind. But we may reasonably expect consistency and probability within the constraints of the fictional world she creates, and when we find inconsistencies, we may investigate their significances. Certainly, this is a major one. If Frankenstein has been conducting anything like scientific research, then writing has been indispensable to his work. Science as we know it simply cannot be done without detailed written records of dates, trials and errors, results, and conclusions. Frankenstein claims that the progressive steps — in other words, the experimental method — of his research are "obliterated" by his success. According to the *Oxford English Dictionary, obliterate,* which only first shows up in the seventeenth century, means to erase anything written. So the generation of the creature as a material being is figured as writing that is erased in the moment of its full signification.

But we need to look more closely at the way "obliterate" takes on its meaning in this context. The "steps" of his experiment had to have been recorded at least in Frankenstein's memory, though most likely in writing. If Frankenstein had been writing as he went, then in spite of what he says, the final discovery could not somehow in itself literally erase that writing. Consequently, it sounds as if he had not been writing as he went and that the discovery must have erased the only other possible record, which would be his memory. With his careful specification—"*all* the steps by which I had been *progressively* led" (italics added)—this latter seems more likely in the sense that it is more believable that a memory could be erased in so total a fashion, though we then have the very unlikely case of a scientific process without writing. In any case, the creature will later find the written record of the "event," so unless this is an inconsistency in the novel (which it may well be; there are others, some caught by Shelley [35], some not [110, 156]), then this passage must mean that his conscious awareness of the written record was obliterated at the time of the big event but that the record still existed. This makes little sense. The only other possibility in the context is that the ugly necessity of dealing with "decay and corruption" (46) in order to generate life has been obliterated from his memory. But then why stress the method, rather than the emotional response? And just before this comment he has spent time explaining how and why he was not disgusted by his work.

Shelley, it seems to me, is aware on some level that she has gotten her hero into a kind of corner, caught in an impossible mix of the oralistic and the written. Since writing is required to do science, then the obliteration seems to mean it must not have been science, which would make this merely a tale of the supernatural, no better than a ghost story. As if to offset just this objection, Frankenstein quickly backtracks, denying that his discovery had to do with "magic." It had to do with solid, directive "information," the kind of information earlier characterized as "facts relative to the actual world" (30) and, again, the "ordinary relations of existing events" (6). And yet, paradoxically, to further make his point he then compares himself to a character from one of the great written compilations of oral story, *The Thousand and One Nights*. He was like "the Arabian who had been buried with the dead, and found a passage to life aided only by one glimmering, and seemingly ineffectual, light" (48). So the great moment of creation is characterized in two intriguing ways: as obliterated, scientific writing and as a written version of a thoroughly oralistic tale. No matter what Frankenstein actually says, he seems to want to think of his act of creation as both science and magic, and as neither science nor magic, and he thinks about all this in the same conflicted, mixed terms expressed about the novel in the preface. In any case, the hideousness of Shelley's progeny is, even in its material creation, a thoroughly divided amalgam of science and magic, alphabetic and oralistic.

⚜III

This amalgam will be manifest in the creature's psychological and emotional nature as well, for he is figured in multiple ways *as* writing. We find this figuration beginning with the way he explains himself. He tells his story verbally to Frankenstein, distinctly as if he is giving testimony in a court of law. "Listen to my tale," he commands, and

> when you have heard that, abandon or commiserate me, as you shall judge that I deserve. But hear me. The guilty are allowed, by human laws, bloody as they may be, to speak in their own defence before they are condemned. Listen to me, Frankenstein. You accuse me of murder; and yet you would, with a satisfied conscience, destroy your own creature. Oh, praise the eternal justice of man! Yet I ask you not to spare me: listen to me; and then, if you can, and if you will, destroy the work of your hands. (96)

Jonathan Grossman has argued that this novel "amplifies an ideological, novelistic conception of modern subjects as necessarily—even in their affective and familial bonds—subject to and produced by the law courts" (81). This holds for the novel in general, but the creature in particular is figured more distinctly in terms of the technology that enabled modern law. As I argue in the opening chapter, the speech that is most like writing occurs paradigmatically in a court of law. From the beginning, then, the creature stages his own spoken biography in terms of the speech that is most like writing.

The creature recalls encountering language when he takes up residence by the De Lacey cabin. He hears its occupants pronouncing what he calls only "sounds" (103). On the evening of that first day he hears the youth, Felix, "utter sounds that were monotonous" (105), lacking the harmony of either human or avian song. This is the creature's first encounter with reading, or the "science of words or letters." As, himself unobserved, he observes the scene, he is struck by what (in a canceled passage) he describes as the "excitements and the aliments of a boundless curiosity" produced in the audience by the monotonous words (105). This scene, "a quintessential family scene of hearthside reading aloud" (Stewart, 120), takes us back again to the introduction and the originating scene of Shelley and her group "crowded around a blazing wood fire," reading aloud from *Fantasmagoriana* (7). The originating story-event of this novel and the original story-event in the creature's psychological existence are both examples of literate people using written texts in the communal way that oral story had always been practiced before writing. In this case, though, it is the creature himself, rather than oralistic story, that is being subsumed into writing.

Next, the creature discovers how the "sounds" can have meaning. He does this by observing that what he does not know—words—produces what he does know—emotional responses—in hearers. This he finds to be a "godlike science" (107). After a time he learns from repetition "the names that were given to some of the most familiar objects of discourse" (107). But words such as "*good, dearest, unhappy*" (108, italics in original), not being names in the usual sense, are more difficult. All of this is of course entirely dependent on eyesight, especially sight of the face and eyes, which cues the creature needs even more than would an actual infant because no one is consciously trying to teach him to speak. Still, in a rough way, this is what infants do as they learn language.

But when he has still only an infant's grasp of spoken language, the creature turns to reading. By watching Felix read and pronounce the same words as he does in speech, the creature conjectures that Felix "found on the paper signs for speech which he understood" (109). The creature immediately wants to comprehend these signs, but reasonably asks, "How was that possible, when I did not even understand the sounds for which they stood as signs?" (109). With this qualifying question Shelley seems to realize that, even within this fantastic fictional world, her creature has made an impossible inferential leap. He has evidently not seen the actual signs on the page, and yet he passes over any notion of the "talking book," which cognitively (and based on Gronniosaw's testimony) would be the most likely initial, nonliterate understanding of the scene. Nowhere does Shelley mention the experience of actually seeing alphabetic signs, and yet her novel is literally thick with images of eyes and elaborately described acts of seeing. Having come upon and stated this problem, Shelley just skips over it. The creature simply goes on to say: "I improved, however, sensibly in this science" (109). It appears that the creature must become literate, or else it will be only a mere monster. But it becomes literate more or less by magic. As with the key moment of his material creation, this key moment of his psychological creation—an impossible mix of the alphabetic and the oralistic—is obliterated.

We have, then, an "infant" appearing to learn to read at the same time as learning speech. But it is more accurate to say we have an "infant" learning "this science" *in order* to speak, for his sensible improvement does not enable him "sufficiently to follow up any kind of conversation" (109), which is what the creature wants. He realizes that he ought not to discover himself to the cottagers until he has "become master of their language" (109). Reading will be his means to that end.

The creature's real language instruction and general education happens because of the arrival of the beautiful Arabian, Safie. As the cottagers instruct her in French, the creature becomes a kind of shadow-pupil, both in and not in the circuit of instruction. Most importantly, he is instructed in the "science of letters as it was taught" to Safie from Volney's *Ruins of Empires* (114). In the two previous usages (105, 109) the "science of letters" has clearly meant writing as a means of representation, rather than some particular content in the readings. So in this meaning it would appear that the lessons are intended to teach Safie how to read.[5] This seems supported because Felix instructs Safie by reading aloud to her, and he has chosen this text because its "declamatory style was framed in imitation of the eastern authors" (114). Evidently it will be easier for her to learn to read a language with which, as an Arabian, she is already familiar. Anyone who goes to Volney's work will find that in diction, vocabulary, and rhetorical flourish it is nearly identical to the prose in Shelley's novel and to the romantic fiction of the day (especially *Werther*). So whatever this may mean for Safie, who already has language, it means that the creature learns a very ornate written language as his first speaking language. The "science of letters" also at times seems to mean the content of the text; Felix makes a point of giving "very minute explanations" of the content, which includes a "cursory knowledge of history . . . the manners, governments, and religions of the different nations," as well as the stories of fallen empires and the conquest of the "American hemisphere" (114–15). After some time of this, Felix apparently teaches Safie from other texts. We are told that while the creature listened to "the instructions" which Felix continued to "bestow upon the Arabian," he learned more or less everything about the "strange system of human society" (115).

Learning the science of letters seems automatically to lead to a certain kind of introspection. "The words" of Felix's instructions, he says, "induced me to turn towards myself" (115). Above, we have discussed the ways that writing separates the knower from the known. If writing separates the knower from the known, then we will come to have a situation in which the self as knower is separated from the self as known. This enables (or causes) a kind of self-analysis that, though found in nonliterate life, is peculiar, in degree, to literacy. Such self-analysis "calls for isolation of the self, around which the entire lived world swirls for each individual person, removal of the center of every situation [the self] from that situation enough to allow the center, the self, to be examined and described" (Ong 1982, 54). Earlier, science gave birth to the creature as a material being, and now the science of letters is giving birth to him as a psychological being. As a result, he is plagued from the very first by this kind of extreme solipsistic self-objectification. He asks, "Was I then a monster, a blot upon the earth?" (116). The creature's own sense of himself occurs in terms of writing. In the figure, the earth appears as the page and the creature as an unreadable and ugly blot on the otherwise clean and clear writing surface. He tries to ignore this realization, but cannot. In fact, he discovers that "sorrow only increase[es] with knowledge" (116). Becoming literate and lettered has brought him a self-awareness he would rather not own as well as the generic, romantic nostalgia that we so regularly find involved with literacy. But whereas typically this kind of nostalgia is for a lost time before the complications of adulthood or civilization, because the creature was born into literacy rather than speech, he laments ever having become conscious at all. "Oh," he exclaims, "that I had for ever remained in my native wood, nor known or felt beyond the sensations of hunger, thirst, and heat" (116).

As Anne McWhir has written, the creature is "trapped by the textual values he assimilates" from all this (74), but if we look closely we find that the more fundamental problem, once again, is the means by which he comes to those values: writing. In concluding the history of his education the creature wonders about his own family. "No father," he says, "had watched my infant days, no mother had blessed me with smiles and caresses; or if they had, all my past life was now a blot, a blind vacancy in which I distinguished nothing" (117). He lacks this kind of past because he is an invented rather than a natural being. This fact gives all the more resonance to his self-description in terms of the technology of writing. For a second time he figures his life as an inkblot. Because of what he has learned about human families, he tries to recall his own past. Failing to find the memories, it is as if that past must have been written but then blotted out. (Ironically, if we recall Frankenstein's earlier claim that the steps of his work were "obliterated" in the moment of success, then the creature is in fact literally correct about his past.) He equates his lost written past with, not just an emptiness ("vacancy"), but an unseeing ("blind") emptiness. In the context, this figure takes on its meaning in relation to old de Lacey, the blind man to whom the creature will soon appeal for succor. Ironically, old de Lacy, the icon of benevolence and simple goodness in the novel, is the case of a blind fullness. In contrast to de Lacy, the creature imagines his past as an emptiness that somehow has eyes but cannot see or, even more exactly, as a nonspatial entity (vacancy) that consists only of unseeing eyes. This would surely be a maximal image of blindness, especially since de Lacey is blind but distinguishes much more than vacancy. The concept of unseeing eyes is equated with blotted ink, which is equated with the creature's unknown past. These images will return later when the creature finally reads his own history.

As the creature is relating the history of the cottagers, he breaks off for fear that Frankenstein will not believe his testimony. "I have copies" of the letters between Safie and Felix, the creature says, "for I found means, during my residence in the hovel, to procure the implements of writing, and the letters were often in the hands of Felix or [his sister]" (119). Like a defense attorney, he does not fail to submit the evidence in its materiality: "Before I depart, I will give them to you, they will prove the truth of my tale" (119). Though Shelley has thought at least to mention the issue of learning to speak and to read, she has made no mention at all of having to learn to write. It is as if reading and writing are simply straightforward byproducts of speaking or of seeing someone read, which is not at all the case. Once again, the creature seems in a way to have been born literate. He seems automatically to know that the written word has the power to validate the otherwise suspect spoken word, an understanding that will be directly supported and even augmented later, by Walton. Though Walton over and over extols Frankenstein's vocal eloquence and persuasiveness, he nonetheless, near the end of the novel, says outright that "the letters of Felix and Safie, which he shewed me, and the apparition of the creature, seen from our ship, brought to me a greater conviction of the truth of his narrative than his asseverations, however earnest and connected" (207). Given the phrasing, it appears that neither the letters nor the creature alone would have validated Frankenstein's story. The written letters carry the same weight as the actual sight of the creature itself. As evidence, letters and creature seem to be of equal substance.

By chance the creature finds a lost portmanteau containing *Paradise Lost*, *Plutarch's Lives*, and the *Sorrows of Werther* (123). Now more than ever we see the representation of a creature who has gone as if by magic straight to literacy. So far we have no evidence that the creature has ever actually spoken words aloud, and yet he can easily read these quite sophisticated texts. With his introduction to epic, history, and the novel, the creature takes an interesting place in the line of fictional characters—from Don Quixote to Catherine Morland to Edward Waverly to Emma Bovary to Ian McEwan's Briony Tallis—who have had their sense of mundane reality corrupted by their (mis)reading. He reads Milton as he had "read the other volumes which had fallen into [his] hands, as a true history" (125), and so he repeats the common misperception that written texts must be true and factual simply because they are written. As with the letters that will validate his oral story, he does not seem to consider the possibility of written language being false or misleading. But though he is similar to these other cases, he is also different in a key way. Unlike the other misreaders, the creature has no previously established, verbal sense of reality for his reading to displace. That is, the other characters can be, and are, responsible for their folly because they were all verbal creatures before they were literate creatures. They all originally developed as human beings apart from literacy. So when they lose their normal, everyday senses to their reading, they have no excuse; whatever the power of writing, they simply ought to know better. And they especially ought to know better than to be misled by oralistic written story. The climactic moment of self-recognition (if it comes) in such stories typically has to do with realizing just this fact. But strictly speaking, the creature knows himself and the world originally through writing. His problem is not so much that he has misread as that he has ever read at all. Since he has no nonliterate self to begin with, he has no core of nonliterate sense to return to.

This conclusion is reinforced when his reading, especially of Milton's epic, induces another inward turn. Being parentless, he compares himself to Adam. But this brings only more despair because of the key difference between them. Adam "was allowed to converse with and acquire knowledge from beings of a superior nature" (125). Even though Adam is imagined in the Bible story as, like the creature, having been "born" fully formed, as already having language, nonetheless he is pictured by Milton as passing from his initial state into an already-established oral community, which would be at least a version of the human norm. The creature never goes through this, but acquires his knowledge almost entirely from the "superior nature" of the science of letters.

The climax of his reading comes with the written record of Frankenstein's act of creation, or what amounts to the creature's birth certificate. The creature reports what Frankenstein presumably already knows: "You minutely described in these papers every step you took in the progress of your work. . . . You, doubtless, recollect these papers. Here they are" (126). But of course we have heard Frankenstein earlier say outright that the moment of revelation "obliterated" the progressive steps of his work (47). Again, this would seem to be an inconsistency on Shelley's part. In any case, the creature presents the papers formally to Frankenstein, makes a point of showing him the material sheets of writing, as if, like the copied letters of Felix and Safie, only the written record will authenticate the oral story he has been telling. Why would he need such authentication with, of all people, his creator? Does he think Frankenstein will simply refuse to acknowledge his own work unless presented with his own writing? But Frankenstein has already admitted being the creature's creator in their first exchange on the glacier (94). Although the creature began his testimony by putting himself on the stand as his own defense attorney and with Frankenstein as the judge, now, much as we have seen with Darcy and Elizabeth, he has turned the tables and become the prosecuting attorney, and Frankenstein the accused. The creature has held the papers until the most dramatic moment of the trial, and he now brings them forth as the maximal condemnation, apparently even more absolute than the immediate presence of his monstrous self.

The essential effect of these writings is their visuality. They "set in view" the "whole detail of that series of disgusting circumstances," the "minutest description" of the results of his creator's work. The language, he goes on, "painted your own horrors, and rendered mine ineffaceable" (126). With this, the earlier imagined figure of a missing, loving, watchful father (117) has been replaced by a painterly fullness ("painted your own horrors") of a present, horrified, watchful father. The previously disembodied unseeing eye ("blind vacancy" [117]) that was the creature's past has not become what it would seem most likely to become now that he has read the written history of himself: an embodied, seeing eye. Rather, that image of his past, too, has been subsumed into the permanent image of his creator's horror. But where the written story of his birth generates an image of his creator's horror as a painting, an iconographic representation of the real, that same story generates an image of the creature's own horror as writing. The *Oxford English Dictionary* reveals that *ineffaceable* only became current in 1802. It has to do with that which cannot be "effaced, obliterated, or blotted out; indelible" (1423). This ineffaceable self-horror is the creature's central psychological quality. Frankenstein himself even refers to the creature in these same terms. When he comes home for Willie's funeral, he mentions that the six years he has been away seem to have "passed as a dream but for one indelible trace" (73), the creature. And finally, near the end, the creature refers to Frankenstein as the "author at once of my existence and of its unspeakable torments" (217). We have, then, a sequence of representations of the creature distinctly in terms of writing: from material birth as obliterated writing, to psychological birth as blotted writing, to "adult" personality as ineffaceable writing.

Taking all this evidence together, we may conclude that Shelley's creature, however she may have consciously thought of it, is hideous in a quite specific way. It carries the conflicted mix of oralistic and alphabetic to an imaginative extreme, for the creature becomes the figure of a most strange impossibility: embodied writing. He seems to spring directly from the obliterated writing by which he was created, as if the writing abruptly becomes material flesh. As we have seen, he himself on some level thinks of himself as writing. His "author" (217), Frankenstein, is explicitly represented to be entirely responsible for his stupendously original creation. Unlike a human infant, embodied writing does not just die if it is abandoned. It is more powerful than its inventor. It goes out into the world on its own in spite of whatever its creator might want. At times it trails after its creator. At times it is simply elsewhere. It outlives its creator. And, most significantly, given the issues we have examined in Shelley's preface and introduction, it literally kills the two representatives of oralistic literature, Elizabeth and Henry, and it becomes the obsessive, unattainable desire of Frankenstein, who is in key ways dissociated from things oralistic. Whatever Shelley may have consciously thought, her text is beset by a fundamental anxiety: it expresses a profound distrust of the technology by which it is created.[6] Writing is the means by which the story exists, but is figured within the story as hideous and demonic, a fantastic invention that becomes destructive of those who invented it. We have seen this essential anxiety in Darcy's letter, and we will see it again. In every case we will be replaying the great paradox first established with Socrates, whose success as a philosopher depends on the writing that he himself rejected.

Clearly, I have here been performing an entirely alphabetic reading, which, before leaving *Frankenstein*, we should balance with a consideration of the more everyday response to this story. Let us return to the preface one last time. No matter what we are supposed to think of this story, and the story itself notwithstanding, Shelley's novel actually succeeds almost entirely as an oralistic fiction, a tale of "supernatural terrors" (6). Shelley, in the act of imitating the most traditional of oralistic story (the German stories of ghosts), takes on the obligatory, alphabetic sense of originality and comes up with a spectacularly innovative tale. The originality of rendering her "monster" into a scientific rather than a supernatural creation can hardly be overstated. This makes the story more, rather than less terrible. It also makes it, like science fiction, particularly appealing to a secular culture. This is also the reason that her creature, rather than her novel, has become a significant modern legend, and exactly in the way that the preface hopes to disallow. The James Whale film version (1931), with aims so utterly different from Shelley's, remains to this day what is popularly taken to be, simply, the story. In it, the hypersensationalized "science" more than makes up for any magic or sorcery, and the creature, far from being an eloquent natural philosopher, is straightforwardly a speechless miscreant.

Especially before the academic revival of interest in the novel in the 1970s, this was a story, much like *Robinson Crusoe*, that nearly everyone knew but almost no one had read, and this is still largely true. The historical comparison to Defoe's novel is instructive. Both novels obviously try to bring in readers by giving something entertaining in the most basic way, something strange and surprising, as Defoe writes in the original title of *Crusoe*. But both writers also clearly do so with an alphabetic sense of literary significance. Although they want to be strange and surprising, at the same time they worry about being dismissed as being *only* strange and surprising, which means, from the alphabetic perspective, having failed to lift themselves above what is taken to be the childish appeal of folktales. And yet the strange and surprising elements of both novels take on an entirely separate existence from the written texts in which they occur. The most sensational, memorable elements of each novel—the lone man stranded for so long on a tropical island and the manmade monster—get lifted out of their stories to operate as postnovel folktales. Like folktales, these stories are known by everybody, though few people would likely recall where or when they ever first heard them. But everybody tends to know that both Crusoe and Frankenstein come from some old novel, even though almost no one has actually read it. As anyone teaching either novel to college students knows, both tend to be disappointing at first (and sometimes to the last), because they are, compared to the popular ideas of the stories, so unsensational and therefore unmemorable. Another way of saying this is that, although both writers set out to delight and instruct, only the "delight" element actually succeeds with large numbers of people over time, and the delight element in both stories is oralistic. The many pages of mundane detail that are the bulk of *Robinson Crusoe*, the many pages of philosophizing in *Frankenstein*, the constant introspection that is, really, the core of both novels—all this is alien to oral story and, not surprisingly, fails to live apart from the text. But men stranded on strange islands and horrifying monsters have been with us since "Homer" wrote down the already-ancient oral stories in his epics.

To sum up, then, Shelley's novel, because of its thoroughly conflicted sense of the oralistic and the alphabetic, is a singular touchstone in the history of story.

CHAPTER FOUR

Letters and Spirits
in *Bleak House*

IT IS EASY TO establish the general importance of the act of writing in *Bleak House*. We have a number of scenes distinctly involving the physical act of writing, most notably Krook in his shop (44) and Sir Leicester after he has had a stroke (576). We have many examples of the materiality of written documents, apart from their content: for instance, the handwritten affidavit in the first chapter (10); the various papers with Hawdon's writing (285); the last letter of Lady Dedlock (611). And of course we have the prominent issue of literacy, most clearly present in the characters of Jo and Krook, but also in several instances of a literate person attempting to teach someone to write: Esther Summerson teaches Charley (325), Caddy teaches Prince Turveydrop (149), the poor bride teaches her new husband (384). As in *Pride and Prejudice*, we again have key cases of a written letter taking the place of speech, not because of distance but because of the emotional quality of the communication. We also have more or less continuously the elaborate linkage of writing and the law. And lastly, we have the recurring case of Esther's narrative being determined by the requirements of written, as opposed to oral, story.

Now, in none of these instances does it appear that Dickens himself had the technological nature of writing as an issue directly in mind. For him, the issues of the novel were, among others, chancery and the law; "rapacious benevolence" (76) of both the philanthropic and religious varieties (Mrs. Jellyby and Mrs. Pardiggle); officious, pompous clergymen (Chadband); and the upper-class "world of fashion" (the Dedlocks). As opposed to these, writing is just a part of the fictional world he set out to represent, and he included it accordingly. But as we found with *Franken-stein*, writing, because of its nature, always has a special significance. Writing in *Bleak House* has been studied before. Since the 1970s critics have claimed that *Bleak House* is about writing or, in a similar conceptual way, about interpretation or about language (J. Hillis Miller, Ragussis), which is to say, the novel is about itself as a representation. But typically, this deconstructive interpretation always finds the text, like any other representation, infinitely self-disestablishing. This kind of interpretation typically discusses an irresolvable, usually unconscious conflict between a theoretically necessary lack of absolute meaning and a meaning that at least putatively presents itself as absolutely full and present.

My understanding of writing and representation does not have to do with this kind of theoretical absolute. Rather, I take language and narrativity as empirically established elements of *Homo sapiens* that do the work they have evolved to do, very well much of the time, but hardly in some exact or absolutely successful way. I take oral story to be the default kind of human storytelling—which of course has no perfect example or pure existence apart from the contingencies of human life but which can nonetheless be reasonably established as a specific category having specific qualities. I take writing to be a historically specifiable technology with specifiable qualities and effects in and on human life. I, too, will discuss signs of a not-quite conscious conflict. The conflict will be necessary, given my founding claims, but it will not be necessary in the rather apocalypto-ontological way of most poststructuralist studies.

In *Bleak House* we have a nearly encyclopedic array of examples of writing. However, instead of attempting an encyclopedic analysis I will consider writing only in relation to three of the largest issues in the novel: the law, literacy, and written story.

I

The relationships between law and the eighteenth- and nineteenth-century British novel have been studied for some time now (Dolin, Davis, Welsh, Bender, Gladfelder, Grossman, Schramm, Posner). One of the most famous readings of *Bleak House*, in D. A. Miller's *The Novel and the Police*, deals with the issue of law enforcement if not law itself, in great detail. But these studies typically take for granted the technology by which law as we know it was originally made possible. There is, however, an area of literary study in which writing does matter in the study of literature and the law: medieval literature. The Middle Ages saw one of the epochal transitions from orality to writing, in England specifically, and in Europe more generally. With respect to the law, the period was characterized by what Richard Green calls a "paradigmatic situation." It involved the shift from the "communally authenticated trothplight to the judicially enforced written contract, from a truth that resides in people to one located in documents" (xiv). Given this and the "pervasive presence of law in medieval English literature" (Steiner and Barrington, 1), it is not surprising that the consideration of writing, literacy, and law would be important in studying this period. But if *Bleak House* is any example, writing remains as integrally involved with the relationship between law and literature in the Victorian period as it did centuries earlier.

Early in *Bleak House* we have in quick succession two crucial scenes that involve writing as a technology, apart from its content, and the law: the scene in which Lady Dedlock swoons after seeing a handwritten affidavit, and the scene in which Esther's godmother dies as she cries out a verse from the Bible. Take the first scene first. The plot for the entire novel is sparked by a singular case of handwriting. We should recall that handwriting in general takes on a special quality as a form of writing. Of the various possible kinds of script, handwriting tends always to have a uniquely individual quality. More than any other kind of writing, it has an element of showing that, while drastically limited, nonetheless comes as close as may be possible to the way the body and the emotions work in spoken language. And this obtains even though the usual methods of writing training try to eliminate individuality. This scene depends on just these qualities.

Lawyer Tulkinghorn has brought some affidavits to Sir Leicester. Lady Dedlock notices the handwriting and asks if it is law-hand. In the nineteenth century *law-hand* was the common term for the writing upon which the practice of the law depended, namely, copying out of all manner of documents by hand in a uniform style. The better the law-hand, the less individualized the handwriting. Law-hand in this sense strove to be like print, to eliminate any visible sign of a particular human writer. Tulkinghorn explains, disapprovingly, that "the legal character which [the law-hand] has, was acquired after the original hand was formed" (10). In other words, to the lawyer's eye this copy is technically flawed because the writer already had an "original" handwriting—one that necessarily carried signs of his individual body—when he decided to take up law-hand. The ideal copyist, then, would be taught law-hand style from the first, so that nothing of the individual would color the writing. Taking this logic even further, the ideal copyist would also be illiterate, for then he would be performing a purely visual task of copying. He would be unaffected by the meaning of what he wrote, would not "hear" the words in his head. He would be as much like a machine as possible. In this novel we will have much to do with just such a copier—Krook, more about whom later. In the present case Lady Dedlock recognizes the signs of a particular person's writing—her old lover, Hawdon—even through the otherwise mechanically uniform law-hand. She swoons, Tulkinghorn becomes suspicious, and we are given the secret whose unraveling will power the plot.

Our first direct focus on writing in the novel is a copy of an affidavit, and it is the material document itself rather than its contents—we know only that it concerns Jarndyce and Jarndyce—that matters. With this, Hawdon, the lost lover, is first figured as he will be throughout the story: all but entirely devoiced and deindividualized into the exactitude of writing. Though he is in a way the key to the whole novel, we only ever hear second-hand reports of any of his few spoken words. Woodcourt, from whom Hawdon has bought opium for a year, only knows him "by sight" (106). Krook, who has rented him a room for eighteen months, has hardly ever spoken to him (106). And one of his neighbors declares at the inquest after his death that she had seen "him speak to neither child nor grown person at any time" except Jo (112). He barely keeps himself alive by copying affidavits, which are precise representations of someone else's oral speech and which are legally binding in the way of speaking on oath in court. If the courtroom is a paradigm for the space in which speech is constrained to be most like writing, then an affidavit is the singular case of that space extending itself and its constraints on speech out into the world at large. Although this particular writing involves us in the particular Jarndyce legal case, we are focused on the script rather than the law, that is, we are focused on the technology that enables the law. A copy of an affidavit must not only precisely preserve the content of the original but also work to look exactly like the law-hand of every other copy. Hawdon must do his best to remove any vestige of himself as an individual human being from both the form and the content of this writing. Furthermore, as simply a copyist, he cannot even sign his name to what he has written. He evidently senses his own disappearance into writing, because he advertises his services in Krook's window under the name *Nemo,* or nobody. But in spite of the exactitude of the legal letter, something of his living individuality is visible, at least to Lady Dedlock.

This one document, then, installs into the novel one of the primary conflicts that accompanies the invention of writing as a technology: the conflict between mechanical standardization and human variation. We take such a conflict for granted in modern times, but writing is one of the great inventions in history that first promotes, or even requires, such standardization. Hawdon's case takes us back to just this basic property of writing; the most successful law-hand would directly achieve the implicit goal of the writing lessons we all begin with when we start school. When we are learning to write, we necessarily have a printed visual model of correct script. The best apprentice writer will be the one whose script is least distinguishable from the printed model. It is in this most everyday way that writing as a technology tends to push toward a mechanical uniformity that is unknown and unnecessary to orality. The unavoidable contingencies of bodily variation and lived life of course tend to prevent the achievement of the desired uniformity. But still, the standardizing effect remains and, as we saw with Samuel Johnson, becomes its own end. This said, we must allow that mechanical uniformity, too, has its benefits, one of them being the certainty that all parties in a legal dispute are dealing with exactly the same facts and statements (we must also admit, though, that without writing there simply would not be the kind of law that would require such exactitude in the first place).

The alphabetic qualities of telepathy and permanence also show up in this example. Because of writing, Hawdon can in effect "speak" to Lady Dedlock even though he is far away and will soon be dead. But this is a truly exemplary case. We should not say that his words speak to Lady Dedlock because, even apart from the fact that writing is not speaking, the words were never his. Nothing of him shows in the content. Rather, the purely visible signs of his flesh and blood hand show up in spite of, and in conflict with, the uniformity required by law-hand. The conflict has been preserved in the act of writing; now it occurs in the two opposed acts of reading (Lady Dedlock's and Tulkinghorn's).

A couple of pages later we find a less direct but equally important scene involving writing. Esther recalls being a little girl and reading to her godmother from the Bible. She specifically recalls "reading from St. John, how our Saviour stooped down, writing with his finger in the dust, when they brought the sinful woman to him" (14). The passage ends with the famous line: "He that is without sin among you, let him cast the first stone at her!" With this, her grandmother leaps to her feet, cries out a passage from the gospel of Mark, and dies. I earlier considered this scene from John. To summarize again, Jesus' response to the Pharisees' question about Mosaic Law makes the point that law put into writing can become inhuman, mechanistic, devoid of any living "spirit," not because of the content of the law, but because of the nature of writing.

In the world of *Bleak House* the law has once again begun to operate according to the letter only. Esther's godmother is the religious instance of this. As John Jarndyce says later in the novel, she had been possessed by a "distorted religion which clouded her mind with impressions of the need there was for the child to expiate an offence of which she was quite innocent" (181). This is a version of the repeated Old Testament idea that the sins of the fathers shall be visited upon the sons, a tenet that Jesus indirectly rejects in John 9:12. So this and the image of Jesus writing in the dust distinctly associate the godmother with the idea that the religious letter "killeth." Lastly, just as she dies she shouts out a verse from Mark 13:35 about the coming of the last times, the implication being that she has held to the letter of the Old Testament law and is now paying the price.[1]

However, the secular law is the overwhelming presence in the novel. As Gordon Bigelow has written, in "the course of [*Bleak House*] we are shown every sort of legal work in law offices of every rank, from the chambers of the Lord Chancellor to the garret of a copyist," the entire enterprise consisting largely of "a vast circulation of paper and ink" (594). The Court of Chancery is most thoroughly associated with writing, and in fact seems constructed of little else. From the very first, the sheer volume of written documents—for instance, each of eighteen lawyers is "armed with a little summary of eighteen hundred sheets" (4)—is mentioned over and over again in many different ways. I will mention only two other examples, though there are many more. When Esther, Ada, and Richard follow Miss Flite down the block to Krook's shop for the first time, Esther, not yet aware of the lane's relationship to Chancery, notices all manner of salvaged bottles. When she comes to "ink bottles," she says, "I am reminded by mentioning the latter, that the shop had in several little particulars, the air of being in a legal neighborhood, and of being, as it were, a dirty hanger-on and disowned relation of the law" (38). In the world of *Bleak House*, ink itself immediately calls to mind not just writing in general but the law in particular. When John Jarndyce explains the lawsuit to Esther, he laments that all "through the deplorable cause, everybody must have copies, over and over again, of everything that has accumulated about it in the way of cartloads of papers." There is a constant need for lawyers, one "counsel appearing for A," another "counsel appearing for B; and so on through the whole alphabet" (73). Even the figurative language of the law depends on alphabetography.

Along with the link to writing comes the relationship of Chancery to common law, which takes us again to the relationship of Jesus to Mosaic Law. Ironically, the Chancery Court was originally created to offset the rigidity of the letter of the common law. It emerged in the Middle Ages, when, as Richard Posner writes, the "Lord Chancellors . . . dispensed justice according to conscience rather than strict legal forms" (143). This kind of justice, called equity, "is more flexible, less hidebound and rulebound, than law" (142). Tellingly, Posner writes of "the spirit of equity —the prudent recognition that strict rules of law, however necessary to a well-ordered society, must be applied with sensitivity and tact so that the spirit of the law is not sacrificed unnecessarily to the letter" (109). However, over time the individual actions of the lord chancellors became "institutionalized in the Court of Chancery," and as a result, almost inevitably it would seem, "the court of conscience [became] the nation's worst example of legal abuses" (143). In other words, the original Chancery adjudication had a distinctive relationship to written law. Any given case would certainly have been based on written law, but the chancellor's decisions were important precisely because they did not conform strictly to the letter. The chancellor would decide a case based on the present facts and people, his knowledge of the law, and his conscience. Early on, his decision-making process itself was not constrained by written protocols or rules or procedures and so was always to an extent ad hoc. Indeed, manifestations of the "spirit" in relation to any written law will always be ad hoc because the "spirit" in this usage always has to do with the immediacy of time, place, and embodied human circumstance as opposed to the permanence and disembodiment of the written sign. Over time the ad hoc "spiritual" decisions of the individual chancellors became institutionalized, which necessarily meant regularized in writing. That spirit, once standardized by writing, became in its turn the new letter. The cure slowly became as bad as, or worse than, the disease.[2]

This consideration of Chancery taken in relation to the scene from the Gospel of John reveals an intriguing quality of the ancient letter/spirit dichotomy. In the traditional opposition of letter and spirit (along with, but also apart from, the New Testament usage), the solid actuality of living human beings in a specific place and time is figured as ephemeral and insubstantial (the spirit) in relation to the relatively permanent solidity of the written word. When we speak of the spirit as opposed to the letter of the law, by "spirit" we mean the lost but recoverable sense of the will and intentions of the living human beings who saw fit to put the given rule or law into written form. By "letter" we acknowledge that because writing is "speech" transformed into an object, it is unchanging, solid, and goes off into the world without the signs of will and intention that visibly and audibly accompany vocal speech. The "spirit" in this sense, then, is generally equivalent to the spoken word (with which spirit is connected etymologically as breath, *spiritus*).

Now, the living human world constantly changes from instant to instant, and therefore, like the voice, is in a way ephemeral in relation to writing. And since a living person in some particular context must write any given text, then writing is always an act of solidifying some instant of living, implicitly oral life. To say simply that in this action the letter "kills" the spirit is an evaluative judgment—the complementary opposite of the positive evaluation of writing that we saw with Gronniosaw and Johnson—toward which the difference between writing and speech seems always to push. But this evaluation, like its opposite (that writing is superior to the chaos of speech), is not true to the facts. The preservation of the spirit in writing is in one way analogous to other preservations of things once living: dried fruit, tanned hides, or an embalmed body. What we have is drastically different from the original, but we do have something tangible. Nonetheless, as we have seen with *Frankenstein*, the sense of the letter as somehow lethal is as endemic to literate culture as the sense of the letter's clear superiority to the ephemerality of speech. As we shall see, though, in *Bleak House* the letter both kills and gives life.

The fatal intertwining of writing and the law begun in the first chapters culminates most pointedly and poignantly much later, when Esther visits Richard after Woodcourt has told her how bound up Richard is with the lawsuit. She finds Richard "poring over a table covered with dusty bundles of papers which seemed . . . like dusty mirrors reflecting his own mind" (526). If the pages are mirrors reflecting Richard's mind, then his mind is figured as an image of the written page, for that is what she must literally see. Our attention is drawn only to the material objects rather than to any specific written contents. And the papers are the only objects mentioned during this visit or the later ones, after Ada has moved in with Richard (619), as if there is no other materiality to Richard's life. The longer Esther talks with him, the more she sees that he is forcing himself to be hopeful about the suit. What she sees in his face changes from the initial image of the mirror. Now she sees a "commentary upon" his forced optimism "indelibly written in his handsome face . . . I say indelibly; for I felt persuaded that if the fatal cause could have been terminated, according to his brightest visions, in that same hour, the traces" of its effects "would have remained on his features to the hour of his death" (527). Richard's face has become the writing surface itself, and the writing is permanent. In the earlier image of conflict between Hawdon's original hand and the letter of law-hand, his flesh at least remained free enough to make its mark in the writing; now the writing marks its presence in the flesh.

II

These examples, then, show us how, although the legal system is the apparent focus of the novel, it is writing—the technological sine qua non of such a system—that is the truly debilitating force in human affairs. We are distinctly in the realm of "the letter killeth." Now, what about the problem of literacy, which, like the law, is an obvious issue in the novel? Literacy is always involved with writing, but the technological nature of writing is usually not considered when literacy is under discussion. Often this will not matter, but as we shall see, it does matter for *Bleak House*.

In *Bleak House* Dickens gives us two major figures of illiteracy: Jo and Krook. From our first introduction, when Jo is summoned to the inquest into the death of "Nemo," he is presented from two related but distinctively different literate perspectives: literacy in relation to the law, and literacy in general. In both cases he is presented as somehow not quite a full human being—which brings us once again to Johnson, whose scorn for "those who cannot read" (Johnson, 75) was mirrored in Gronniosaw's experience of not being accepted as fully human. At the inquest, we are told that Jo doesn't know about home, his own name, his own origins; doesn't know the origins of the knowledge that he does have. He has no sense of a larger order of ideas, such as the morality of truth in relation to falsehood, and therefore no sense of negative consequences being anything other than what should naturally happen. For instance, he knows it is wicked to lie and that to lie brings negative consequences. He "can't exactly say what'll be done to him arter he's dead if he tells a lie . . . but believes it'll be something wery bad to punish him, and serve him right —so he'll tell the truth" (113). His other deficiencies aside, the coroner rejects Jo as a witness because "'Can't exactly say' won't do. . . . We can't take *that*, in a Court of Justice, gentlemen. It's terrible depravity" (113). Poor Jo is "depraved" because he lacks the literate sense of precision upon which the law is based. Now, the narrator relates this scene with great irony throughout. He is clearly making fun of the coroner, the jurymen, and the entire business of the official inquest, in much the same way as he does all of legal officialdom throughout the novel. So in this case we may take it that the narrator is not presenting his own opinion of Jo's condition. Rather, everything about Jo in this scene has been presented from the perspective of these particular officials.

But our next encounter with Jo is significantly different. In the "Tom-All-Alone's" chapter the narrator discusses the "connections" that could possibly bring together the various segments of London culture. He turns at this point to a generalized (not only legal) excursus on Jo's illiteracy (168). In this passage the literate narrator sets out to imagine Jo from the inside, to imagine what it must be like to be illiterate. As a result we learn as much about what the narrator assumes of literacy—his own internal, normative state—as about what he imagines of illiteracy. Once again, reading the passage requires a close attention to the narrator's use of irony. For instance, he begins, "It must be a strange state to be like Jo!" We can sense the hyperbole, the overdramatization. Looking at Jo from the literate perspective, the narrator seems to be willfully exaggerating the difference between illiteracy and literacy. From that perspective, to be illiterate is to "shuffle through the streets, unfamiliar with the shapes, and in utter darkness as to the meaning, of those mysterious symbols, so abundant over the shops, and at the corners of the streets, and on the doors, and in the windows!" (168). Illiteracy affects not just the mind but also the body: the very activity of walking is reduced to a "shuffle" for those who cannot read. To the illiterate as imagined from the literate perspective, written signs have to do with both light and darkness. Jo can see the signs all around him, just as any literate citizen can see them. But for the literate person these signs light up automatically with meaning. The result is that, for Jo, even utterly mundane signs are as mysterious as nature-spirits are to an animist; in a sense, Jo can only see the material letters, not the spirit of meaning. With this imagery the irony is not quite so plain. It is hard to be sure whether this is hyperbole or simply the way the narrator imagines Jo to be.

We continue on, to find that Jo can see "people read, and . . . people write," but he is "stone blind and dumb" to "all that language." Writing "speaks" visually, but Jo, blind and in darkness, sees only objects instead of representations of oral words; he has no "voice" with which to speak in return. The narrator imagines Jo watching people with Bibles on their way to church. Jo must be puzzled "to think (for perhaps Jo *does* think, at odd times) what does it all mean, and if it means anything to anybody, how comes it that it means nothing to me?" (168). Jo, being human, necessarily thinks; so the hyperbole in the parenthesis at this point seems to work as irony. We have the sense that the narrator wants to chastise and correct those who scorn the illiterate as somehow subhuman. And just when this moralistic attitude seems surest, the narration slips from the third person to the first person, as if the narrator's sympathy has brought him into some kind of closer identity with Jo. Speaking as "I" now, the narrator wonders how "everybody overlooked me until I became the creature that I am!" The implication is that society is responsible for Jo's illiteracy and its consequences.

But then we read that it "must be a strange state, not merely to be told that I am scarcely human (as in the case of my offering myself for a witness), but to feel it of my own knowledge all of my life!" Whatever Jo himself might think or feel, the narrator, imagining himself as Jo, takes it that illiteracy automatically entails an interior sense of being subhuman, apart from what literate culture may directly say about such a condition. It is hard to see how this attitude can be ironic in the same way as the hyperbole just mentioned, especially because more of the same follows. The narrator imagines Jo seeing "horses, dogs, and cattle" going by, and knowing that "in ignorance I belong to them, and not to the superior beings in my shape, whose delicacy I offend!" To the literate mind, the illiterate person identifies more with animals than literate human beings. The animal connection now takes over the narrator's imagination entirely. He thinks of Jo beginning his day. As the town awakes, "all that unaccountable reading and writing, which has been suspended for a few hours, recommences. Jo, and the other lower animals, get on in the unintelligible mess as they can" (169). Reading and writing seem to have become all of waking life for the literate, and therefore life itself is an unknowable chaos for the illiterate and the animals. As the morning progresses, Jo and a sheepdog listen to music. The dog is "an educated, improved, developed dog, who has been taught his duties" by his master "and knows how to discharge them." Once again we have an ironic commentary on the failures of society to provide education, something even the dog has had from his master. But then the dog and "Jo listen to the music, probably with much the same amount of animal satisfaction; likewise, as to awakened association, aspiration or regret, melancholy or joyful reference to things beyond the senses, they are probably on a par. But, otherwise, how far above the human listener is the brute!" (169).

Here again, it is hard to see how the irony works in accord with a sense of moral outrage. In other words, the narrator is outraged that society has produced such a person; but this seems to be the narrator's actual opinion of the status of that person, as if illiteracy really does entail a condition of subhumanity. Evidently, the brute is superior to the human listener because he has at least been educated to follow orders successfully. But if we turn "that dog's descendents wild, like Jo," then, "in a very few years they will so degenerate that they will lose even their bark —but not their bite" (169). Without education by a master, dogs will eventually become as Jo is now. The outcome for society at large, which must mean literate culture, will be dangerous. Unlike, presumably, a literate lower class, an illiterate lower class will possibly turn on its masters and, though deprived of a voice by illiteracy, still be able to do damage.

To sum up, the narrator expresses a sense of moral outrage at the failure of society to teach all its citizens to read and write, which is, given the context of a literate culture, in itself a good thing. But the idea that being human is only possible for those who can read and write is something else again. In clear contradiction to the earlier biblical allusion, the letter now gives human life, and the "spirit" seems to be only available to the literate. To equate full humanity with literacy in this way is a truly pernicious conflation of writing and spoken language, especially because the power of writing has often induced even those who are illiterate to accept the value judgments that come with the conflation. We are taken directly back to the case of Gronniosaw. The narrator, then, is thoroughly and unwittingly caught up in the ongoing conflict in, and of, writing. On the one hand, he obviously sympathizes with Jo and feels that leaving Jo out of literacy is an inexcusable social failing. But on the other hand, though he apparently does not know it, he himself must take writing to be what speech actually is in human life—the verbal ability that is fundamental to our species—and as a result he takes Jo to be less than human.

In contrast to the young, entirely illiterate Jo, we have another dweller in the precincts of Chancery, old Krook. Both "Jo and Krook . . . live in a world in which signifiers are forever unreadable" (Lougy, 483); but though Krook is illiterate, still, he "writes." Krook, "Lord Chancellor of the Rag and Bottle shop" (337), is figured as the parodic opposite of the real lord chancellor, and accordingly is much involved with writing and documents. He has been designated lord chancellor by his neighbors because of, among other things, his large stock of "old parchmentses [sic] and papers" (40). We have already mentioned the prominence of ink in his shop. Weevle says of Krook that "it's a monomania with him, to think he is possessed of documents" even though he can read none of them (345). But along with these details we regularly see Krook "writing," that is, copying out letters. This begins with the bizarre scene in which Krook chalks out the names *Jarndyce* and *Bleak House* on the wall for Esther. To the literate Esther, he has a "very curious manner" of writing, "beginning with the end of the letter, and shaping it backward" in law-hand style. He will write only one letter at a time, spelling out the words "without once leaving two letters on the wall together" (44). He must have Esther's verbal verification of each letter as he goes, because, he says, he has "a turn for copying from memory" but in fact "can neither read nor write" (44).

Later, we learn why he will only write one letter at a time. As Krook is spontaneously combusting, Weevle tells Guppy that, try as he might, Krook will "never read. He can make all the letters separately, and he knows most of them separately when he sees them . . . but he can't put them together. He's too old to acquire the knack of it now" (342). What exactly does Krook know? He can link a vocal sound with its visual sign to the extent that with most letters he can speak their oral equivalent correctly on sight. He can hold at least some whole words in visual memory, but not really as words in the alphabetic sense. Rather, they are mental pictures of clumps of letters, and because he lacks confidence in his actual command of each letter, he will not trust himself to write more than one letter at a time. He cannot himself generate written whole words out of his own mind and body. He is, then, stuck at the first step of literacy, like a schoolchild having just learned by rote his ABC's but not yet having learned how alphabetic signs work. This puts him closer to literacy than is Jo. Accordingly, though he is closely associated with his malicious cat and generally characterized by animal imagery, there is no sign that the narrator himself sees Krook as subhuman in the way of Jo.

Also unlike Jo, Krook has a sense of the need to be literate. During another trip to the shop, this time with John Jarndyce along, Krook is discovered trying to teach himself to read and write. Jarndyce asks if it would not be easier to be taught by someone else. "Aye," Krook replies, "but they might teach me wrong! . . . I don't know what I may have lost, by not being learned afore. I wouldn't like to lose anything by being learned wrong now" (153). Krook has already absorbed to the letter, so to speak, both the literate sense of the absolute importance of writing as well as the alphabetic sense of exactitude, and as a result he is caught in a parodic double bind that prevents him from becoming literate. He has confused the kind of precision that writing enables (or requires) with writing itself. Though he shares Jo's inexactness in one way—he "can't exactly say" what he has lost—nonetheless he has a notion of a precise thing in the world, "writing," which, if not learned exactly correctly, will cost him grievously and in ways he cannot even know. Humans are neither adequately precise nor trustworthy to teach him in the correct way, which again, paradoxically, is an alphabetic understanding of human beings: compared to the precision of the technology, human minds and bodies are hopelessly undependable. Therefore, he cannot trust anyone else to teach him exactly the thing itself. On the one hand, writing is, relative to speech, thoroughly noncommunal, even isolating. But on the other hand, being a technology (and unlike speech), it must be systematically taught, and so the learning of it necessarily involves other human beings as conscious instructors. Krook is committed to ruling out the one distinctly interactive aspect of writing. Like his own manner of writing letters, he is an inverted, backward case, embodying the most inhuman qualities of writing along with being illiterate.[3]

The relationship between Jo and Krook as images of illiteracy continues most intriguingly with their respective deaths. In the long and dramatic scene in which Jo is dying, he feels guilty about having infected Esther with smallpox. He asks if Snagsby, the stationer, is "able to write wery large p'rhaps" (490). When Snagsby says yes, Jo asks him to "write out, wery large so that any one could see it anywheres, as that I was truly wery hearty sorry that I done it" (490). Jo is asking for an epitaph in a specific kind of law-hand, which we have encountered earlier in the novel. Nemo had advertised himself as "a respectable man aged forty-five [who wants] engrossing or copying to execute with neatness and dispatch" (38). To engross meant, at least until 1875 (the last citation in the *Oxford English Dictionary*), to write out in law-hand in very large letters. Jo's dying wish is to be "engrossed" in writing, which Snagsby agrees to do. Further, as Jo actually expires, we return to imagery that we have encountered before. Things begin to turn "wery dark," Jo says, and then asks, "Is there any light a-comin?" (492). This is of course the very traditional imagery of the heavenly light that follows the darkness of this life. But then, just after Jo's last word, from the Lord's Prayer, the narrator tells us that the "light is come upon that dark benighted way" (492). With the narrator's prior vision of Jo wandering the streets in the "utter darkness" of illiteracy and Jo's own dying desire to be inscribed into enlarged law-hand, it is as if he has died into the glowing heaven of writing, where presumably he finally becomes fully human.

If Jo expires into the heavenly light of writing, Krook and the letters with which he is so strongly identified combust into hellish cinders. As Weevle and Guppy come to Krook's room at midnight in search of Hawdon's letters, the imagery of evil and decay is all around: the "snarling" cat, the "smouldering suffocating vapour," the "dark greasy coating on the walls and ceiling" (346). Weevle recalls his last sight of Krook, "turning the letters over in his hand." Not just the letters, but the tools of the copier's trade are specifically mentioned, for Weevle spies on the floor "a dirty bit of thin cord that they tie up pens with. That went round the letters" and has survived the combustion that destroyed the copyist. They soon discover two piles of ash: one a single piece of bone, the other some "tinder from a little bundle of burnt paper . . . seeming to be steeped in something" (346). The paper letters and Krook's entire body appear to have been roughly equal as combustible substances. Though we are not told what exactly the, to Krook, unreadable letters must have been steeped in, it appears that they were somehow the cause of the combustion, which would be the strongest case of "the letter killeth" in this novel.

The narrator ends this scene with one of the most declamatory of his several declamatory speeches. This lord chancellor, he claims, "true to his title in his last act, has died the death of all Lord Chancellors in all Courts, and of all authorities in all places under all names soever, where false pretences are made, and where injustice is done" (346). Now, though Krook has all along been presented as a pretty nasty character, he is, as others have noted, "actually fairly harmless" (Hack, 136). He can hardly be seen as an authority figure; and the only thing he has actually done that could have to do with false pretences or injustice would be taking the letters from Hawdon's room, refusing to bring them forward at the inquest, and trying to sell them for profit. In Krook's favor, though, Hawdon had once said Krook was "the nearest relation he had," and Hawdon died owing Krook six weeks' rent (106). The phrase "last act" is a bit ambiguous. It could refer to the spontaneous combustion or, more likely, to the plan to sell the letters. Either way, the obscure, illiterate copyist who would make a petty profit from someone else's personal writings is equated with the immense social evil of the Chancery Court. The only significant qualities Krook and the law actually share are their obsession with writing and documents. So Krook seems to be who he is in the novel simply because of his relationship to writing. Illiteracy, then, involves being subhuman, on the one hand, and just plain demonic, on the other. Whatever Dickens' conscious intentions, with these two figures he has rather perfectly captured literate culture's conflicted attitudes about the communications technology by which it defines itself.

❧III

To investigate writing and our third major category—written story—we turn to Esther's narrative. Much has been said about the double-narrative structure of *Bleak House*.[4] Because I am concentrating on writing itself, I will be concerned only with Esther's narrative, but she as a narrator is necessarily contrasted with the narrator of the other chapters. That narrator is presented rhetorically as an entirely classic written version of an oral storyteller, very much in the tradition of, say, *Tom Jones*. Such a teller combines both a first-person sense of personality and a third-person sense of omniscience. If we compare this to oral story, we can see why this narrator would be so appealing. In the default scene of human storytelling we always have a living, embodied narrator physically before us in full possession of the story. This means we have the "first-person" regardless of whether the teller actually uses the word *I* in a given telling or not. As discussed in chapter 1, in the act of conforming story to writing, early novelists worked to compensate for the loss of that embodied telling by presenting as personable and distinctive a first-person teller as possible. They felt little conflict, at least early on, between staging the narrator as an identifiable first-person speaker and as having a godlike knowledge of the story world. Over time, though, as story conformed more and more to the technology, this manner of telling was superseded (though it never disappeared entirely) by the notion of story as "untold" report, story in which signs of the teller are reduced as much as possible.

With these ideas in mind, we can read *Bleak House* as an intriguingly mixed case. It combines an image of a teller who is ostensibly speaking directly to the reader and an image of a teller (Esther) who is plainly beset by the necessities of writing her story. The unnamed (unless we simply accept the narrator as Dickens) omniscient narrator is presented as being entirely self-confident, opinionated, sarcastic, witty, and oratorically grand. He never says anything at all about the fact that he must be writing his words rather than speaking them; the illusion of an oral teller is maintained from start to finish. Esther is the opposite in all ways. She tells both her story and the story of writing her story. First let us examine Esther's telling and then consider the effects of this mixed case as a whole.

As Chris Vanden Bossche has noted, Esther is "agent of her own narrative self-making" (26) in the sense that she at least has the ability to write out her own story. But this agency is forced upon her by the requirements of putting her story into writing. Very much unlike the other narrator, Esther experiences a distinct lack of authority, at least at first. She begins by telling us she has a "great deal of difficulty in beginning to write my portion of these pages, for I know I am not clever" (11). Interestingly, she backs up this self-deprecation with the story of being a child and talking to her doll. The doll had a "beautiful complexion," like Esther before her illness, and would sit "staring at me—or not so much at me, I think, as at nothing—while I busily stitched away, and told her every one of my secrets" (11). It seems odd for an adult woman to claim she "thinks" a doll was staring at nothing, but a confusion of the child Esther and nothing is suggested, as if there were little difference between them. Esther would always begin the "conversation" by saying outright: "I am not clever," but because her "secrets" were only the details of her day away at school, it is not so easy to see what cleverness would have been involved. Still, this is the memory she chooses to help illustrate her present predicament as a grown woman and a writer.

To explain her lack of alphabetic cleverness she gives us an image of a kind of oral diary. As a child she had felt a sense of not being clever even when reporting to an obviously nonjudgmental, imitation-human about the day's affairs. Where must the sense of inadequacy have come from? We have to conclude that the little girl was projecting onto the doll something of her Old Testamentary godmother, who was the only other person in her life and was nothing if not judgmental. And then we must conclude that even now, as an adult of twenty-six, on some level the unknown "audience" to whom she writes must in her mind still be like the doll, carrying the disapproving weight of the godmother and seeing Esther as "nothing." Esther is now setting out to do in writing as an adult what she did orally as a child, and with much the same sense of inadequacy. Right here at the beginning, she conflates written story and oral story.

Later in this first of Esther's chapters she interrupts her story. "It seems so curious to me," she says, "to be obliged to write all this about myself! As if this were the narrative of *my* life! But my little body will soon fall into the background now" (20). Having to accommodate her story to writing is producing a couple of entwined effects here: both the problem of arbitrariness and the necessity to tell in detail because writing cannot show. We can see that Esther writes "with an air of having been commissioned or compelled to narrate" (Buzard, 25), but she seems also to think of herself as having to write somebody else's life story, as if she were a biographer. At this point it is not so clear who else that could be, and it does not become altogether clear even after we have met the other main characters: Ada? Lady Dedlock? John Jarndyce? Everyone she mentions? In any case she feels surprised and uncomfortable about having to include herself so much in someone else's story. The implication is that someone might accuse her of arbitrarily and therefore selfishly turning the focus on herself when, evidently, the story is supposed to be about someone else. It appears that in growing up she has added to the little-girl sense of inadequacy about not being clever: with the doll she did not feel any hesitation about making herself the focus of the story, as she does now.

One reason for this change is the other side of the arbitrariness problem. A storyteller will always have to provide at least some context for a story, but the more intimately the teller knows the audience, and the closer the physical proximity of their lives, the less context will typically be necessary. Little Esther, imagining the doll as an actual member of the household, could set the context for the doll just as she could for a sister or a mother. She would have only to say, for instance, "this morning at school the teacher . . ."; and time, place, and two major characters, Esther and her teacher, would be thoroughly established without any further elaboration. But generally a storywriter can have no such intimacy or proximity to the reader. Therefore, a much more elaborate setting of context is often required simply to make the subject or focus of the story understandable. To get her story into written form Esther has been required to go on at length about herself in order to set the context for what she takes to be the story of others, something that as an oral storyteller she did not have to do. Still, she takes some relief from knowing that soon her "little body" will disappear into the "nothing" observed by the doll. Her surprise with all this shows that she is still operating under the basic idea of an oral story, even though she is writing. And of course only an oral story could involve her "little body" (as opposed to just the hand) at all. But at the same time if it were actually a case of oral story, her body could not possibly fade into the background because it is the source of the narration. She is conflating the written content about her with her embodied self, as if they are the same thing. As we have seen before, in itself this conflation would not usually be of consequence, but in this novel the consequences are significant.

The next meta-narrative interjection comes right after the scene with Mrs. Pardiggle and the illiterate brickmaker's family. Esther begins her chapter:

> I don't know how it is, I seem to be always writing about myself. I mean all the time to write about other people, and I try to think about myself as little as possible, and I am sure, when I find myself coming into the story again, I am really vexed and say, "Dear dear, you tiresome little creature, I wish you wouldn't!" but it is all of no use. I hope anyone who may read what I write, will understand that if these pages contain a great deal about me, I can only suppose it must be because I have really something to do with them, and can't be kept out. (85)

The problem is much the same as before, but now her sense of it has changed. Although she still seems to think in terms of her exchanges with the doll—the "Dear, dear" quote is very much the tone and language she used with the doll in her first chapter—now she no longer seems to be unconsciously figuring her reader as the doll. Rather, she now figures herself as both the teller and the doll listener, which, since a doll cannot hear, was the actual case in the childhood scene. She overtly acknowledges an anonymous but real, literate reader out in the world ("anyone who may read"). Before, she felt an obligation to write about herself, and it was so unexpected that it only struck her as curious and surprising, an anomaly that would quickly go away. Now, since her "little body" has not fallen into the background after all, she begins to consider the situation. She feels vexed because the written version of her own memories of other people is requiring her to write things she does not want to write. But the more she has written, the more the story has taken on the kind of distancing that writing regularly brings; and the more she can step back and observe it as removed object. In a way she herself has become one of "anyone who may read." In doing this she has been forced to take the side of the written story's requirements against her own interior sense of her own memories. The writing has now convinced her against her wishes (she "can only suppose") that she must in fact be central to the story. She does not say "cannot be left out" but says "cannot be kept out"; her first narrative motivation has been to forcibly keep herself out, but the external force of written story has overcome her desire.

Later, Esther inserts this kind of authorial commentary again, just after passing a negative judgment on Richard's failings. "I write down these opinions, not because I believe that this or any other thing was so, because I thought so; but only because I did think so, and I want to be quite candid about all I thought and did" (173). We have once again the unexplained sense of some obligation to be writing all this out in the first place, even when it requires her to say negative things about other people. But the act of writing has led Esther to accept that she is important to the story: she no longer feels uneasy in the spotlight. The act of writing also requires her to imagine her words going out into the world to "anyone who may read," without her little body to inflect them. She worries about a censorious reader, one who will object to this kind of negative judgment. The phrasing of this passage again makes it sound as if Esther thinks of herself as writing some kind of factual history. To be exact, the phrasing sounds like an affidavit. If she thought of herself as writing fiction, then she would not have this concern at all. She is worried that her opinions will be taken as statements of objective fact or as, we might say, the law. And as if she were on oath, she feels the need for full disclosure, not just of the letter of the written content, but of the spirit of her immediate motivations for writing.

The written narrative requires her to go against her wishes again later. She pauses in the story of her recovery at Mr. Boythorn's. "I had better mention in this place," she writes, the event of Hortense offering to be her maid (242). Why "had better"? Why the sense of obligation? She says nothing negative about Hortense in the scene, so the requirement is not the same as the previous ones. Indeed, this is the most purely alphabetic obligation so far. The only reason to feel the need to mention this scene is so that the reader will understand the meaning of later, negative events. Without this preparation, the murder of Tulkinghorn will seem to have come from nowhere, to be a deus ex machina. Including this information at this time shows that, though she accedes to the requirements of the written story, she has not yet fully given herself over to the written from the oral mode. If she were in full writer mode, she would insert the scene with Hortense but would have no need to justify it with the "had better." For a writer, it would just be the normal way to tell the story.

As her writing progresses, Esther becomes ever more accustomed to the realization that she is writing in general and that she is writing her own story in particular. She also slowly loses the sense of the negatively judgmental "anyone who may read." She becomes so self-assured that, no longer worried about full disclosure, she willfully withholds, and admits to withholding, information from her reader. After reading of Woodcourt's "gallant deeds" as a sailor, she writes: "And now I must part with the little secret I have thus far tried to keep," that she had hoped, before illness disfigured her face, to be loved by him (380). With this, we can see how much she has changed since that first insecurity about not being clever. This confidence shows up again a few pages later when she holds back some of her mother's letter from the reader: "What more the letter told me, needs not to be repeated here. It has its own times and places in my story" (389). The earlier sense of full candor about the story seems to have given way to a judicious, authoritative sense of confidence; and now, rather than keeping the rest of the letter an entire secret, she says right out that she will decide when its contents should be revealed. This is the first time she has used the phrase "my story." The writing has by this point convinced her that this is her story instead of the one she had originally set out to write.

In Esther's last comment about her own writing we read: "The few words that I have to add to what I have written, are soon penned; then I, and the unknown friend to whom I write, will part for ever. Not without much dear remembrance on my side. Not without some, I hope, on his or hers" (663). In the classic manner of a memoir, Esther finishes in the present moment. Her language about parting figures the friend as having been in one way or another in her actual presence during the writing, but at the same time invisible and unknowable on the other "side" of the script. She expects she will have dear remembrance of that unknown friend, even though there is no way for this to be literally the case. She must mean (whether she realizes it or not) that she will have a dear memory of the feeling of companionship generated by the act of writing the story. We have an example in which occupying both sides of the communicative interaction operates quite positively. The writer's audience, as Walter Ong has written, is always a fiction (1977, 53–82). Over the course of this story that audience has changed. But since the audience has been a fiction, it must be that Esther has changed and that she has experienced that change as if it were happening to someone else. As we have seen, earlier the imagined reader was evidently harshly judgmental (like her godmother) about any mention in general of herself, and then especially about her own critical judgments of others. But the act of having to conform her personal memories and opinions to the requirements of written story has changed her as an individual, the paradoxical sign of which is the change in the "reader" of her writing. For Esther, writing has been therapeutic. It has brought her from the infantilized victim of her abusive godmother to someone who, on the last page, can write "Me" twice with a capital, in the middle of a sentence, and without explanation or shame (665).

With Esther's "story" we have yet another take on writing in *Bleak House*, one that seems altogether positive after the lives and deaths of Jo and Krook, and of Hawdon and Richard. But having noted all this we need to step back and consider how this therapy has worked, for it has been definitively literate: individualized, noncommunal, nonvocal, disembodied. It is hard to imagine a possible corollary for this particular kind of psychological process in a purely oral cultural setting. We have to wonder, given the nature of writing as it appears in both the world at large and in this novel, whether, or at least to what extent, Esther could have undergone this change without writing. We must conclude that although she was necessarily disembodying her spirit into the writing, the writing itself at the same time inspirited her anew, and in such a way that she could thrive in the social world around her.

"Thrive," however, hardly captures Esther's success. Even allowing for her scarred face and the tragic death of Richard, Dickens still gives us as rosy and sweet (or saccharine, depending on one's taste) a Victorian ending as he ever wrote. In contrast to the linkages of writing and death earlier, it seems that Esther has written herself directly into a living, material version of the heaven that illiterate Jo could only get to by dying. Unlike Hawdon and Richard (not to mention the Pharisees), she has conformed herself to the letter of writing without dehumanizing herself. So it appears that at least in written story, letter and spirit can work together dialectically instead of in simple opposition. Still, as always, this is both good and bad: good that, given the nature of literate culture, there exists a writing that can be therapeutic rather than lethal; but bad that human life should have ever come to the point of needing or requiring such therapy in the first place.

Taking all this together, *Bleak House* seems to have enacted its own version of the scene from the gospel of John. Dickens both condemns the letter, but gives us right here in the text the image of the letter as saving rather than only killing. Considering the novel as a whole, the unnamed narrator casts the first stone at writing; but Esther is the writing in the sand.

CHAPTER FIVE

The De-Composition of Writing
in *A Passage to India*

W E HAVE SEEN already that the conflicted relationships between orality and writing, between oral story and alphabetic story, show up in novels otherwise quite different from one another. With E. M. Forster's *A Passage to India* added to our sample we may begin to feel ever more secure in our sense that, as a genre, the novel is of its nature distinctively bound up with this conflict. And we may also begin to feel more secure with a general conclusion that this conflict will often underlie other important conflicts. This last certainly holds true with *A Passage to India*. I choose this great novel in part just because it has so often been examined in terms of its concern with the nature of language. To name only a few examples, essays by Malcolm Bradbury, Molly Tinsley, David Dowling, Doreen D'Cruz, John Colmer, Michael Orange, and Robert Barratt discuss language in the novel. And it hardly needs arguing that Forster himself was thinking deeply about issues of language as he wrote. But typically in critical discussions, writing and oral speech are lumped together with little regard for the significance of their empirical and historical differences, and in nearly every case the poststructuralist understanding of writing frames the interpretation. For this reason *A Passage to India* provides a particularly strong example of how the present consideration of writing and speech can offer new insights into already-studied texts.

 I

It has of course been noticed that *A Passage to India* gives us "unbridgeable divide[s]" not just "between British and Indian cultures" but between various factions of Indians as well (Armstrong, 377). But the divides between British and Indian are consistently represented in certain ways that are not common to the divides between the Indians. The more firmly we keep these divides in mind, the less likely we are to derive inaccurate generalizations about such large categories as literature, language, civilization. For instance, Doreen D'Cruz shows how conflicts in conversational exchanges thematize a general "inadequacy of language" (195). But I would argue that sense of inadequacy is peculiar to the British, not a general case. Our distinction of alphabetic and oralistic will help us be more specific with such conclusions.

We begin with a look at key issues that seem on the surface rather far removed from the effects of writing. Early on, a primary distinction between British visitor, Anglo-Indian, and Indian appears in two opposed notions of the public and the private. On the surface, this opposition simply has to do with senses of physical space: by British standards domestic privacy, for example, hardly exists in India. But Forster gives this opposition most notably in terms with which we are now familiar: the oralistic and the alphabetic.

In chapter 2 we meet native Indians in their own environs, apart from the physical presence of the British. Right away, Aziz, the main Indian character, is characterized as enthralled by the poetries of the Indian subcontinent. He spontaneously launches into a verbal recitation before his friends, who "listened delighted, for they took the public view of poetry, not the private which obtains in England. It never bored them to hear words, words; they breathed them with the cool night air, never stopping to analyze" (12). As mentioned earlier, poetry—historically closely aligned with music, chant, and the speaking voice—is in some ways the preeminent and original form of oral literature. Fielding will, toward the end of the novel, mention that Aziz had used poetry as "incantation" (308), and perhaps that is just the word for the recital and its effect. From the way Forster brings in this and similar, later scenes, he seems especially intent on the idea of oral performance itself and on the engagement of embodied emotions through literature that both shows and tells rather than on any particular content. Even though he mentions specific poets, he does not include quotes of the verses. Thus, our first image of the Indians includes this archetypal tableau of oral performance and the communion it creates. Though the scene invokes an oral archetype, the group is entirely literate, trained, in fact, in British-style schools. Nonetheless,

Forster makes a very distinct point of putting them in this scene and describing them in these ways. And he both directly and indirectly sets all this in opposition to the British, who will later be associated with prose (160, 256).

The "public view" of literature clearly means oral literature, and contrasts with literature that is read in private. The mention of boredom takes us back to our earlier claims about the issue of oralistic versus alphabetic notions of the "same." It appears that Aziz is performing works already known to the listeners—which would raise the possibility of boredom—and that in spite of this (and unlike the British), they do not get bored. Aziz is necessarily showing with his voice and body as he tells, so there can have been no performance quite like this one before. In line with this Forster stresses the hearing, not just of content, but also of the spoken sounds in the air: "words, words." The bodies of all are actively involved, as they are said to "breathe" rather than only to hear the words. The "text" is pointedly not something to be analyzed in the way that alphabetic readers will do: by "stopping" the experience of the performance. No one feels the call to step apart from their emotional involvement in the text in order to make rational judgments about it. The nostalgia of the narrator for this ancient literary mode—now lost to the British—is apparent. The Indians are nostalgic as well, but for a time in history rather than a kind of literature. Experiencing the poetry as a public telling, "they regained their departed greatness by hearing its departure lamented" (12).

Later, Aziz is on his sickbed, being visited by his Indian friends. Once more, he recites a poem. It has "no connection with anything that had gone before" in their conversation, "but it came from his heart and spoke to theirs" (113). The stress on the random eruption of the poem again pushes the divide between the oralistic Indians and the hyperliterate narrator. In the same way that conversation, when judged by the standards of writing, can veer and switch by whim or impulse, the poem simply appears. Only the narrator notices this. To the Indians it is simply the normal way of talking. And because the recitation is oral, Aziz achieves the kind of intimate communication that is impossible with writing. Aziz's very "heart," the central organ of his physical body, "speaks" to the hearts of his friends. And although, except for Hamidullah, Aziz's listeners have no particular appreciation for poetry, nonetheless "they listened with pleasure, because literature had not been divorced from their civilization. The police inspector, for instance, did not feel that Aziz had degraded himself by reciting, nor break into the cheery guffaw with which an Englishman averts the infection of beauty. . . . The poem had done no 'good' to anyone, but it was a passing reminder, a breath from the divine lips of beauty" (114).

In India, unlike England, civilization and "literature" still form a kind of matrimony, a sacrosanct union, as if one could not exist fully without the other. This notion of "literature" must go back to oralistic literature. Literature is woven into the life of oral culture in ways that it cannot be woven into the life of literate and especially hyperliterate cultures. The strong, literate distinctions between poetry, story, history, myth, and religion only become possible once there is writing. Otherwise, literature is all these things at once. The implication is that at some time in the past this matrimony was also true of England. In India, still oralistic in spite of literacy, the recitation is pleasurable even to the most unlikely of people: the representative of law enforcement (the "police inspector"). Furthermore, in the narrator's mind the poem retains a kind of sheer fleshly authenticity because it is put to no political or moral or other utilitarian purpose. It does "no good to anyone" beyond a kind of communal rapture inspired directly in the listening audience (114).

Each of these examples has to do with a definitively alphabetic nostalgia, a nostalgia that underwrites well-known romantic and modernist images of the "primitive." We have a straightforward positive valuation of the kind of communality and intimacy that literate cultures perceive as what-has-been-lost in becoming, precisely, literate. The narrator feels this nostalgia while fully aware that the sense of communion lasts only as long as the poetic event itself. The antagonisms of class, religion, and politics resume almost at once. In a way, though, this makes more sacred the act that can, for however brief a time, create such unity.

On the other hand, it matters to see the other side of this value judgment. The very "divine" beauty that literate culture has lost, but that oral culture retains, is also perceived by literate culture as an "infection," an esthetic disease. We have not really seen this valuation of orality in our study so far. In *Bleak House*, Dickens made the case that illiteracy reduces humans to animals, that a right-thinking literate culture ought to be ashamed of (and anxious about) this, and that something should be done about the problem. But in Forster's novel the conflicts between orality and literacy are not really of the kind that can be resolved by social programs or political policies. In fact, this story is particularly intriguing because of the way it brings out the other side of the demonic vision of writing that we have seen in *Frankenstein* and *Bleak House.*

From the literate perspective, oral literature as well as orality more generally are at times mythically positive; they possess an original authenticity lost to the workings of an invented technology. This would be the necessary opposite to any vision of writing as demonic or corrupting. But at other times oral literature and orality are seen as mythically negative: savage, uncivilized, primitive, etc.; Samuel Johnson's sense of speech in relation to writing invokes this valuation. At still other times, as in *A Passage to India,* they are seen both ways at once. In other words, the "beauty" in the quote above, like beauty in general, is positive and desirable; but it is also negative. Since orality is the default nature of human life, then the beauty of oral literature is the original literary beauty. Evidently, in the transformation from oralistic to alphabetic culture, that beauty sooner or later transforms into an infection, or to use the other term, sooner or later gets divorced from its original culture as that culture becomes more alphabetic. An infection occurs when the body is invaded by invisible carriers of disease. But while the image figures oralistic beauty as a biological threat to the literate cultural body, it also figures it as a social-psychological threat, something that can be averted by laughing at it instead of taking it seriously. Plainly, literate culture is *dis-eased,* if not diseased, by oralistic literature. Why should this be?

To begin to answer this question, we turn to the key passage concerning one of the novel's major themes: "invitations." Once again Indians are physically apart from the British. Turton, the Collector, has sent written invitations to a select group of Indians to attend a "bridge party." The Indians, without Aziz this time, discuss the meaning of, and possible responses to, the invitation. The setting is a "little room near the Courts" (32). As we have already seen, courtrooms, testimony, affidavits—things having to do with the speech that is most like writing—tend to come with an automatic extra weight in alphabetic texts. The Indian men are speaking, then, just outside the site of the most alphabetic form of speech, "where the pleaders waited for clients; clients, waiting for pleaders, sat in the dust outside. These had not received a card from Mr. Turton. And there were circles even beyond these—people who wore nothing but a loincloth, people who wore not even that . . . humanity grading and drifting beyond the educated vision, until no earthly invitation can embrace it" (37).

The courts in this case have been imported from England. At the center of the "circles" of Indians sit the courts. Only those Indians (the pleaders) given a voice in and by the courts are qualified to receive invitations, as if of all the English-speaking Indians only these are allowable or even knowable. Away from the legal center we gradually lose all sense of individuality, as if there is no speech at all and therefore no individual identity outside the center of alphabetic speech. In fact, outside the courts, everyday speaking human beings are perceived—automatically it would seem—only according to their visible bodies, as if they are somehow all nature with no culture. Since we know those outside the center do in fact speak but are utterly apart from the courts, the great mass of unincludable Indians becomes a figure of orality as such. We hear and see named pleaders (Ram Chand, Mahmoud Ali), but then are given a lump of anonymous "clients," and then "people," and then just "humanity," which in fact means Indian. This great nebulous "humanity" is visible only as deindividualized bodies to the "educated vision," which in this context must mean the literate British way of seeing. It finally becomes so disembodied that "no earthly invitation can embrace it" (37). Now, "earthly" would most commonly be opposed to heavenly, and the paragraph immediately following will take it this way. But again given the context, "earthly" must mean written in English, because as Forster makes very plain, only the British have this particular educated vision and only the British send out written invitations.

We must pause to wrap our minds around the word *embrace,* for it leads us into two of the novel's key thematic issues: the unsatisfiable desire for unity and the threat of what I will call nihilistic relativism. It would appear, paradoxically, that there exists some desire on the part of the literate culture to overcome these separations, to gather into its figurative arms (embrace) all the infinitely retreating circles of those who have been dis-voiced. The last words of the passage lead us directly into the next paragraph, in which we read the novel's definitive statement on invitations, and it too involves an unsatisfiable desire for unity. "All invitations must proceed from heaven perhaps; perhaps it is futile for men to initiate their own unity, they do but widen the gulfs between them by the attempt" (37). Following this, Forster gives us a kind of parable about this problem. In specifically Christian terms we get the religious dilemma over what portion of the material world will be invited, "welcomed and soothed," by "divine hospitality" into heaven. As with the unembraceable circles expanding away from the courts, this maximal desire to be inclusive—argued over by the missionaries, Mr. Graysford and Mr. Sorley—gets confounded by an ever-retreating earthly limit: from human beings to "monkeys" to "jackals" to "wasps" to plants and finally to "mud . . . and the bacteria inside Mr. Sorley" (38). But with desire carried to the point of inviting the carriers of infection (bacteria), a limit is reached, at which point we read: "No, no this is going too far. We must exclude someone from our gathering, or we shall be left with nothing" (38). It turns out that the stronger the Christian desire to embrace inclusively, the more we inevitably approach (a certain understanding of) relativism, as a result of which the basis for certain kinds of value judgments is lost. And this entails, at least from the literate perspective as presented in this novel, that we be left with nothing at all. By direct contrast, the religion most featured within the novel is Hinduism, which, whatever else may be said of it, willingly invites in all the world. Not surprisingly, the great celebration in the Temple section seems like chaos.

This theme of unsatisfiable desire having been established in Christian theological terms, it goes on to find its largest elaboration in terms of a specific example of oral literature: the "religious song" that Godbole will later sing at the tea party. The scene is yet another version of oral performance, but this time the audience is mixed, and it includes all the main characters: Aziz, Fielding, Adela Quested, Mrs. Moore, Ronnie Heaslop, as well as the servants nearby. In the song, which echoes from beginning to end of the novel, the earthly maiden yearns for the heavenly Krishna to come to her, but he never does (85).[1] This song is the pre-eminent example of the oral literature regularly associated with India as opposed to the alphabetic British; and in conjunction with the "Temple" section, which concludes the novel, the song makes of Godbole and his Hinduism the maximal images of orality. Clearly, both are also maximally opposed to other large-scale elements of British and European culture: the various (by comparison) rigidly structured scientific, legalistic, and moral-religious systems of thought and action.

At the end of the song, doing her best to embrace its strangeness, Mrs.

Moore asks if Krishna comes to the maiden in some other version. Given her sense of story, she naturally wants that "proper" ending. But she, like the maiden, is never satisfied. Equally, the British esthetic is unable to embrace the work's form: the uncertain rhythm and the "illusion of a Western melody." It baffles what the narrator simply calls "the ear" (84), as if the British ear is the universal ear. But then "the servants," who are presumably illiterate, do understand—with oral literature, the audience need not be literate—and one, like Aziz and his Muslim friends earlier, is entranced "with delight." Evoking the immediacy of bodily response to oral literature, the song seems to summon him physically from his work to come toward it: he is "gathering water chestnuts" but comes "naked from the tank, his lips parted with delight, disclosing his scarlet tongue" (85). The song ends incorrectly to the British ear, and that incorrectness comes in terms of standard, written musical notation: "apparently half through a bar, and upon the subdominant" (85). But, most significantly, the disjunction between the British "ear" and the song is not simply a matter of taste. Adela will later specifically credit the "haunting song" (86) with inaugurating the catastrophe that reaches its climax at the Marabar caves (266). Lastly, the song is apparently physically infectious, for it mysteriously leads to the illness of all the participants except Fielding (though this does not imply that Fielding simply appreciates the song; we find out his opinion much later, when he declares that "Hindus are unable to sing" [309]). Indeed, this most oralistic song "haunts" and "infects" this entire novel.

Taking all this into consideration (oral literature as infection, the courts, the vanishing circles, the attempted embrace, the song of heavenly refusal), we find emerging in *A Passage to India* an alphabetic worry that, again, we have seen in different ways all along. Writing removes speech from the body. The direct and indirect benefits of this are so vast as to be difficult to summarize, but, as with any technology, there are negative outcomes as well. In this novel the disembodiment of speech is nowhere more negatively affective than in literature, because it privatizes, interiorizes, and silences what is otherwise one of the fundamentally public, social, and oral-aural forms of art. One outcome of this takes us back to issues we have already discussed with respect, specifically, to oral and alphabetic story: the novel's enabling disability, namely, its inability to show. Given oral story as the paradigm of human story, in a sense all other story desires to achieve the communicative efficacy—the simultaneous showing and telling—of that paradigm. This means that for story that cannot show but can only tell, the fullness of oral story is a constantly receding goal. Whatever the quantity or quality of contextual detail, evocative language, exclamation points, italics, etc.; however convincingly realistic the tale, showing cannot happen at all or, if it does, can happen only in a very artificial way. Attempts to establish the context in which represented speech might come closest to oral story will always be up against the reality that context is infinitely dense in a speech-act. Thus, the "heavenly" fullness of oral story retreats infinitely from alphabetic story's attempted embrace. On the one hand, this is a perverse blessing because written story achieves its greatness in large part just in trying to achieve what it cannot achieve. On the other hand, the impossible object of desire can easily be seen as a curse—or an infection—rather than a blessing.

In *A Passage to India* Forster seems to be taking all this to the level of alphabetic literature in general (not just alphabetic story), and perhaps more importantly, to the level of alphabetic culture, which is "dis-eased" if not diseased by the constantly receding, "heavenly" fullness of orality. Obviously the divide in the novel is not simply between literate and non-literate because both the British and the relevant Indians are literate. The divide is between those who seem to have themselves become alphabetic, fully in conformity with the technology, as opposed to those who have not —at least not yet.

Having said this, it is important that we not see all this, dismissively, as mere nostalgic fantasy, which tends to be the case with readings based on a deconstructive understanding of speech and writing. It is undeniable that writing has induced fundamental changes in fundamental cultural practices, and those changes happened largely as unexpected, unintended effects of the technology. As to *how* one deals with the too-late understanding of what has been changed, that is another issue. But the change itself is not a fantasy.

II

If our understanding of the technology of writing is to prove truly useful, it will, as would any approach to this novel, have to provide insight into the trip to the Marabar caves and especially its aftermath, which Forster calls "the decomposition of the Marabar" (287). His choice of words is perhaps more exact than he knows. The "of" refers both to what happens to the event as it fades into the past, as well as what the event does to—the decomposing effects upon—those who experience it; and with this latter meaning, decomposition begins to shift to de-composition, as in de-writing.

I have already noted that before or without writing, the voice and the ear together form the sensory nexus of the definitively human body-mind and that the eye takes on a much larger relative weight with writing (Ong 1967, 1982; Havelock, 1986; McLuhan). I have delayed studying the implications of this issue because *A Passage to India*, especially the caves scene, is such a rich case in this respect. Plainly, the caves are places of the oral-aural, alien to the seeing eye. Though there are two distinct images of light connected to the caves, both undermine the primacy of sight. The one mythical highest cave "mirrors its own darkness in every direction infinitely" (138), and the one instance of actual light—the striking of a match—inverts the normal relationship of seeing eye to seen object. The match produces a glow that is itself "eternally watchful," as if it is the subject rather than the object of vision. The one most marked sensory experience of the cave is the "terrifying echo" (162). In fact, echo, which is directly or indirectly mentioned at least nineteen times in the novel, comes to be a natural-world acoustic counterpart to the human vocality of Godbole's song.[2] As we have seen, the song reveals the disconnection between the earthly British literature and the heavenly, but infectious Indian oral literature. And since Forster so strongly associates literature with civilization (as in the image of the divorce of literature from civilization in modern England), we may generalize that the novel's invocation of orality, and particularly Godbole's song, reveals the disconnection of the alphabetic British *culture* from the *culture* of orality. With the caves we find a parallel disconnection, what Benita Parry describes as a "sensory and intellectual detachment from the empirical world" (181). This time, the British are debilitatingly disconnected from what we may call the *nature* of orality.

In terms of writing and speech, echo holds a unique, intermediate position between the speaking voice itself and the technological representation of that voice in writing. Echo repeats the spoken word apart from the actual body, but this occurs as a function of the natural world; no technology is involved. Echo is a bringing-back to the ear of speech rather than a representation of speech through another medium, and therefore echo remains within the oral-aural sensory domain. So we may say that echo disembodies the voice, estranges the voice from its original source. But because it returns within the oral-aural realm from which it departed, it also affirms the voice; the otherwise evanescent, instantly dissolving voice is not so evanescent after all. Strictly speaking, an echo is only an echo if we recognize the returning sound as a repetition and affirmation of the original.

In first introducing the echo, Forster's narrator makes sure to mention "some exquisite echoes in India" (163). These are the kinds of echo that have always fascinated human beings. We have the echo that whispers "round the dome at Bijapur," making a circuit of sound (163). And then even more definitively we have the "long, solid sentences that voyage through the air at Mandu, and return unbroken to their creator" (163). Though echo always involves elements of both estrangement and reassuring recognition, Forster here gives us only the latter. The repetition of echo, unlike writing, does not break the voice out of the circuit of orality. Echo in general is not "terrifying" at all.

But the echo in the Marabar caves is something else. We must notice that, although Forster writes as if there is only the one kind of echo in the caves, in fact only Mrs. Moore and Adela seem to hear it, at least in any remarkable way. Fielding hears it, but is, at least in his conscious mind, unimpressed (175, 185). Insofar as we can tell, none of the Indians notices it, and we know that Godbole, the man most familiar with the caves, "had never mentioned an echo" (163).

Mrs. Moore being the original respondent to the echo, we turn to her first. Unlike the normal echo, the one Mrs. Moore hears is "entirely devoid of distinction." The "same monotonous noise" replies no matter what the originating sound or voice. So in this case Mrs. Moore hears only the estrangement of the sound's departure. The affirming return does not happen. Again, strictly speaking, this is not really an echo, and yet we have just this word for the event. Our framework of the oralistic-alphabetic distinction can help us see in a rather precise way what to make of this. The issue is not as it is commonly taken to be, "the equivocal and uncertain nature of language" in general (D'Cruz, 195). For next we read that "'boum' is the sound as far as the human alphabet can express it" (163). This first climactic moment in *Passage* reveals the failure of the technology upon which written story—including this written story—absolutely depends. The echo is such that even alphabetography, which again imitates sounds, not concepts, fails at its essential task. The actuality of the real-world sound, at least as heard by Mrs. Moore's ears, remains outside the embrace of alphabetic writing. And in this way the moment of the echo takes up its correlation to the infinite regress we have examined above. Why emphasize "human" alphabet? What other kind could there be? Because of the way literacy and orality have operated in this particular novel and because of the way alphabetography appears at this particular moment, the human alphabet becomes another figure of the general alphabetic failure to embrace orality, paralleling the figure of the earthly maiden who constantly fails to embrace the infinitely retreating god. The British are again linked not just to writing but now, pointedly, to alphabetic writing, and alphabetic writing is linked to the theme of unfulfillable desire.

With an echo, if the secondary sound is anything other than the originating sound, the initial estrangement is pumped up to the level of the uncanny, much as it would be if one looked in the mirror and saw someone or something other than oneself. If this kind of event occurs in the natural world, it must mean either that the natural world is no longer natural in the way that it had been or that the perceiver is no longer a part of that world, as had previously appeared to be the case. Since the echo is apparently normal to everyone else, it must be Mrs. Moore who has been removed from the natural world. The echo comes to her not as a repetition but as a "comment" (165). The content of the comment may be explained in more than one way, but certainly it most straightforwardly makes the statement that nihilistic relativism—the negative understanding of the absolute lack of absolutes—is the factual nature of human life. "Pathos, piety, courage—they exist, but are identical, and so is filth. Everything exists, nothing has value" (165). Now, the realization of this understanding of relativism need not in general be peculiar to literacy as opposed to orality, but Forster presents it that way here. He has specifically prepared for this moment in the earlier argument between Mr. Graysford and Mr. Sorley. Whereas in that earlier scene relativistic nothingness loomed only as a conceptual shadow at the end of a theological dispute, now it becomes quite real. For Mrs. Moore, the moment of being estranged from aural-oral nature decomposes the literate world and all its complex social, esthetic, moral, and religious forms by revealing that they are just that: forms, rather than essences. Therefore there exists no solid basis by which meaningful distinctions of value may be made.

Not coincidentally, the full effects of the echo come upon Mrs. Moore only when she sits down to compose letters to her children back in England. Mrs. Moore manages to write only "Dear Stella, Dear Ralph" before the echo begins to surge over her. She finds that she can forget the actual sensory "crush and the smells" of the event in the cave, "but the echo began in some indescribable way to undermine her hold on life" (165). The normal repetition of the voice as echo has failed, and now a maximum case of the writing most like speech—a personal letter to her children— begins to fail her as well. Later, Adela tries to get Mrs. Moore to explain the nature of the echo. This the older woman refuses to do, and the talk turns to the upcoming trial. Mrs. Moore angrily rejects anything to do with "the witness-box." "I have nothing to do with your ludicrous law courts," she says (222). In the end the echo undoes her investment in both the writing most like speech and the site of speech most like writing.

But the effects of the uncanny echo go further still. Mrs. Moore is characterized with two primary traits: being the only British character in the novel with any true sense of spirituality and being a mother thoroughly committed to her children. From the early scene with Aziz in the mosque, Mrs. Moore has been a uniquely spiritual figure in the midst of the otherwise prosaic, pragmatic British. When the echo first strikes her as she begins to write to her children, she tries to shirk off the feelings of "despair creeping over her," tries "to go on with her letter," but she cannot. For the echo goes on to undermine "poor little talkative Christianity" (166). Now, Christianity is one of the world's three great religions of the book (along with Islam and Judaism), and yet just at this moment the single British character associated with spirituality thinks of Christianity in terms of the voice. And the voice is represented as having no power: it is poor and little and merely talkative as opposed to the oracular Word typically associated with sacred texts by the believers in those texts. She goes on to think that all of Christianity's "divine words from 'Let there be light' to 'It is finished' only amounted to 'boum'" (166). The originary sacred texts of the religions of the book attain their unique status in part because they consist of the only writing that represents nonhuman, that is, supernatural language. Whereas from the beginning, the technology of writing both succeeds and fails because it disembodies language, "holy writ" (again, to its believers) differs from all other writing because it does not originate from a fleshly body. Of all writing, sacred writing is taken to be uninfected by the vicissitudes of the natural, material world. But the revelation of the echo has abruptly reduced even the uniquely powerful writing of the divinely spoken words to mere talk.

At the same time that she loses Christianity, Mrs. Moore is also separated from her other great connection to life: her children. For at the end she realizes that "she didn't want to write to her children, didn't want to communicate with anyone, not even with God" (165). Finally, the echo detaches Mrs. Moore from the oral-aural world in the maximum possible way; as she failed to hear the affirmation of the echo, now she finds that her own voice has become detached from her body. At the last, all "the affectionate and sincere words that she had [earlier] spoken to [Aziz] seemed no longer hers but the air's" (165).

To summarize what the oralistic-alphabetic distinction has so far shown us about the decomposition of the Marabar: the echo has revealed literate culture's disjunction from oral nature; the revelation of this disjunction so dislocates the literate self-identity that the writing closest to speech, the writing that most connects literacy to lost orality (the personal letter) fails; the social speech that is closest to writing, the speech over which writing can most assert its representational power (court testimony) must be rejected; the writing of the divine word falls to the lowly level of everyday conversation; and the very voice itself seems to become literally, not just representationally, disembodied. De-composition has become de-writing with a vengeance.

III

Adela's response to the echo also links directly to the oralistic-alphabetic conflicts, though this time the Marabar decomposes British rationalism rather than British spiritualism. Unlike with Mrs. Moore, the effects of the cave are as much involved with Adela's body as with her mind. Adela is rational to the point of being a kind of polar opposite to the emotional, poetic, oral-aural Indians, and especially to Aziz. Having associated with "advanced academic circles" in England, she has come to India in order to make a "reasoned conclusion about marriage" (88), and it seems to occur to her only by chance that matrimony should possibly have something to do with love (168). She considers any tears of emotion to be "a negation of her advanced outlook" (215). Until the event at the caves, she has hardly sensed herself as an embodied being: "Hitherto she had not much minded whether she was touched or not: her senses were abnormally inert and the only contact she anticipated was that of the mind" (214). After the experience of the caves, this abnormality shows up as unnatural, as if her self-identity has all along depended on offending her own flesh: "Everything now was transferred to the surface of her body, which began to avenge itself, and feed unhealthily" (214). Clearly, she is directly in contrast with the Indians as figures of orality.

Though Mrs. Moore tends to represent British spirituality, and Adela British intellectuality, still we find many strong parallels between their experiences of, and responses to, the cave. For instance, when Mrs. Moore is in the cave, she feels attacked by "some vile naked thing" (162), which turns out to be an innocent baby. When Adela is in the cave, she is "assaulted" by an Indian man who turns out not to have been there at all. Whatever actually happened in the cave, as with Mrs. Moore, the echo is from the beginning the effect that most remains with Adela: "The echo flourished, raging up and down like a nerve in the faculty of her hearing, and the noise in the cave, so unimportant intellectually, was prolonged over the surface of her life" (215). The irony here is that it is exactly the intellectual unimportance (akin to the earlier unimportance of "poor little talkative Christianity") that most gives the echo its weight. Again, as with Mrs. Moore, the echo comes as a "comment" (215), and it specifically undermines Adela's sense of her intellectual self. Of the consequences of the echo, she says that all "the things I thought I'd learnt are just a hindrance, they're not knowledge at all" (219). Most ironically, especially in light of what we have seen with Mrs. Moore, "after years of intellectualism" the echo leads her to resume "her morning kneel to Christianity," though she does so purely for practical reasons (234). Before the scene of her testimony in court, Adela explains that in the cave she created the echo, "and before the comment had died away, [Aziz] followed her, and the climax was the falling of her field glasses" (215).

With this event, which, as it turns out, is purely acoustic, the oral-aural nature of the caves now decomposes the primary physical sense associated with Adela: seeing. It is Adela's original desire "to see the real India" that initiates this entire story (22). Given the promotion of the visual sensory domain in the literate world, and given the tensions between literacy and orality in this novel, it makes sense that Adela, the figure of maximum alphabetic rationality, would also be the figure most associated with this particular idea of "seeing." Further, the association is powerfully reinforced by two physical objects, each from opposite ends of what we may call the technology of seeing. We have the binoculars in the cave. Later, we find Miss Derek and Mrs. McBryde spending hours and hours examining Adela's skin "through magnifying glasses" (214). Adela, then, becomes as maximal a figure of literacy as Godbole is of orality, for now her association with hyperliterate rationalism gets compounded by her distinct association with the technology of seeing. It is not surprising that she is particularly upset when the echo amplifies the "faculty of her hearing." Most revealing of all, she describes the "falling of her field glasses," not the (imaginary) assault by Aziz, as the "climax" of the event in the cave.

Taking all this together, we can see that Adela's experience in the cave and the following echo has led to the figurative collapse of her literate self and that the novel has represented the sickening of alphabetic intellectual culture through a kind of demonic infection by oral nature. And here again the specter of nihilistic relativism looms up as a result. It comes upon Mrs. Moore as she sits down to write letters to her children. It comes to Adela during her court appearance. Before getting to this moment of "catastrophe" (255), though, we must consider the context in which the fall into nihilism takes place. In the colonial setting the courtroom is a singularly conflicted sociocultural space. It tends to be quite opposed to just those qualities that the narrator finds healthiest and most positive about the Indians. Both Ronnie and Mrs. Moore refer to the court case as "machinery" (229). It is true of courtroom scenes in general that the "official decorum of trial is always at risk of disruption from the unpredictable world gathered into its midst" (Franken, 117). In this case, the whole of India is the unpredictable world. The British "machinery" is established to prevent disruptive emotions from infecting the systematic search for the facts. Many of the British arrogantly assume that this machinery will guarantee the innocence of Adela and thereby of all things British. Accordingly, when Adela withdraws her charges, Superintendent

McBryde looks "at his witness as if she was a broken machine" (256). This, more than any other space, is the space of what the narrator calls "verbal truth" in the British sense (76), that is, the purely literal, informational content of words. Forster stresses this fact (including the British naiveté about it), even to the point of including the most common cliché: "Adela had always meant to tell the truth and nothing but the truth" (252).

In the opening testimony McBride makes no "emotional appeal" and speaks with a "studied negligence," which in its very lack of spirit enrages the Indians in the audience. In Adela's testimony she and McBryde speak in rigorously "monotonous" tones, "employing agreed words throughout," as if speech in this context is a kind of hireling, instead of an authentic human expression (254). This kind of unemotional, direct, purely informational speech is consistently represented as alien to the Indians. Earlier, when Aziz and his friends ask Fielding to talk about colonial politics, he gives them a very straightforward and honest answer, but his response —not the content, but the mode of speaking—leaves them "bewildered." Unlike the British, what the Indians "said and what they felt were (except in case of affection) seldom the same. They had numerous mental conventions and when these were flouted they found it very difficult to function" (121). Even in its attempt at acceptance, this attitude is still condescending, as if for the British, by contrast, informational content and emotional inflection are always working in unity. Still, we get many examples of this; for the narrator it is a general truth about the Indian people. British characters are shown to be distinguished by their ability to appreciate and maintain this difference in their speech, and they are often bewildered when the Indians say one thing but mean another. Not surprisingly, at the tea party academic Adela takes Aziz's words as "verbally true," which will ultimately lead to the necessity of the Marabar caves expedition. And also not surprisingly, at the same tea party Fielding is characterized as the one Englishman who has "dulled his craving for verbal truth and cared chiefly for truth of mood" (76). So in placing the second climactic scene of the novel in a courtroom, Forster has taken us as far in the other direction from the space of the caves as possible in colonial India. It would seem to be the most accommodating space of all for Adela.

When in the courtroom, however, it is just the most Indian element that strikes her: the punkah puller. He and Mr. Das, the "cultivated, self-conscious, and conscientious" Indian embodiment of the British court of law, are staged symmetrically "opposite" each other, both on raised platforms at either end of the "central gangway" (241). Mr. Das is officially in charge, but to Adela, the punkah puller, though "humblest of all who were present . . . seemed to control the proceedings" (241). Since the punkah puller has no legal, political, or even social status in the court, we may wonder what about him seems to Adela so powerful. He is described as a kind of embodied "god" on earth, having the "strength and beauty that sometimes comes to flower in Indians of low birth." He is also portrayed as a barely conscious being, entirely remote from the scene, much like that nebulous humanity that receded infinitely beyond "the educated vision" earlier (37). It is with such specimens, we are told, that "nature . . . [proves] to society how little [society's] categories impress her" (241). This is phrased as a universal truth, but in the context it must be specifically British culture's categories that are undone by such a monument of human nature. Certainly Adela takes it this way. His physical beauty seems to infect her as soon as she enters the room, causing her to wonder: "In virtue of what had she collected this roomful of people together? Her particular brand of opinions, and the suburban Jehovah who sanctified them—by what right did they claim so much importance in the world, and assume the title of civilization?" (242). The decomposition of the Marabar has in a sense climaxed with a trial, not just of Aziz, but of English "intellectualism" and in some ways of the entire "triumphant machine of [British] civilization" (234). Not surprisingly, it is in "hard, prosaic tones" that Adela withdraws her charges (256).

Lastly, we must consider Fielding in relation to our examination of *A Passage to India*. Fielding is rather precisely positioned as a mixed case in terms of orality and literacy. As the teacher in the British-style schools, he is the primary purveyor of British literacy and literature. Yet apart from his obvious sympathy and alliance with the Indians, he is specifically praised by Aziz as "a celebrated student of Persian poetry" (67). As mentioned above, of the participants in the tea party only Fielding does not fall ill after listening to Godbole's song. Similarly, we have seen that Fielding does hear the echo but is unimpressed. And yet for him, too, echo becomes the sign of decomposition. In his final summation of the situation of the British in India, he concludes that, unlike in the past, "Everything echoes now; there's no stopping the echo. The original sound may be harmless, but the echo is always evil" (307). No matter his own experience, this statement describes what both Mrs. Moore and Adela experienced in the Marabar caves. At first glance it would seem that Fielding possesses a superior insight into all this, a conscious awareness of what the two women experienced but could not really comprehend. But the narrator immediately tells us that this "reflection about an echo lay at the verge of Fielding's mind. He could never develop it. It belonged to the universe that he had missed or rejected" (307).

The universe that he has missed or rejected takes us directly back to an earlier key moment in the book, when we get Fielding's primary response to the Marabar hills as a natural phenomenon. At the end of the climactic day of the outing, he stands on the club's verandah, looking at the hills in the distance. Just at dusk they are "exquisite"; but rather than pleasing Fielding, the beauty leaves him feeling incomplete and dissatisfied and sounding like another version of Adela: "After forty years' experience, he had learnt to manage his life and make the best of it on advanced European lines, had developed his personality, explored his limitations, controlled his passions. . . . A creditable achievement, but as the moment [of the hills at dusk] passed, he felt he ought to have been working at something else the whole time,—he didn't know at what, never would know, never could know, and that was why he felt sad" (212).

Related to this moment, we find Fielding, too, being assaulted by nihilistic relativism. When Aziz speaks of demanding monetary retribution from Adela, Fielding suddenly loses "his usual sane view of human intercourse, and felt that we exist not in ourselves, but in terms of each others' minds—a notion for which logic offers no support and which had attacked him only once before, the evening . . . when from the verandah of the club he saw the fists and fingers of the Marabar" (278). Interestingly, Fielding, who would seem to be the most generally aware character in the novel, is not fully conscious of what has happened to himself. For the narrator's comment refers to Fielding's experience of seeing the hills at dusk, quoted above, and as we have just seen, nothing overtly like this occurs in Fielding's conscious thoughts. It must be that Fielding experienced the assault of relativism only unconsciously in the earlier moment. Is this the means by which, compared to Mrs. Moore and Adela, he is saved from the devastating consequences of relativism? In any case, we are left with all three major British characters having a negative, relativistic understanding thrust upon them by the echoing "decomposition of the Marabar" (287).

I have claimed that *A Passage to India* holds both the mythically negative and the mythically positive view of orality as seen from the alphabetic perspective, and I have attempted to show this with respect to oralistic literature and culture and oralistic nature. All this tends to work in one evaluative direction; namely, literacy taken to the all-embracing level of the English is debilitating to human existence in some fundamental ways. But, as has been inevitable since Socrates and his amanuensis, Plato, the expression of this happens in writing. Further, given our earlier explanations of the qualities of alphabetic story, this novel is most thoroughly alphabetic. I would argue that it is even more alphabetic than *Pride and Prejudice*. Only by spending hours alone with the text, by constantly rereading and "stopping to analyze" have I been able to read the novel in something like the detail in which Forster wrote it. The more alphabetic, or to use the text's word, the more "advanced" the reading, the more the reader will have engaged in just the kind of hyperliterate literary experience that the novel itself seems to find so unnatural. And yet such is the ongoing paradox of any critique of writing: "Once the [spoken] word is technologized, there is no effective way to criticize what technology has done without the aid of the highest technology available" (Ong 1982, 80). Ong was speaking of Plato and discursive arguments about the technology, but given what we have seen in our texts so far, it seems that the novel—evidently both empowered and plagued by the anxieties built into alphabetic story—tends to do, from within and in not fully intended ways, just what Ong describes.

CHAPTER SIX

The Waves

Disembodiment and Its Discontents

⚜I

VIRGINIA WOOLF'S *The Waves* makes a likely choice for the present project because it deals so directly with the situation of creating stories and because of its particular experimental nature. Woolf's novel is unusual by any generic standard. Its plot—ultimately involving a writer's discovery of the end of writing—is, thematically at least, as alphabetic as we can find. Six named characters alternate "speaking," always in the present tense, always in the first person, and always in quotations. From this, we can see that the novel is trying in a way to be like a drama, trying not to tell a story through a narrator but rather to show it (as much as can be done in writing) by putting on display a record of vocal communication. However, it makes little pretense at being an imitation of any actual conversation between actual people. It often reads like some kind of telepathic communication, at other times like a spontaneous soliloquy. The voices tell of their interwoven experiences over the course of their lifetimes, so that we have, taken altogether, "one" story with a beginning, middle, and end told from six points of view.

Because this is a written story, we can see no bodies speaking the words; so unless we have some purely graphic means—systematically different fonts, for instance—of distinguishing speakers, we must be given some "teller" apart from the speeches in order to track who is saying what. An omniscient narrator is present for this purpose, but in the most reduced way possible. It is only the barebones identifier—the "Bernard said" or "Rhoda said"—of the speakers. It does not occur in any other way. Usually, master third-person narrators provide the reader with, at least, the context within which to make sense of the action of the story. If we are given only dialogue, we must infer the context from the content of what is said, but we cannot really do this with *The Waves*. Except for the last chapter, Woolf has written so that we cannot, for example, infer from the content any real world situation in which these words might be said. And though the speeches are recognizably about the real world, their quite poetic language bears little resemblance to any actual speech. All this produces the unusual effect of stories being told by an array of named, but strangely disembodied voices. Of course, all written story is always a disembodied telling, but some forms of written story force this fact on our attention more than others. *The Waves* has this effect.

There exists, though, what we must take to be a different omniscient narrator, who gives us the brief, very poetic italicized passages that act as prelude to each of the nine chapters, and the lone italicized final sentence of the novel. This narrator tells us a story, if we can use that term at all, only in the most minimal sense. It gives us a gradual, dawn-to-dusk description that is centered on what is seen looking from an unspecified beach out across the surf to the horizon. It also at times describes various equally unspecified natural and domestic scenes. It never reports speech, and when it does, occasionally, mention humans or human affairs, it makes scrupulously sure that they are presented on the same level as any other element of the described world. This narrator comes across as quite objective, at least with respect to what it chooses to notice. In fact, with respect just to content, it gives us a kind of report. We have, compared to any human story, no drama, no tension. But at the same time the descriptions themselves are the opposite of objective in any informational sense. Rather, they are extraordinarily (and to my mind quite beautifully) poetic throughout—a kind of poeticized report.

We will do well to consider in more detail how this portion of *The Waves* works. The first text we read in the novel begins with an omniscient teller, and yet, unlike the other, identified speakers, this narrator does not really come across as a disembodied voice. Why not? This brings up the larger question: Why does the usual third-person narrator *not* typically come across as what it plainly is—a disembodied voice? The reason is more than just a literary convention. It has to do with the telepathic effect of writing. In the normative third-person telling of written story —the standard narrative form for an immense number of novels—the telepathic effect of writing induces us to receive the story without much thought about the actual nature of the "speaker." As with written texts more generally, we tend, unless we have evidence to the contrary, to assume the otherwise unidentified telling voice to be that of the author, and we take this as unproblematic. Of course there are special cases. Modernist or postmodernist experimental fictions willfully try to upset this effect. But just the special, experimental case verifies the norm. Professors of literature are often careful to teach students not to assume equivalence between third-person narrator and writer, but the need to consciously teach this also proves the normative response.

Readers normally take the presenting voice more or less as it seems to take itself: it is simply there, telling a story. Strange as it is, we generally have no problem accepting that there is no one actually speaking the words. Indeed, in this situation disembodiment works quite positively. With no showing available to us, all our attention tends to go to what is being told: the content. If we did not more or less automatically and regularly do this, it is hard to see how we could successfully accomplish the primary task of getting the story. We do just this with the italicized narrator, and especially with the minimal narrator that identifies each speaker. But since the other voices are presented within the unnamed, third-person narrator's story, they automatically require some kind of embodiment—not necessarily human, just some identifiable entity in charge of the "saids"—to be understood, precisely, as *in* the story, rather than as beginning an altogether different story.

Since the italicized text has an omniscient narrator, we tend to read just for the content of the story. How does this story work? The various introductory interludes all read sequentially over the day, so they could be taken out and run together as one continuous, freestanding text. But it is hard to imagine that text being successful. It would read in one way like lyric poetry, but, the poetic, descriptive beauty aside, the piece would go on too long to work as only that. Because of the length and the way it begins, a reader coming into the text will automatically be thrown into the normal narrativistic "anticipation of retrospection," as Peter Brooks has called it (23). If a narrator (omniscient or first person, writing or speaking) begins by describing a dawn in detail, an automatic suspense, an automatic question, arises: What makes the beginning of this particular day worth telling? What conflict or tension or risk will occur along the way that will, at its end, cause this day to be both the same day we started out with, but also fundamentally different? Woolf does install patterns of imagery in the piece, which we can certainly read for a kind of change. But apart from the poetic language, she seems to work quite consciously not to include anything plot-worthy. The question of what makes this day worth telling is never answered within the italicized text itself. The description simply ends with darkness and the waves still breaking. There has been nothing special about this day; it might have been any other.

As a consequence of this report-like content, the italicized text as a whole depends for its success as a text on being broken up into short lengths and placed between the moments of the speaking voices. Otherwise it will fail because it lacks a story; it is only a sequence. Said another way, the text of the speaking voices could work without the italicized text, but not the other way around. The speaking voices may be disembodied; but although none of the six lives is especially dramatic or memorable, still, the voices necessarily present at least the conflicts, joys, and anxieties that all humans experience. The italicized font itself in fact seems to be trying to overcome this lack of story content by making the descriptions *look* dramatic, exciting, special.

So we have both disembodied voices and a poetic nonstory. Since the two kinds of telling are juxtaposed in one novel, we are plainly meant to read them as parts of a whole. As we shall see, that whole is very much about two closely related issues of alphabetic story, issues we have encountered before: disembodied telling and story-worthiness.

II

As with all our sample texts, there are more relevant elements than we can attend to. I choose to focus specifically on the character Bernard, who is Woolf's most elaborate fictional portrait of a writer. As Howard Harper has noted, the novel "favors Bernard from the beginning, and at last seems to embody itself in him entirely" (237). Bernard is represented as a born storyteller, telling stories having been his primary characteristic from childhood on. He describes himself as if he has his own theory of cognitive linguistics and narrativity; he was born, he says, "knowing that one word follows another." He spends his life "finding sequences everywhere," even when he tries not to (267). Presumably, he must mean certain kinds of sequences—that is, stories—here, since *sequence* in general means only a series. Any human whose attention and memory are functioning normally will automatically perceive sequence: the simple fact of one item following another. Bernard would have no reason to feel special about just this. But it matters that he conflates sequence and story in this way. It happens again when Neville early on says of Bernard: "Let him describe what we have all seen so that it becomes a sequence. Bernard says there is always a story. I am a story. Louis is a story" (200). Unless Neville is operating with a very serious—in fact, incapacitating—cognitive malfunction, he does not need Bernard or anyone else to describe everyday reality so that it "becomes" merely a sequence. It would appear that by *sequence* he must mean a specifiably meaningful series that would not otherwise be apparent simply in terms of everyday attention and memory. *Story* would seem to be the word he wants, and he soon he switches to that term. But in conflating the terms he conveys more than he realizes. On some level he takes it that awareness in general requires some manifest form of actual story in order to apprehend sequence at all; as if, were Bernard not there to tell some specific tale, there would be no sense of sequence, and no *I*.

We should notice another not-so-clear distinction, one being made between the everyday storytelling in which most children engage and something significantly different, something more formalized and self-conscious. Bernard stands out from the others because of this uncommon ability. But even at a young age—as far as we know, before he can write—Bernard already thinks of himself primarily as a story-*writer*. He prophesies of himself: "When I am grown up I shall carry a notebook—a fat book with many pages, methodically lettered. I shall enter my phrases. Under B shall come 'Butterfly powder.' If, in my novel, I describe the sun on the window-sill, I shall look under B and find butterfly powder" (199). In order to write—and, for him, to write seems always to mean a novel—his experience of the world will have to have already been arranged according to an alphabetographic methodology. Literally from the beginning, the sense of story that seems to come so naturally to him is being determined by the technology of writing: all along, for Bernard "story" means written story.

As a boy Bernard feels compelled to make up tales. "I must open the little trap-door," he says of himself, "and let out these linked phrases in which I run together whatever happens so that instead of incoherence there is perceived a wandering thread, lightly joining one thing to another" (208). This idea takes us back to the conflation of sequence and story. Bernard takes it for granted on some important level that there is either story or incoherence. Now, in one way this is true. Story can be considered as an element of our cognitive apparatus, as a built-in means by which we know ourselves and others in time. Certain specific kinds of brain damage can disrupt this cognitive capacity, and anyone suffering such disruption can reasonably be described as beset by incoherence. Otherwise, the story capacity works like our vision or our speaking or our hearing or, perhaps the better analogue, our theory of mind. These functions are, if working normally, the constituents of consciousness. We have no choice but to perceive sequence (as opposed to some specific story), so there can be no conscious "must" about it in the way Bernard intends. Bernard is already doing this successfully or he would not be able to "speak" as he does. However, in a given situation, there may be an obligation to create a given kind of story. Bernard is conflating an everyday sense of storytelling with story on the cognitive level. A parallel with language might be, "I must have language or else incoherence," when in fact by "language" is meant, say, oratory. To say I must have language or incoherence is true, but, except in a case of impairment, we cannot make a choice about this. Oratory of course is a different matter. Because from the beginning Bernard constantly uses "story" (or sequence) when he means written story, in this defining case he is conflating a cognitive ability and written story. Obviously, human life does not require *written* story to be coherent.

And yet Bernard seems to see things just this way. In an effort to prevent incoherence he finishes the above statement by offering to tell a story of a figure from the group's childhood: "I will tell you the story of the doctor," he says. Since it is "the" story of "the" doctor, and since "you" in this case most directly means the five other speakers, he is going to indulge in some oral history, as opposed to an entirely made-up story. The pleasure in hearing the tale would be quite communal in the sense that the audience ("you") already knows the content well. Like oft-repeated family stories, just the telling and hearing of what has been known commonly to all gives the story its quality and value. And he charges up the sense of community by narrating in a first-person plural: "Let us follow him as he heaves through the swing-door to his own apartments" (208). He begins a description of the doctor by picturing him alone in "his private room" (208) and describing his most mundane actions as he undresses. So now Bernard must be making up a fictionalized episode from the real doctor's life.

And yet, though he is verbally "telling" this story, he appears to be thinking, whether he knows it or not, as a story-writer. We can see this when, in parenthesis, he says of the details he gives: "(let us be trivial, let us be intimate)". Since he has just described the man unfastening "his sock suspenders," it is plainly evident that he is being trivial and intimate. Why would he feel the need for the parenthesis unless he feels some negative response emerging in his audience as he goes into these minor, very undramatic descriptive details? What must be the violated audience expectations that he is trying to account for (we recall Eliot facing a similar situation in *Adam Bede*)? If it matters that the group be told that he is doing this intentionally, he must be worried that they will think he has turned to such detail unawares, the implication being that they will find him to be just a poor storyteller.

Continuing on, Bernard imagines the doctor with "both arms stretched on the arms of his chair," doing nothing, lost in reflection. Once again Bernard inserts a parenthetical comment: "(this is his private moment; it is here we must try to catch him)" (209). But then, as happens with literally every story Bernard tries to tell, he cannot get to an ending. He simply breaks off, confessing that "stories that follow people into their private rooms are difficult. I cannot go on with this story" (209). We may ask, difficult compared to what? difficult how? to which the first answer would presumably be: difficult compared to stories that follow people who are taking actions in their public life.

This brings us to an aspect of alphabetic story that perhaps no one thought more about than Virginia Woolf. In my opening chapter I explained that one function of accommodating story to the technology of writing is the diminished need for oralistic content: content that is spectacular enough to be easily held in an audience's memory. As the technologization of story evolves, this initial, diminished need becomes a need to be as different as possible from oral story. A major outcome of this is the turn to the real as the basis for story. From the oralistic perspective, content of the realistic type now associated with the novel would not really count as story-worthy. It would read more as a report on, a description of, the everyday real. If that tendency away from oralistic content were carried to its (techno)logical maximum, then story would become indistinguishable from description, even for a literate reader. Such a story would give up even the relatively modest alphabetic need for specialness of content, some element of drama or tension or conflict that distinguishes the realistic fiction from a report or a sequence. It would not be clear why the word *story* would matter for such a document. Bernard seems to be maximally conforming story to writing, to be disappointed with the result, but not to understand why.

Woolf, as is well known, consciously wanted to take story out of its traditional forms and contents. In one of her most famous essays, "Modern Fiction," she thinks of herself as rejecting certain contemporary novelists —"materialists," as she called them. With their kind of novel, the writer "seems constrained, not by his own free will but by some powerful and unscrupulous tyrant who has him in thrall, to provide a plot, to provide comedy, tragedy, love interest, and an air of probability embalming the whole" (1984, 149). Despite what she may think, she is in fact rejecting story in general here. Of course, such experimentalism is allowed (and can be quite interesting, though primarily to the hyperliterate reader, including myself), but a price will have to be paid for leaving behind these story essentials. She cannot expect to appeal to the common reader in any broad sense, though the prologue to the book of essays in which "Modern Fiction" is included suggests that she may think of herself as doing so (1984, 1–2). In *The Waves*, she seems to acknowledge in two ways that a "story" of this type will not really work. First, she has created just such an experiment in the italicized interludes. The necessary splitting up of that sequential whole into italicized parts suggests, in spite of its poetic language, that it cannot succeed on its own. And then within the novel she gives us an image of a writer trying to create a "story" lacking all those tyrannical requirements, and the results seem fairly plain. Bernard gives up on the doctor, not because of some intrinsic difficulty with this particular story, but because the kind of "story" he wants to tell is not interesting enough to hold even his own attention.

The loss of a common reader is immediately backed up by a comment from Neville. "Bernard's stories amuse me," he says, "at the start. But then when they tail off absurdly, and he gapes, twiddling a bit of string, I feel my own solitude" (209). Neville expresses what Bernard seems unable to grasp about his "difficulty." If what is put forth as a story beginning simply tails off, then it becomes merely a sequence. Said another way, without an ending predetermining why a beginning is necessary, we will not have a plot. The invocation of the private moment could possibly work, but if it does not become part of a plot, it fails to satisfy on a basic level. It seems simply absurd, random, not a story. Further, since Bernard is at this point telling orally, rather than writing stories, his beginning instantly generates the little community of teller and listener. Accordingly, when the "story" fails in this essential way, it forces a distinctly negative sense of private "solitude" on its unfortunate audience.

As a figure of the story-writer, Bernard is more important for what he thinks about his art than for any art he actually produces, and his thinking is regularly split between notions of orality and writing. For instance, at one point he is on the train to the university when a stranger gets into the car. He feels uncomfortable having no social contact with another person in such close physical proximity. "I instinctively dislike the sense of his presence, cold, unassimilated," he says. "I do not believe in separation. We are not single. Also I wish to add to my collection of valuable observations upon the true nature of human life. My book will certainly run to many volumes embracing every known variety of man and woman" (221). Quickly, Bernard works to get a conversation going, thereby "bringing [the man] into contact. The human voice has a disarming quality" that creates a kind of spontaneous unity (221). So this sense of the warmth and inclusiveness of verbal interaction matters to Bernard. But at the same time he seems, as always, to experience the world in terms of written story or, more precisely, in terms of a fantasy of written story. He wants the interaction of speech as much for its use in a future written story as he does for its immediate sense of unity. He assumes that in his writing he will achieve a maximum in terms of both quality and quantity; not just some truth but "*the* truth of human life," and not just some characters but "every known variety of man and woman." He is still a young man at this point. His sense of the writer he will become appears to be youthful idealism. But he will carry much this same notion of written story throughout his life.

Once the conversation barrier is broken, Bernard begins, silently in his imagination, to compose the kinds of details and specifics required for an alphabetic, fictional sketch:

I furbish him up and make him concrete. He is indulgent as a husband but not faithful; a small builder who employs a few men. In local society he is important; is already a councillor, and perhaps in time will be mayor. He wears a large ornament, like a double tooth torn up by the roots, made of coral, hanging at his watch-chain. Walter J. Trumble is the sort of name that would fit him. He has been in America, on a business trip with his wife, and a double room in a smallish hotel cost him a whole month's wages. (221–22)

As has happened regularly in our explorations so far, writing seems to take on more substance than an immediately present, living person. Rendering the living man into the form of written fiction, it appears, solidifies him, makes him "concrete" in a way that even conversation and actual physical presence do not.

And yet, having begun to concretize the man in a story, Bernard quickly faces his usual failure to conclude. Before he can come to an end, he has to change trains. "These are the things," he says, "that forever interrupt the process upon which I am eternally engaged of finding some perfect phrase that fits this very moment exactly" (222). Throughout the novel, Bernard's use of *phrase* is like the use we have already seen of *sequence* and *story*. *Sequence* does not normally default to the meaning "plot" or "story," because, though all stories are sequences, not all sequences are stories. Similarly, though all written phrases are phrases, not all phrases are written phrases. We would usually need to directly specify "written phrase." But Bernard consistently—always, as far as I can tell—uses the general term *phrase* to mean consciously composed words that will at some point constitute a written story.

What might be the nature of such a perfect phrase? We can see reverberations of the generic desire of written story to achieve the communicative efficacy of oral story, but this is not quite the same case. Let us consider an answer in terms of the letter-and-spirit dyad that we introduced in our discussion of Dickens. We have the actuality of the experienced event on the train, and we have the phrase, the written letters, that Bernard expects will preserve the spirit of that event—the cognitive and emotional qualities of the experience—for a later human reception. The very possibility of such exact preservation of past moments in such precise detail is originarily a function of writing. Otherwise, we have only living memory or the archive of oral history by which to revisit the past (even a pictorial preservation that shows an experienced moment requires an accompanying oral telling to have meaning for later viewers). The ability to preserve the spirit in letters at all automatically brings along the idea of an increasingly precise preservation. Bernard seems to have become obsessed with the possibility of the letter getting ever closer to the quality of the spirit on the micro-level—the instant of experience. But experience is embodied and writing is disembodied, so this cannot work. He does not seem to understand that the letter's desire to get at the spirit cannot be satisfied.

At least he does not seem to understand this consciously. He has just expressed a sense of the problem of content in writing. Next, in a scene that is in many ways paradigmatic of the nature of writing (and is densely metafictional), he expresses a sense of the problem of form. He imagines being a "dashing yet reflective man" composing a "letter to the girl with whom he is passionately in love" (228). "I am writing the first thing that comes into my head," he says, "without troubling to put the paper straight. It is going to be a brilliant sketch which, she must think, was written without a pause, without an erasure. Look how unformed the letters are—there is a careless blot . . . I will write a quick, running, small hand" (228). As we know, another reason that writing cannot get at experience is that it can only tell, not show, its content, although, as I have discussed with respect to *Bleak House*, handwriting is the kind of script that shows the most individuality. Bernard seems intuitively to understand that however great the passion of the writer, and however great the passion of the content, the emotion, the embodied spirit, just will not be communicated without some kind of showing. Consequently, he imagines writing that will show as much of the body as possible; writing that, as with the italics in the poetic interludes of *The Waves*, will *look* passionate.

With this desire Bernard becomes part of a very old tradition, most famously following the seventeenth-century *Letters of a Portuguese Nun*, which purported to be the love letters from a nun to a French soldier-lover. The content of the nun's letters is melodramatically passionate, but formally they are written as if "the Nun was dashing her unpremeditated thoughts down on paper as fast as they came, an effect which was enhanced by the use of dashes and sudden exclamations, the absence of rhetorical subordination or periodic sentence structure, and a jerky, nervous style" (Day, 34). This style, as much as the overt content, was responsible for the extraordinary popularity of this text. But of course, as Robert

Day points out, both the author and the audience "forgot to observe that the time-consuming physical and mental effort of putting ideas on paper offers an almost insuperable barrier to rendering them exactly as they first occur in the mind" (34). This kind of effort is in direct contrast to the great majority of speech-acts. Most of the time speech is so easy that it seems to flow out of us, without anything like alphabetographic preparation. Compared to speech, just the physical act of using the technology (putting "the paper straight") is troublesome. Specific, concentrated work is necessary to get the reader ("she must think") to believe the writing has been casual and spontaneous. Extra work is required to force writing to appear to flow, like our usual "quick, running" chunks of speech, "without a pause."

Earlier I discussed how the technology of writing induces mechanical regularity of form and exactness of content. Handwriting works against this mechanization, but it is still much more mechanical than speech, which by contrast seems almost "unformed." To leave a "careless blot" on the page is a conscious decision to appear as unconsciously casual about formal precision as we commonly are in speech, where an unimportant accident of form would hardly be noticed. In an attempt to overcome the lack of embodied audience, Bernard consciously imagines his reader and the specific ways he wants her to respond. "I want her to say as she brushes her hair or puts out the candle, 'Where did I read that? Oh, in Bernard's letter.'" He goes on about all this at some length. He seems, now, to be searching very pointedly for the visual image of the perfect script (as opposed to the perfect phrase) that will fit his mood exactly and communicate it exactly to his intimate reader.

Despite his diligent efforts to make his writing visually embody his feelings, it begins to fall "flat. It peters out" (229). Because he is writing, he immediately thinks that he could "rewrite it" with just this failed attempt in mind to shape a better letter. But he seems to feel that revision would ruin even further the passionate spontaneity he wants. She will think that he "is posing as a literary man." So the perfect visual form of writing, like the perfect content, escapes.

Still undeterred from trying, he immediately begins again, giving a quick, clearly novelistic description of a stay in the countryside, including spoken "quotes" from an unnamed, imaginary woman. After some lines of description, he says, "I can sketch the surroundings up to a point with extraordinary ease. But can I make it work? Can I hear her voice—the precise tone with which, when we are alone, she says 'Bernard'?" (230). His question sounds rhetorical, but it is not. These problems worry Bernard. The question takes us back to his notion of the "perfect phrase that fits this very moment exactly," and of course the answer to the question is no. To "sketch the surroundings" in the way he does is the kind of detailed context-setting that written story often requires. Bernard feels no discomfort with this element of the story. For this kind of thing, simply telling can be relatively satisfactory. But when he gets once again to the kind of exactitude that writing makes at least imaginable—the "precise tone" of her voice when they are alone—he feels the failure of being limited only to telling. The situation is entirely paradoxical. It is because of writing that he can imagine a story that could possibly represent her precise tone, and it is because of writing that he cannot represent just that tone.

I want to be clear. I am not arguing that an oral or other telling could possibly precisely imitate the woman's voice in the private moment, although oral telling, itself a vocalization, could come closer than could any possible writing. What I am arguing is that the worry about this kind of precision only occurs in the first place because of the kind of precision that writing enables. Because both writer and reader can go slow, stop and start again, revise, and reread, a story-writer can provide descriptive detail on an entirely different scale than can any oral storyteller. A listening audience would simply not be able to keep in memory the kinds of detail that are standard in many novels. And because written story can be so much more detailed and, therefore, precise than oral story can, its communicative possibilities can seem limitless. Nonetheless, it is still always and only telling. Therefore, when it comes to those elements of experience apart from the words themselves, written story will always fail on a fundamental level in relation to story that can literally show: oral story, drama, or film.

What can we conclude from our examination of these scenes? Bernard is experiencing failure and lack in *written* story, but he does not really think of it consciously this way. He feels simply that he himself fails to find, variously, the right words with the "perfect phrase," the right visual form with the love letter, and the right way to "make it work" with the woman's voice. He is conflating a fundamental, built-in human ability to tell story in general with an ability to produce story accommodated to an invented communications technology. As a result, he feels that he is failing at storytelling in general rather than at story writing. This also links to the conflation of sequence and story earlier. To fail at creating "good" stories of some specific kind is not the same as failing at the fundamental cognitive work of finding sequence in the world around us. Similarly, to fail at finding the right descriptive written phrase for a moment of experience is not the same as a general failure to be able to describe. In each case an alphabetic perspective is being assumed as the only, and the normal, perspective, which automatically leads to a rather profound sense of inadequacy. We can draw a comparison with, say, argumentation. Failure to write a successful argument does not entail an inability to reason in general. And yet, because of the nature and power of writing, the alphabetic standards of logical disputation—like the alphabetic standards of storytelling—tend to become the only and obvious standards, the result being that "illiteracy" is often simply taken for stupidity. Bernard is entirely caught up in this kind of writerliness, and as was the case in *A Passage to India*, it is not a healthy state of being. Still, the signs of an unconscious awareness of the problem do hold out some possibility for change.

As Bernard grows older across the course of *The Waves*, his doubt about his own abilities as a writer slowly change to a doubt about the idea of story itself. At the time of his engagement and the splitting apart of the circle of friends, he says that "sometimes I begin to doubt if there are stories" (276). Later still, as a middle-aged man visiting Rome, he thinks: "I have made up thousands of stories; I have filled innumerable notebooks with phrases to be used when I have found the true story, the one to which all these phrases refer. But I have never found that story. And I begin to ask, Are there stories?" (306). This recalls his childhood prevision of himself carrying "a fat book with many pages" of phrases that would become the text of his novel (199), and then later his sense of himself constantly writing down "valuable observations upon the true nature of human life" (221). But now his desire for the perfect phrase, which will capture private experience on the micro-level, has grown into a desire for the perfect story, which will capture private experience on the macrolevel. Once there is writing, we have the idea of a perfectly exact inscription of the moment. Once there is written story, we have the idea of a perfectly exact inscription of, for instance, a life—the one grand, integrating whole of which the many smaller stories are necessary parts. Clearly, Bernard is thinking of an impossible, Platonic ideal of written story. And yet he appears to take this ideal as if it were a real possibility. This, again, seems to lead him inexorably to question, not just some particular story or kind of story, but the idea of story in general.

Having asked this question—"Are there stories?"—he then looks out across the view from his room and imagines creating stories from what he sees. "I could break off any detail . . . and describe it with the greatest ease," he says. He begins making up stories, but then stops to ask: "But why impose my arbitrary design? Why stress this and shape that and twist up little figures like the toys men sell in trays in the street? Why select this, out of all that,—one detail?" (306). At this point Bernard's disillusionment becomes most revealing. It takes us back to the issue of arbitrariness and originality that we encountered in our discussions of Shelley, and especially Eliot. In a sense Bernard takes to an extreme the problem that bothered Eliot. She sensed the oralistic story tradition accusing her of arbitrarily putting forth her own individual version, or "design," of people and reality. She turned that accusation around, charging that the oralistic tradition, unbound by the real, was in fact arbitrary. But still, she understood that the charge of arbitrariness was not simply empty, which is why she felt the need to give her oath that she was being as true as possible to her perceptions and understandings of the real. Woolf's character, Bernard, does not need anyone to accuse him of arbitrariness. His own involvement with written story has led him to accuse himself. Unlike Eliot, Bernard does not feel that honesty and sincerity are sufficient to overcome his sense of arbitrariness. Said another way, he feels the charge of arbitrariness much more extremely than did Eliot, and for good reason. Bernard is involved with alphabetic story when, in part because of writers like Eliot, considerably more of what Ong calls the "residue" of oral story has been eliminated from the novel. We know this because of the kinds of story he constantly plans to write, which tend toward report or description. It is as if, the more technologized the story, the more compelling the sense of arbitrariness.

This brings us once again to consider Bernard in relation to the statement from "Modern Fiction" in which Woolf rejects all the basic elements of story; it seems that he is abiding by Woolf's statement more than she herself did. Unlike Bernard, Woolf nearly always gives us at least a bare-bones framework of beginning, middle, and end; some version of a love interest; some kind of plot involving a conflict that, though not tragic in the Aristotelian sense, nonetheless leads to some kind of self-recognition; and even some comedy (these are all certainly true of, for instance, *Mrs. Dalloway* and *To the Lighthouse*). But Bernard seems to want to create "stories" that are extreme versions of the ideas Woolf put forth in "Modern Fiction," as if Woolf is experimenting with her own idea of experimental fiction. In any event, he pays a heavy and symptomatic price for taking things this far, not just in theory (like Woolf), but in practice. His case is symptomatic because his own conflation of written story with (oralistic) story in general leads him to the nihilistic conclusion that there are no stories, that story in general is arbitrary and therefore of no real value. But he will get past this conclusion.

Though Bernard's speaking alternates with that of the other five characters for most of *The Waves*, the last chapter is entirely his, followed only by a culminating one-sentence return/completion of the omniscient, italicized narrator. For the first time we have a consistently inferable real-world situation for a character's speaking. The entire chapter takes place in a restaurant as Bernard, now an older man, has dinner and tries "to sum up" his life to a never-named "you" across the table. To "make you understand" a human life, he says, "I must tell you a story." But then he says that "there are so many, and so many—stories of childhood, stories of school, love, marriage, death, and so on; and none of them are true" (341). He evidently uses "story" in the sense of an oral telling and also in the sense of factual reality communicated in narrative form, as with biography and history. In other words, a simple list of the sequence of events will not do to make "you" understand the human reality. But then he actually means written story because he goes on to lament the need to come up with "ridiculous, flamboyant, beautiful phrases," something not usually required of oral history. As before, he seems to be thinking that because certain kinds of written story fail in certain ways, story in general is simply untrue. "How tired I am of stories," he goes on,

> of phrases that come down beautifully with all their feet on the
> ground! Also, how I distrust neat designs of life that are drawn upon
> half sheets of notepaper. I begin to long for some little language such

as lovers use, broken words, inarticulate words, like the shuffling of feet on the pavement. I begin to seek some design more in accordance with those moments of humiliation and triumph that come now and then undeniably. Lying in a ditch on a stormy day. . . . Of story, of design I do not see a trace. (341–42)

As always, "phrases" means written story here. When he says simply "design," he must mean written design, though he still conflates writing and orality. And yet with this, we find signs of a major change. Instead of simply stating the problem of finding the perfect phrase that fits a given moment exactly, he now begins to say what it would take to get what he wants. The earlier childhood sense of story has reversed itself. Before, (written) story was good because it established order instead of incoherence. Now, he rejects that very sense of order as untrue to the real. In fact, the dialectics of the technology are continuing. Having earlier come to the dead end of alphabetic story, he is now emerging out of that end. Life, he can now see, is misrepresented by written story, by "beautiful" phrases and "neat designs" on notepaper. Accordingly, he begins "to long" for orality, "some little language such as lovers use." What could be a more certain case of the rich immediacy that is possible only in an actual speech-act? Lovers develop a shared idiolect, with tones and phrases that carry nuances of meaning understandable only to the other. The shared bodies, the shared looks, the shared memories, the shared emotions, the shared thoughts, the shared material contexts and experiences are all contributing to this exchange. No writing can hope to communicate in this way. Of course this language is not perfect, but it works uncommonly well. But why call it a "little" language? What is the standard in relation to which such language would seem "little"? The standard must be those beautiful written phrases that we put on paper.

And so we have a perfect paradox: Bernard unwittingly reinforces alphabetic superiority just in the act of admitting that writing is inferior to speech. From this beginning, he goes on to imagine other possibilities that move ever further from writing, words that, though "broken" and "inarticulate," can still communicate because of a living human speech situation. Then, as the logic of getting as far from written language as possible continues, he imagines the rudimentary aural "communication" of hearing human footsteps. If there is to be "some design" that is true to life, then it must include what his earlier attempts at story did not include: dramatic conflict involving emotional "humiliation and triumph." Having begun to seek something other than written story, he ends up concluding that such designs seem entirely detached from experiential reality; more precisely they are detached from bodily experience. And yet at this point, though he may have reversed his sense of the value of story—from that which saves us from incoherence to that which distorts the real—he still conflates written story and oral story, making them the same thing, and so he still makes the same debilitating category mistake as before. It is true that if we look at the natural world, we may not see design in the sense either of a specific fictional story or of a "story" of scientific explanation; it is not true, if we are of reasonably sound mind, that we see no design at all.

As Bernard works to retell the story that we have already passed through in the previous chapters of *The Waves*, the sense of failing to get at the historical thing itself continues to plague him. Recalling his first, teenage love, he suddenly interrupts himself: "these flagging foolish transcripts—how much too deliberate! How much too reasonable!—which attempt to describe the flying moment of first love." From this we can see that he is beginning on some level to attend more and more to the differences between writing ("transcripts") and speech. What is the use, he demands, "of painfully elaborating these consecutive sentences when what one needs is nothing consecutive but a bark, a groan?" (350). Now, we have an expression of *need*, rather than simply of longing. The need is most revealing. He has shifted to a quite specific notion of orality; not any human language in the usual sense, but rather the kind of vocalization that achieves its meaning precisely because it is the oral, but nonlinguistic, expression of a linguistic creature. A bark or groan, when made by a human instead of an animal, would always be made in special, usually uncommonly emotional circumstances. Stereotypically, this kind of sheer vocalization (as opposed to verbalization) is taken to express directly an inner state that is dominated by emotion or physiological condition, rather than by the "deliberate," "reasonable" processes that usually govern our speaking. In fact, a bark or groan is more code than language. This kind of vocalization is akin to blushing or getting goose bumps or breaking into a "cold sweat." So if speech in general is always corporeal, for a human the bark or groan is maximally so, a kind of visceral vocalization. And if writing must in general fail to equal the communicative efficacy of spoken language, its failure is even starker when compared to this kind of oral expression. Bernard has begun, though he does not consciously think of it this way, to work actively against the disembodiment that comes with writing.

So Bernard has a conflicted notion of biography. Though "life" is such that only a story can adequately explain it, at the same time, the story that will make life tellable is false to the factual real. He more directly addresses this issue as his sense of failure grows. At one point he creates imaginary quotes from his own written biography. "That," he says, "is the biographic style, and it does to tack together torn bits of stuff, stuff with raw edges. After all, one cannot find fault with the biographic style if one begins letters 'Dear Sir,' ends them 'yours faithfully'" (356). He makes an important concession: biography is not simply a fiction. But then he justifies the concession through a negative comparison to the formulaic beginning and ending of a business (or at least a formal, nonpersonal) letter. We write "dear" in such a text though we may not know, or may even despise, the addressee. We write "faithfully" without necessarily having any thought at all of actually being faithful. If we can accept these, Bernard claims, then we ought to be able to accept biography as life-writing. But the comparison is false. Biography is a subset of story in general; the business letter is not. Biography in general is a direct function of the storytelling aspect of human being; the business letter is not. Still, biography as we know it is certainly a function of writing (as its etymology makes plain). Ironically, only because of the kind of exactitude and detail that comes with writing could Bernard feel the extent to which biography fails to achieve the possible goal that it enables. He is gradually, and inconsistently, becoming more conscious that writing itself is the problem. Soon, he will concede that life "is not susceptible perhaps to the treatment we give it when we try *to tell* it" (362, italics added). He seems to mean "*tell*" in the most general sense, but of course all of the telling he has actually mentioned has depended on the idea of written story.

At the very end Bernard goes through a climactic (by Woolf's standards) moment of self-dissolution and reconstitution, after which he finds himself walking "alone in a new world . . . unable to speak save in a child's words of one syllable; without shelter from phrases" (376). His dependence on "phrases," it turns out, had sheltered him from an authentically human apprehension of the material world itself. Rediscovering that world apart from phrases takes him back to a state of entirely preliterate speech. Accordingly, he feels separated from the alphabetic self he has been since he was a child. We recall that he dreamed of growing up to carry a "notebook . . . methodically lettered," in which, he said, "I shall enter my phrases. Under B shall come 'Butterfly powder.' If, in my novel, I describe the sun on the window-sill, I shall look under B and find butterfly powder" (199). But now he says: "He is dead, the man I called 'Bernard,' the man who kept a book in his pocket in which he made notes —phrases for the moon . . . under B, butterfly powder, under D, ways of naming death" (379).

And finally, we read that his

> book, stuffed with phrases, has dropped to the floor. . . . What is the phrase for the moon? And the phrase for love? By what name are we to call death? I do not know. I need a little language such as lovers use, words of one syllable such as children speak when they come into the room and find their mother sewing and pick up some scrap of bright wool, a feather, or a shred of chintz. I need a howl; a cry. When the storm comes across the marsh and sweeps over me where I lie in the ditch unregarded I need no words. Nothing neat. Nothing that comes down with all its feet on the floor. . . . I have done with phrases. (382–83)

Obviously, he is at first talking about writing: a book stuffed with phrases. As before, he feels the failure of writing to get at authentic human experience. From this, he moves on beyond the little language of lovers to the even "littler" language shared by a toddler and its mother, to, once again, an example of nonlinguistic verbalization. This time, though, he seems to pump up the emotional charge because he needs a howl or a cry, instead of a bark or a groan. But having begun the rejection of writing, he cannot stop until he has gone all the way to its dialectical opposite. At the end he needs only that which is constitutively left out of writing—the body itself as the living ground of experience.

If we consider all this together, what can we conclude? *The Waves* explores, among other things, the price to be paid for the extreme technologization of story by writing. It does this by telling the story of a man who is not a born storyteller but a born storywriter and who, until the end, does not understand any real differences between the two activities. In coming to understand the effects of writing, he comes to discover that he has been in a sense cut off from his own body, disembodied without quite knowing it. And he embodies himself in the act of understanding the effects of writing. Further, this happens both within his story and on the level of *The Waves* as a whole. With Bernard, the last chapter finally gives us an embodied first-person speaker. It is no longer simply a voice speaking but a voice of an identifiable person in a material situation who recounts a powerful moment of crisis and self-recognition. It is as if the novel, too, has experienced the effects of its own recognition of writing. Woolf seems to have experimented with her own experimental ideas and, ironically, to have reaffirmed just what her theory wants to deny. And the inescapable other alphabetic effect occurs as well: only through writing can the differences, positive and negative, of writing from speech be revealed.

CHAPTER SEVEN

"Why a story at all?"

The Writing of The Golden Notebook

⚜ I

DORIS LESSING'S *The Golden Notebook* famously involves a consciously *mise en abyme* form of plot. It opens in one way like a traditional, omnisciently told novel, with what appears to be a chapter heading: "Free Women." But this turns out to be a novel within the one we are reading, for later we shift into writer Anna Wulf's private writings, separated into five notebooks. Along the way we discover that what we now know is a novel, *Free Women*, is about Anna's own experiences. Within the notebooks, she begins another novel, told in the third person, that is another retelling of her experience of writing a novel. Near the end we learn that *Free Women* has also come out of her notebooks and is the story of her life after the period that is the content of her one published novel, *Frontiers of War*, about which she writes in the notebooks, etc. The ostensibly separate writings "bleed into one another" (Henstra, 6). All this makes it difficult to gain a sure foothold on any governing point of view that can be the foundation in relation to which we may judge other points of view.

In a sense this kind of telling is maddeningly disorienting, carrying a "Möbius strip" quality (Hite, 22), and over the course of the novel, Anna passes into and out of her own madness. A number of reasons for her insanity show up in the novel, most prominently the anxieties of living in the Cold War geopolitical world of MAD: mutually assured (nuclear) destruction. Lessing's novel makes the case that, given a world gone crazy, there is a certain valid self-discovery in encountering and passing through madness, rather than rejecting it categorically as an inauthentic state of mind. But writing, the practice by which Anna constantly believes she can save herself, turns out to be an essential cause of the decay of her identity. Her story distinctly reminds us of Woolf's Bernard. We recall that over a long period of time the arbitrariness-effects of writing brought Bernard to a critical moment of despairing doubt about story in human life. In a real sense, Anna's story is a several-hundred-page elaboration of the crisis that Bernard experiences in a few pages at the end of *The Waves*.

Lessing's novel has been discussed in relation to issues of writing and writerliness before, but always in terms of poststructuralist notions of writing, representation, and subjectivity (Greene, King, Krouse). I would argue that these understandings—indeed, like Anna's understandings in this novel—regularly confuse what can be validly claimed about writing with what can be validly claimed about language in general. In order to show how the concept of writing as a technology can help us interpret *The Golden Notebook*, we need briefly to review a few key ideas.

I have explained the kind of self-skepticism that writing can—in some senses must—engender because it requires a word-for-word sense of originality and responsibility that is only true of certain special cases of speech. Along with this, alphabeticized content stakes itself on an appeal to the real and therefore to individual perception. This entails, as George Eliot realized, that sincerity and precision about one's own perceptions become all important. Realism as established in the nineteenth-century novel involves fictional story that works to represent the real. Writers feel free to include fictionalized versions of events of their own lives in their novels. But the tendency toward the real (and toward what must be solipsism from the oralistic perspective) reaches a limit with the idea of story that Anna Wulf seems to take for granted: only the actual events of her own life can provide authentic content for story. Woolf's Bernard thought of story this way but could never make it work, even to his own satisfaction, much less to anyone else's.

By contrast, Anna has written this kind of "story," and she has profited from it. Earlier in her life, she published a successful novel—*Frontiers of War*—that is the "story" of time she spent in Africa during World War II. But although she can satisfy others with such a story, she cannot satisfy herself; this, too, is an outcome of conforming story to writing. We are taken back once again to Eliot, who realized that her account of "men and things" would be "doubtless defective" (150), but since she was writing fiction, she did not have to judge the account in relation to the real in the way that, say, a biographer or responsible journalist would. Said another way, notwithstanding Eliot's commitment to the real, she still accepted a basic distinction between fictional story and story as report. Because Anna has taken the alphabetic idea of story to a limit, she only considers her own actual experience as legitimate content. This entails a number of consequences, the most important of which is that she always faces a debilitating conflict: the differences between her experiential memory of the lived reality and her own written account. This is a rather profound outcome of writing as a technology, and one that we need to look at more closely.

In their early considerations of writing Goody and Watt wrote about the "homeostatic tendency" of primary oral cultures (33): their tendency to change according to immediate social needs and conditions. Oral-cultural notions of history are a good example of this. Typically, "history" in oral cultures has to do with genealogies and monumental events. We (literate folk) might assume that these verbal records would be permanent and unchanging; they are, after all, the only record of blood lineage and important events of the past. But this is not the case. Oral cultures do not use genealogies as "faithful historical records of times past" (33). They use them as a means of conforming the past to the needs of present life. Genealogies, for instance,

> operate within an oral rather than a written tradition and thus tend to be automatically adjusted to existing social relations as they are passed by word of mouth from one member of the society to another. The social element in remembering results in the genealogies being transmuted in the course of being transmitted. . . . One of the most important results of this homeostatic tendency is that the individual has little perception of the past except in terms of the present; whereas the annals of a literate society cannot but enforce a more objective recognition of the distinction between what is and what was. (33–34)

This effect has to do with the permanence and disembodiment of writing. Without writing, all human institutions and customs are necessarily social in a way that is not quite the case with literate cultures. Laws, religions, and knowledge of whatever kind emerge as a result of the actual practices and beliefs of living, interacting human beings. Memory and verbally handed-down stories are the only means of judging present cases by past precedent. Since memory and verbal communication cannot be precise or permanent in the ways that writing can, culture tends to change in a relatively ad hoc manner, as needs require, without anyone necessarily making a conscious decision to abandon the older for the newer or vice versa. Oral culture, from the literate perspective, depends on forgetting because forgetting enables adjustments to present realities without the feeling of contradictions with the past. As a consequence, change happens, from the literate perspective, more or less constantly in tiny ways. Large-scale change would be uncommon and would typically be a result of immediate external circumstances: drought, plague, invasion, and the like. Goody and Watt use the term *homeostasis* to describe this kind of roughly automatic self-adjustment to the ongoing conditions of the present.

The appearance of writing drastically affects this foundational human situation. As we have seen in our discussion of the letter/spirit dichotomy, writing preserves an instantiation of some earlier reality indefinitely past its living existence. The present, which will have changed from the past according to the usual contingencies and necessities of life on earth, must accord itself with this now-fossilized piece of its own earlier living reality. This means that writing makes almost certain a regularly occurring conflict between the present and the past senses of self. A literate culture not only can but almost certainly will experience purely internal conflicts over the inconsistencies between its immediately present self-identity and its written version(s) of itself. Nation states with written constitutions clearly show how this works. The original written documents that constitute such a state never themselves change as long as they exert power. The states themselves always change. National history is, in a sense, the ongoing work of squaring the spirit of present actuality with the letter of the written constitution.

What Goody and Watt described on the macro-level of culture is also true on the micro-level of the individual. The understanding of the past, be it oralistic or alphabetic, can only ever occur in terms of present identity. But with writing there arises, first, the possibility of making a conscious, ongoing record of the present as a diary or journal. Beyond this, any writing whatsoever that is preserved will necessarily be a "lettering" of the writer's "spirit" at the time of its writing. Any present reading of the past writing will necessarily involve some sense of the self now looking at the self then as a different personality. This is a generic conflict, produced more or less automatically with writing. But *The Golden Notebook* is very much about this conflict. In Anna's case the generic conflict becomes the specific source of her breakdown.

II

Anna's compulsion to write down her life leads her to create four notebooks. "I keep four notebooks," she explains late in the novel, "a black notebook, which is to do with Anna Wulf the writer; a red notebook, concerned with politics; a yellow notebook, in which I make stories out of my experience; and a blue notebook which tries to be a diary" (475). Now, Lessing's novel is overtly about the splitting or disunification of the modern psyche. The compartmentalization of experience into different notebooks is one of the most straightforward manifestations of this theme. Of course, all manner of historical forces, especially the Cold War, are the causes for this splitting. But whatever the cultural and historical causes, all the splitting depends on a certain hypertrophied self-scrutiny. With Anna, our otherwise natural and definitively human meta-cognitive ability—our ability to think of our thinking, of our words, of ourselves as if from another's perspective—has become debilitatingly powerful. And it has become so because of writing.

We can see this emerging even in her description of the notebooks, first with the very idea, in the black notebook, of writing about her writing. Humans in general have a basic ability to consider their own words and themselves as speakers, but without writing or other technological recording devices, the only record of our speaking is memory. So our self-scrutiny is limited accordingly. By contrast, a writer has his or her preserved, materialized words to examine at leisure, in detail, over and over again, quite as if they were someone else's words. I have already explained how writing automatically requires the writer to take on the role of the missing "other" of a speech-act. To write about one's own writing is to materialize oneself as at least one written version of that "other." Because the one writer becomes the written origin and the written "audience" to the one set of words, this act comes perhaps as close as possible to a maximum conformity of the self to writing. This can be self-revealing and beneficial because the writer has the opportunity to see meanings now that could not have been seen at the time of the writing. The same set of words by the same person now carries a different significance, and this shows, for better or worse, an increase of (self)knowledge. The writer has become wiser. But then each act of writing necessarily reproduces the original situation. A newly original writing occurs that can be responded to in its turn, implicitly ad infinitum. This sense of infinite regression has a sense of distinct, material possibility with writing, as opposed to only a vague, hypothetical possibility with speech. The technology enables a unique kind of self-objectification. Given this, we can see why Anna herself says that the black notebook has to do with "Anna Wulf the writer," as if she were speaking of someone else.

Over the course of the novel Anna writes of having become disillusioned with the Communism that she had earlier believed in and worked for. Much of this she writes into her red notebook. Marxism in general has to do with an ongoing self-scrutiny in the sense that one of its primary aims is to bring to consciousness the economic and social forces that form the unconscious grounds of identity. For Anna this means not just experiencing and talking about politics, but writing about the experience and the talk. As we shall see, the ways in which she reads her own writing and thinks about writing in general are strongly affected by her Marxist commitments.

The similarities and differences between the yellow and blue notebooks are perhaps the most revealing in terms of writing. Anna thinks of herself as a novelist, and yet she seems never to imagine making up a story from scratch or from some event she has heard or read about. For her, to fictionalize means simply and only "to make stories out of [her] experience" (475). With this, we can see the polar reversal of the meaning of story as it occurs in oral culture. That which would be only gossip in oral culture is taken as the obvious right content for a novel. But along with the yellow notebook, she writes the "blue notebook which tries to be a diary" (475). So, we may wonder, what is the difference between writing private experience into story and keeping a diary? The evident answer would be that private experience is fictionalized in the one and simply recorded as a report in the other. Interestingly, the blue notebook only "tries" to be a diary, as if compared to the three other kinds of writing, this one is least likely to succeed at what Anna wants it to be.

Much of Anna's writing seems to be aimed at generating another novel, to follow the success of *Frontiers of War*. In working toward this, she regularly expresses her opinions about her own novel and about the novel as a genre. We need to consider these opinions, often thoroughly contradictory, at length. At one point, for instance, she recalls having been a reviewer, "reading ten or more books a week" (60). She discovered that modern novels differed in kind from "Thomas Mann, the last of the writers in the old sense, who used the novel for philosophical statements about life" (60). She takes "the quality of philosophy" as an obvious, definitive requirement: "the quality a novel should have to make it a novel." In contrast, modern novels are books "of reportage" that "we read . . . for information about areas of life we don't know," in much the way we read journalism. Sounding like T. S. Eliot thinking about the metaphysical poets, she attributes the informational quality of the novel to the contemporary "fragmented society, the fragmented consciousness" (61). She now looks back on her own commercially successful novel as a failure for just these reasons. Though she can realize this historical fact about the novel, she cannot herself somehow overcome it, and this causes her to feel that she is an unsalvageable failure: "I am incapable of writing the only kind of novel that interests me: a book powered with an intellectual or moral passion strong enough to create order, to create a new way of looking at life" (61). With all this, Anna seems to have a very grand, highbrow notion of the novel in the great-tradition sense, made famous by F. R. Leavis. Since she never shows any doubt that her own experience must be the content of what she writes, we must assume that she fails to express her own experience in the forms of the great tradition.

But this standard and her consequent sense of failure are in conflict with another standard. Considering the differences between her present memory of the lived time in Africa and the written version of that time in her novel, she remembers the original motivation to write. The "pulse beat, violently," she says, not because of the particular story she had to tell —"The 'subject' was almost immaterial"—but simply because she knew she "would write" and "could write" (63). It is the activity rather than the content that most compels her (an alphabetic urge that we examine in more detail in chapter 8). But now she wonders:

> Why did I not write an account of what happened, instead of shaping a "story" that had nothing to do with the material that fueled it? Of

course the straight, simple, formless account would not have been a "novel," and would not have got published, but I was generally not interested in "being a writer" or even in making money. I am not talking now of that game writers play with themselves when writing, that psychological game—that written incident came from that real incident, that character was transposed from that real one in life, this relationship was the psychological twin of that. I am simply asking myself: Why a story at all—not that it was a bad story, or was untrue, or debased anything. Why not, simply, the truth? (63)

Like so much of Anna's thinking on the nature of writing and the novel, this important passage is rather packed with confusion and contradiction. By "formless" she must mean reportlike rather than novelistic, datalike rather than esthetically designed. And she does not mean reportlike in the sense of disguised autobiography or *roman à clef*, which would still be examples of the real shaped by story. But at the same time she does seem to mean a narrative of some kind, not just a strictly documentary record, a list of events and thoughts. Revealingly, in spite of her sense that her novel fails as an account of the events, she says that it is not "untrue." In fact, she makes a point of repeating this just afterwards: "I said nothing in it that wasn't true." This implies that her questions do not have to do with truth to the factual real after all. In searching for an answer to her questions, she decides at last that the problem must be the "emotion [the novel] came out of," which she now sees as a kind of nihilistic desire "for license, for freedom, for the jungle, for formlessness." This apparently means that the particular representation of the lived events was colored in a certain emotional way and that now she finds that emotional coloring, not untrue, but as she next concludes, "immoral." She cannot read the novel now "without feeling ashamed, as if I were in a street, naked" (63). The emotional coloring, then, was true but so deeply personal that it was wrong to make it public in writing.

This notion begins to skew the idea of truth in yet another way. If the novel is true to the real, and if the emotion it came out of was the actual, necessarily private emotion that she felt, and yet she feels the novel fails because it is immoral, then we must conclude that only novels that are colored by some publicly sanctioned, morally correct emotion will pass muster. Being true to the factual real is required unconditionally, but being true to the factual emotion is constrained by a rather didactic-sounding sense of right and wrong. She does not explain what an alternative, rightly true emotional coloring would be. However, she does immediately begin a ninety-page telling of the events and people in Africa, which we must take to be an attempt at writing the content as she wishes she had originally done. In the process of this retelling, she discovers the contradictions that led to her questions about her novel.

In order to begin, she claims that she must consciously "switch something off" inside her: "Now, writing about [that time], I have to switch it off, or a 'story' would begin to emerge, a novel, and not the truth" (65). She can feel the stories automatically begin to form, and she feels that the same emotions as before compel them to happen: "nihilism . . . a longing to become part of dissolution" (64). This nihilistic emotion, she laments, unconsciously feeds into her readers: "That is why I am ashamed, and why I feel continually as if I had committed a crime" (64). With this, we must recall the sense of transgression that we encountered so often in the novels already considered. Anna's case is similar, but it has its own distinctive inflection. Since the emotional affect she feels about this past time is still plainly with her, we must assume that it is quite real, quite solid in terms of her individual life. But her sense of certain yet-unexplained moral obligations of written story requires her to split herself apart from her emotion in order to write the truth. As she writes this text, she will worry continually about this problem.

At one point, for instance, as she feels herself "falling into the wrong tone," she declares, "I will try to put down the facts merely" (65). Later, in retelling this story she goes for help to some of her own written journals of the time. She finds a set of opposing character traits she had listed while trying to understand one of the characters, Willi. Looking back on this, she realizes that data-type lists are "meaningless" and "irrelevant" when it comes to people. Rather, only storylike descriptions of the person in a specific time and place doing specific things can capture personality. But then she thinks that in rejecting data for story, she is "accepting amorality." Not colorless data, but literary description is amoral. And "I do accept [amorality]," she continues, "the moment I start to write 'a story,' 'a novel,' because I simply don't care. All I care about is that I should describe Willi and [other characters] so that a reader can feel their reality" (71).

Clearly, truth to her private emotions and to her private perceptions is the storytelling impulse that drove her original novel. But now she seems to understand why she has condemned that work. The moral disapproval comes from her Communist politics and her "twenty years' preoccupation with this question of morality in art" (71). It turns out that what appeared to be a universal notion of truth in the question, "Why a story at all—why not, simply, the truth?" is in fact a Marxist notion of artistic truth; "this question" is a Marxist question. In abiding by that truth she comes directly into conflict with two of the effects of writing upon story: truth to the individual real and to sincerity. She cannot be true to the real or be sincere if she is, for ideological reasons, not allowed to get her actual emotions into the text. At this point she does not quite know what to do with the split between her Marxist commitments and her thoroughly alphabetic sense of story. She writes: "So what I am saying is, in fact, that the human personality, that unique flame, is so sacred to me, that everything else becomes unimportant?" (71). The sentence form of this notion perfectly captures her ambivalence. She begins with what reads like a statement of fact, but she seems compelled to back away from its political significance by closing the statement with a question mark. Then she simply drops the question and continues her story.

At one point, sounding unexpectedly like Dickens' Esther Summerson, Anna finds herself questioning her value judgments about the people she had known in Africa, about describing someone as "good" or "nice" (109). These are words, she decides, that one would only "use in talk . . . these are not words you'd use in a novel. I'd be careful never to use them." And yet, she says, any ten people picked at random off the street and somehow made a part of that original group of people would "instantly" agree with her classification. Evidently she thinks of the writing she is doing at this moment as "the truth" in relation to a novel and also as no different from speech. As we have seen all along, this is standard literate thinking about writing.

But within the context of this particular novel this particular example takes on a specific weight. Since Anna does not think of herself as writing a novel at the moment, and yet she automatically judges herself according to "a novel," it appears that some concept of "the novel" constantly hovers over whatever writing she may be doing. This concept of the novel links to the earlier, Marxist concept. She realizes that the value judgments bother her because of all the reigning theories about personality: "Heaven knows, we are never allowed to forget that the 'personality' doesn't exist anymore" (109). It is "the theme of half the novels written, the theme of the sociologists and all the other -ologists." But she continues: "Yet when I look back to that group under the trees, and re-create them in my memory, suddenly I know it's nonsense." All of "this anti-humanist bullying, about the evaporation of the personality becomes meaningless for me at that point when I manufacture enough emotional energy inside myself to create in memory some human being I've known" (109). And then she gives a descriptive example of what she means. The description is plainly a function of written story, not simply memory. So, though she speaks of memory, she really means writing, only not what she takes to be novelistic writing. Again, she seems to be taking this present writing as "talk," the "formless" form she hinted at above. As before, the element of the emotions seems to be the crux of the conflict.

Since Marxist theory is famously "anti-humanist," we must assume that once again she finds herself resisting a Marxist literary-value system. In her mind, that esthetic requires that human individuals be represented without overt examples of the writer's private value judgments, much as we would normally expect of a social-scientific text. The linkage to sociology matters. The Marxist esthetic operates as a conscious, even programmatic implementation of writing's effects on story: the move toward a neutral, objective, disembodied observer. The more alphabetic the story, the less visible will be signs of a specifiable human teller and the less we will have of overt emotional coloring in the narrator's "report." But the individual writer's private values will always determine whatever story gets written, if only because that writer chooses what to tell and how to tell it. Even a Hemingway story is a function of idiosyncratic desires and choices.

Since a literally objective telling is impossible, Marxism provides (in some cases stipulates) a telling that is avowedly not neutral in the everyday sense of the word but is, rather, "scientifically" neutral. This seems to take the disembodiment effect to an extreme. After all, there is a difference between a putatively neutral telling that is still unproblematically a function of a unique, private perspective and one that depends on a conscious allegiance to an organized system of thought external to the individual. The Marxist goal, of course, is to institute openly a publicly acknowledged, conscious "neutrality"—one that is cognizant of capitalist ideological functions—in place of the otherwise relatively unconscious value systems that color whatever kind of neutrality a (non-Marxist) writer might want to practice. As represented here the Marxist "novel" appears to have thoroughly and finally removed the individual teller from the tale. However, Anna, who has been much involved with Marxism, is split between this esthetic and her sense that story should have to do with authentic emotions.

But then, as Anna thinks about the conflicts between her memories, her emotions, and her Marxist sense of "the novel," the great-tradition concept reappears, though in a different way. She writes that remembered images come into her mind as in "a slow-motion film" (110). "The moments I remember," she writes, "all have the absolute assurance of a smile, a look, a gesture in a painting or a film. Am I saying then that the certainty I'm clinging to belongs to the visual arts, and not to the novel, not to the novel at all, which has been claimed by the disintegration and the collapse? What business has a novelist to cling to the memory of a smile or a look, knowing so well the complexities behind them? Yet if I did not, I'd never be able to set a word down on paper" (110). Her memories have a quality of showing, of making content visible to her inner eye in such a way that emotional value is simply built in. "The novel" has in its greater past, before being "claimed by the disintegration" of Cold War modernity, evidently been able to express that emotional value with at least some degree of success, otherwise Anna would not feel the sense of nostalgia for the way the novel used to be. But then she goes on to ask questions that pertain to a much broader area than simply the contemporary novel. For "the kind of certainty" she wants is impossible in the novel in general, not because of some sociohistorical collapse but because of the nature of writing. To lament "the complexities" that a novel cannot capture compared to a visual representation, especially a film, is to mistake a technological necessity for an artistic failure; it would be like lamenting the living motion that bronze sculpture cannot possibly capture because it cannot move. Not even Thomas Mann could have captured the "absolute" quality of emotional memory.

As Anna continues writing "the truth" of the time in Africa, she comes to suspect her memory just as much as she has suspected "the novel." This takes us directly to the self-objectification mentioned above. Her memory consists of discrete episodes, "like beads on a string" (137), but she wants to remember even the "intervening" connective, cause-and-effect events between the episodes. Because she experienced the past time continuously, she thinks that the full memory is "there in [her] brain" and should be accessible. But human memory does not operate this way. Only with a written record does such fullness and permanence even become imaginable as a serious possibility, and because writing does enable at least this possibility, Anna is now "appalled" at what she failed to notice about events as they happened. In other words, the relative precision of the written record that she does have, as opposed to the imagistic, episodic, emotional quality of her memories, automatically means there could have been a fuller written record that would have gotten more of the possible perspectives onto the page. This leads her inexorably to question her memory as a whole: "How do I know that what I 'remember' was what was important? What was important was chosen by Anna of twenty years ago. I don't know what this Anna of now would choose" (137). We must be reminded again of Woolf's Bernard, who was struck by the sense of arbitrariness of choosing what to put on the page.

But where Bernard was conflating writing and speech, Anna's despair is a necessary result of conflating writing and memory. She herself admits this, though she does not grasp its full implications. She says: "The experiments with the notebooks have sharpened my objectivity to the point that (but this kind of observation belongs to the blue notebook, not this one)," and then she drops this line of thought. She is correct in one way. Systematically putting herself into writing has induced a thorough self-objectification. But in fact she has been brought to a self-canceling position. It is always possible to review the (remembered or written) past and discover that we failed to see something that was important at the time, but rightly or wrongly, we necessarily made choices based on our then-current knowledge and perspective. This is how humans operate. Our present perspective is necessarily different from that past judgment, constituted in part by that past judgment and also based on our current knowledge and perspective. It, too, can be more or less right or wrong, but only in relation to some possible, specific real-world perspective(s).

To condemn memory and current perspective as hopelessly and catastrophically partial is to judge memory and perspective from an impossible, omniscient point of view. Writing is not in itself required to generate this notion of "objectivity," but Anna's case is represented as in a fundamental way caused by writing. She is a paradigmatic example of the peculiarly alphabetic conflict between present and past. Anna takes the conflict to a maximum when she is led to the false generalization about memory—and it is writing about her writing that almost brings her to recognize this fact. But just as, earlier, she came right up to the edge of a transforming realization about Marxist esthetics, so she now comes right up to the edge of the same kind of realization about the technology of writing. Something inside her prevents either realization from taking effect.

The relentless alphabetic self-objectification never stops. When she finishes this version of her time in Africa, she writes that "the two 'stories,'" *Frontiers of War* and this current retelling, have nothing in common (153). Some months later she rereads this version and declares that it is "full of nostalgia, every word loaded with it, although at the time I wrote it I thought I was being 'objective'" (153). With her unexamined notion of objectivity in mind, it is hard to see how she could ever feel satisfied with what she writes of herself.

This same notion of rereading the texts of the past and discovering now what must have been unknown but important then gets transferred to the present. In her yellow notebook Anna begins a novel called *The Shadow of the Third*, in which a main character, Ella, clearly modeled on herself, begins to write a novel. The story involves a young man who lives an apparently organized and planned life but comes to the point of committing suicide. At the moment of death he can see that his life had been constantly progressing toward suicide, though he had not been able to see that end as his life moved along. That the manifest story is not what it seemed only becomes visible at death. This novel about Ella and her novel is, of course, directly taken from Anna's life. She breaks out of the novel to write: "It as if this novel were already written and I were reading it. And now I see it whole I see another theme, of which I was not conscious when I began it. The theme is, naivety" (211). Again, if only because of the limitations of memory, this kind of detailed, analytical self-objectification is impossible without writing. Though of course self-analysis, written or otherwise, can be useful and therapeutic, in this novel it tends, because it is taken to obsessive extremes, to be self-destructive. Anna seems unable to feel sure of any knowledge at all unless she gets it from writing. She reports, for instance, that she had never "analyzed" her sexual relationship with her husband of five years until she "sat down to write about it" (215). By analyzed, she seems to mean: to think about seriously and directly. But in fact she means: to think as the act of committing her thoughts and her experience to alphabetography.

The Shadow of the Third, not surprisingly, fails to satisfy Anna's desire to get at the truth. This time she decides the fictionalization of her own experience of love, marriage, and breakup "is untrue" because the beginning and middle of the story are determined by the end that she already knows before starting to write. But while "living through something one doesn't think" in terms of the unknown ending yet to come. The ending comes as, relatively, a surprise, in the way of the suicide story she had imagined earlier. What she most desires is to write a story that would operate as experience itself operates, moment by moment. But she herself knows this is impossible. The ending is what must "give the [story] its shape. Otherwise it would be chaos" (228). (Actually it would not necessarily be chaos, but it would not be what is usually considered a story.) "Literature," she decides, "is analysis after the event." Story in general depends on a sense of "afterness," but the more alphabetic the story—that is, the more dependent on private perception—the more acutely the writer experiences this effect. She realizes what is missing. "To show a woman loving a man," she goes on, "one should show her cooking a meal for him or opening a bottle of wine for the meal . . . but that isn't literature. Probably better as a film. Yes, the physical quality of life, that's living, and not the analysis afterwards, or the moments of discord or premonition. A shot in a film," she concludes, and describes an imaginary example. Though this is confused in the way Anna's thinking is always confused, we can see that what she misses is story that shows, rather than only tells.

This turn, once again, to film gives us another perspective on the extremity of Anna's case. We have all along seen how, as story is conformed to the technology of writing, there occurs a shift away from the oralistic and toward "story" that is, from the oralistic perspective, a report. We have seen Woolf's Bernard and, earlier in *The Golden Notebook*, Anna bound up with, but also confounded and disappointed by, this alphabetic notion of story. But another, recently invented technology—motion pictures—enables Anna to think about story in general and the novel in particular in a way that seems never to have occurred to Bernard. Obviously, film existed at the time of both *The Waves* and *A Passage to India*, but it was still a new medium in the 1920s, hardly the massively successful storytelling form it had become by the 1960s. Anna's alphabetic crisis seems automatically to occur in relation to film. In fact, we may wonder to what extent the advent of film itself, rather than what she sees as the disintegration of the novel as a genre, is causing her anxiety. In any case, if the novel seems to have reached some end, film is now on the scene to pick up the storytelling slack. Ironically, though, because she is from the beginning so thoroughly "inscripted," we may say, by writing, she automatically thinks of film as the ideal form for alphabetic content. If she somehow thinks a filmed story can escape the necessity of being end-governed, she is of course wrong. Still, of all story-telling media, film can be most successful at conveying the unstoried real as content because it has the technological ability, not just to tell, but to show; and further, not just to show but to show change as it happens.

The appeal of showing to human beings cannot be overstated, and that appeal finds its maximum with a moving image. As anyone who has been in a room with a television program they are not interested in watching knows, a moving image more or less automatically draws, even compels the eyes' attention. The eye itself, be it nonliterate or hyperliterate, is drawn to the moving image in a way that it is not drawn to writing, unless the writing itself is in a moving image. Obviously, our visual capacity is involved both in reading text and in viewing film. But with writing we consciously direct our eyes to move methodically over a static, noniconic visual representation that changes only in very small, entirely prescribed ways. Even a noniconic moving image draws the eye, and an iconic image draws the eye as does movement in everyday life. The eye is designed for this kind of input. This means that a filmed "story" of the everyday real can at least possibly appeal in a way that no written story of the real, however detailed, can hope to do. The recent popularity of what we call reality TV makes plain that this basic idea can hold a broad audience, even when the audience is aware that they are not seeing the real "real." Both Anna and the audience for reality TV express the peculiar story-desire that emerges historically only with the advent of the novel: the desire for story that is not story. Anna seems to want the maximum version of such a story, and she intuits that only film makes this kind of story doable in a way that can possibly be satisfying. We can speculate that film as a medium might have on its own induced the desire for the nonstory story, but alphabetic story had already institutionalized that desire by the time film arrived on the scene. Indeed, reality TV is an example of alphabetic story content in moving-picture form. Anna, rather ahead of her time, wants this kind of story.

In spite of this desire, however, Anna cannot stifle her storytelling urge. Even after having written about the experience of rereading her first novel, and after writing, and writing about, *The Shadow of the Third*, which is the story of Anna's own marriage, she cannot somehow will herself out of making the real into story. She witnesses a scene between her flatmate Molly and Molly's son, Tommy, that strikes her as something that should be written down. She goes upstairs to do so, and "instantly [begins] to turn it into a short story . . . without even planning to do it" (228–29). This, she decides, "must be an evasion. Why not," she asks herself once more, "write down, simply, what happened between Molly and her son today? Why do I never write down, simply, what happens?" (229).

The alphabetic senses of privacy, arbitrariness, sincerity, and honesty that we discussed with Eliot, Shelley, Dickens, and Woolf have come to their most debilitating extreme. If the only story-worthy content is the individual experience of the real, then ultimately it will follow that to fictionalize at all is to be dishonest about one's own personal experience, and the question quickly arises: What is the meaning of such dishonesty? Eliot worried about getting her own perceptions of the world wrong, but she had not come to the point of doubting fiction in general. Woolf's Bernard came to the point that Anna has come to, doubting the idea of story, but he did not take self-skepticism this far. When he asks "why impose my arbitrary design?" (306), he has come to the same end as Anna. But whereas he concludes that life "is not susceptible perhaps to the treatment we give it when we try to tell it" (362), Anna looks to herself for an explanation; and given her understandings of story, she seems bound to hold herself, not story or life, responsible. Anything but description of the real must be arbitrary, and since she herself chooses the elements that are arbitrary, she must do so for a reason. Since she has not consciously made the choices, then the choices are being made by her, but unconsciously. The only conclusion is that she is managing to deceive, not some public, some reader, but herself. In an effort to avoid her compulsion to fictionalize, she decides that she "shall keep a diary" (229) in a blue notebook, the implication being that if she consciously thinks of writing a diary she will not automatically begin to write stories.

This decision made, she is, as always, driven to take it as far as possible, to "write down, as truthfully as [she] can, every stage of a day" (331). But when the chosen day has passed and she begins to write its record, she necessarily wonders whether having chosen "to be very conscious of everything that happened yesterday changed the shape of the day" (331). "Conscious" here, like "the novel" and "the truth" earlier, seems to have just a very general, everyday meaning, having to do with willfully directed attention. But in fact Anna means it quite specifically: willed awareness of her experience as what will have been conformed to writing. "Inscripted" as she is by writing, she seems unaware of the significance of this condition. In spite of her self-suspicion, she sets out to write the truthful, detailed record, just "to see how it looks." At one point during the day she discovers that her period has begun. Writing about this gives her pause because, she says, "as soon as I write the word 'blood,' it will be giving a wrong emphasis, and even to me when I come to read what I've written" (340). The phrasing captures what she misses in her unaware usage of the word *conscious*. To whom will "it" be giving a wrong emphasis if the diary-writing is directed toward herself only? The "even to me" implies some other reader who would likely be more affected by menstrual "blood" than the writer of the word. And as she writes, she even looks upon herself as an "other" reader. Plainly, being "conscious" of putting her experience into writing, even in diary form, forces her to imagine her words going out into the world apart from her body. The outcome of this kind of being "conscious" is that she objectifies her own experience as it happens.

To understand this, we return once more to Eliot. She realized that taking the real as story content entailed that she and her reader would be dependent on her personal perceptions and understandings, which she readily admitted would be "doubtless defective" in some ways. But she felt no need to mistrust her perceptions in general; she could take her experience and her understanding as reasonably dependable givens from which fictionalizing could begin. The challenge was being true to experience and understanding in the act of writing. As we have seen, Anna has from the beginning thought of her experience in terms of writing. But the decision to write a diary seems to force things up a notch. Before, as with the experience of Molly and Tommy, she would at least let a given experience strike her spontaneously as needing to be written, though she would then suffer the sense of failure to get that experience down truthfully. Now she treats her experience, as it is occurring, like writing. With her period, which after all happens every month and is a part of her being as a woman, "the idea that [she] will have to write it down changes" the otherwise normal way she experiences the event, "destroying the truth" (341) of it as raw experience. Still, this does not stop her from writing out the day. But when she is finished, she scores through the many pages we have just read, and then writes: "No, it didn't come off. A failure as usual" (368). She does not explain why it is a failure, but then writes a one-paragraph summary of the day, much as might appear in a more record-keeping sort of journal. Presumably this is not such a failure.

Anna slips into a kind of insanity across the course of the novel. Though she seems to think of writing as therapeutic, and though writing can truly be therapeutic, in her case it appears to be at least a significant cause of her madness. Gradually, the alphabetic self-division that has been more or less normal for her becomes more and more pronounced. At one point, as she writes the diary details of the one day, she wonders, "who is that Anna who will read what I will write? Who is this other I whose judgment I fear; or whose gaze, at least, is different from mine when I am not thinking, recording, being conscious?" (351). The lack of quotes around the "I" shows just how completely she is beginning to objectify herself as another person. Neither of the two different "I"s in the passage is written as merely a hypothetical or supposed entity. "Being conscious" must in the context mean thinking of herself as the content of a written text, though she takes it as meaning being conscious in some everyday sense. The "other I" would apparently be herself apart from alphabetic consciousness, and that "I" is beginning to seem like an antagonist.

Later, as she resumes writing the character, Ella, we read: "I see Ella, walking slowly about a big empty room, thinking, waiting. I, Anna, see Ella. Who is, of course, Anna. But that is the point, for she is not. The moment I, Anna, write: Ella rings up Julia to announce, etc., then Ella floats away from me and becomes someone else. I don't understand what happens at the moment Ella separates herself from me and becomes Ella. No one does. It's enough to call her Ella, instead of Anna" (459). Her mental decay is explicitly expressed in this failure to distinguish between herself as writer and herself as the subject of writing. Ella is, as usual, a fictional creation, modeled directly upon Anna. Anna knows this. But in alphabetic story the character is always necessarily both a function of the writer's private individuality and also cut off from the writer because of the nature of writing. "Ella" floats away because of the means by which Anna chooses to write her story.

Anna continues her blue notebook diary for a year and a half as a list of dates and events with no commentary whatsoever. But it turns out that the "blue notebook which [she] had expected to be the most truthful of the notebooks, is worse than any of them" (468). It fails because she had expected "the terse record of facts to present some sort of pattern when [she] read over it" at a later time (468). It is unclear what kind of pattern Anna might think she means here. All she can say is that the record of the facts is no "more real" than her other records, in which she wrote what she "thought." As her story continues, it becomes clearer and clearer that on some level Anna wants to produce writing that both is and is not a representation. On the one hand, she seems unable to conceive of living without representing herself in writing; on the other hand, she wants there to be no difference between writing and its content. There is in all this a desire to "overcome reference" (Fuoroli, 150). In her case this dead-end desire is complicated by the way writing causes her to self-historicize. Because she writes only from her own experience, she is always both recording and analyzing the present moment in her writing. But she also always writes with the idea that she will reread her own words later, not to recover the kinds of facts that will normally be lost to memory, but to understand "the truth" about what will have been her past self. As a result, her writing radically disjoins her from the immediacy of the present.

Now, human beings in general have the capacity to be disjoined from the present, at least to a degree. We can always think ourselves into an awareness of how the present may possibly look as the past of some future present, and also of how the present actually looks compared to what we had imagined of it in the past. The ability to think of ourselves from this removed temporal perspective can be a powerfully positive thing in life, enabling us in the most basic way to plan wisely and to learn from our mistakes. It is essential to the specifically human sense of the present: we "know" the present as no other animal does because we have this sense of time. There is a tragic edge to it as well, though, because we become aware that we are always in a sense hopelessly "out" of time, always knowing too late what we needed to have known earlier. But Anna's near-absolute faith in the power of writing is causing an otherwise normal human state to become psychologically cancerous.

Earlier, I noted how literate cultures, deprived of forgetfulness, are bound to experience conflict between their present sense of identity and the identity preserved in their written pasts. Anna is profoundly in conflict with her present identity because she experiences the present itself as an uneraseable, already-written past. We can see this in her reaction to this portion of her blue notebook. After rereading and being disappointed by the factual record, she goes back and crosses out every page with "a thick black cross" (467). This recalls Elizabeth Bennet's inability to destroy Darcy's letter. Why not destroy the notebook, or at least those pages? Why not erase them? Evidently this action would feel like destroying the past itself, which she cannot do. An inked cross at once rules them out and leaves them intact. The comparison with Elizabeth is instructive in other ways as well. Like Elizabeth, Anna experiences a conflict between a written record of the past and her own memory of the past. But since the written record is Anna's own, the conflict is entirely, solipsistically private. On rereading her notebooks Anna says, "I didn't recognize myself. Matching what I had written with what I remembered [the writing] all seemed false" (476). Fully inscripted into writing, fully taking up the roles of both experiencer and recorder, of writer and reader, she lacks what Elizabeth took for granted: a public "other," even an imaginary one, in relation to whom she could at least possibly measure her own judgments. It is in this way that writing itself is a fundamental cause of Anna's madness.

Anna's madness begins to reach its climax with a final return to her past, a final review of her experience as if it were another's. This time, though, she does not do so in writing. She goes through an extended, more or less hallucinatory episode. At one point, as she moves in and out of this state, a kind of controlling inner consciousness demands that instead of "making up [written] stories about life, so as not to look at it straight, [she] should go back and look at scenes from [her] life" (616). Immediately the scenes from Africa reappear, but this time as in a film being run by "an invisible projectionist" (617), who is plainly a projection of herself. This figure is also verbally "directing" her along the way (634). He becomes, then, both artistic and technological director of this phase of her experience. As she has been all along caught up in being both writer and reader of her own experience, now she is both filmmaker-projectionist and viewer. Interestingly, she imagines the show as being controlled both by the projectionist and by the cinematic machinery. At first the projectionist willfully runs the film at a "speeded-up" pace. Then abruptly he (Anna says "he") stops showing Africa and begins "running a new part of the film." But it "was running slowly, because there was a technical hitch of some kind, and several times he . . . turned back the film so as to go through it again" (617).

She can grasp, at least in a general way, a fact about film that she never seems to grasp about writing: a technology is determining the nature of "story" in both cases. With all this, we are also given an image of how film is like and unlike alphabetic story. Because of its technological nature, film, like alphabetic story, can be attended to at variable paces, can be stopped and started at the viewer's discretion, and can be reviewed in its exact form as many times as desired. Unlike alphabetic story, film enables all this with story that is shown to the eye in moving images, rather than told in alphabetic signs. For these reasons film marks the next major epoch in the history of story after the novel. That this particular character's great crisis should occur in terms of film seems to acknowledge this. It is as if the novel as a genre is expiring into film. Still, as always, even the turn to film comes to us in a novel. So even if film is the next event in the history of story, this does not mean alphabetic story will somehow disappear.

This interior film episode goes on at some length. Sometimes it runs continuously, and then it becomes "perfunctory. Scene after scene flicked on, then off" (618). Images of a long list of people from her past appear "briefly, distorted with speed." Then they vanish, and the film "[breaks] off, or rather [runs] down, with a jarring dislocation" (619). Now the projectionist challenges her just as she has always challenged herself about her stories. He asks, "And what makes you think that the emphasis you have put on it is the correct emphasis?" He then begins "running the film through again, or rather, the films, for there were several." Having been asked the great critical question, she becomes a critic and passes much the same judgment as she has passed on *Frontiers of War*. "They were all," she says, "conventionally, well-made films, as if they had been done in a studio." Then, viewing the credits, she discovers that she herself had made the films. The projectionist even keeps "running the films very fast, and then pausing on the credits" just to drive this fact home. She denies having made the film, but then the projectionist calls into her mind her usual dilemma: "The material had been made by me to fit what I knew, and that was why it was all false" (620). He challenges her to tell the Africa story from one of the other character's point of view. This she does by beginning to write. Since the only story she has actually seen is her own, she can only write, as opposed to show the film of, another's story. But again, as always, her written words disappoint her. They read "in the style of the most insipid, coy women's magazine" (620). The projectionist scorns her once more, and just as he is about to start the film again, she wakes out of this dream state.

Even fully awake, she remains constantly aware that "the projectionist [is] in wait for" her (633). And when she sleeps again, he does return. This time the showing of the film bears an even greater resemblance to the qualities of what we have earlier called alphabetic reading. "Patches of the film," she says, "slowed down for long, long stretches while I watched, absorbed, details I had not had time to notice in life." She watches "for an immense time, noting every movement" of the film's content. As she can slow down and re-view, so she can at times speed past content. She views and re-views this film as Elizabeth Bennet read and reread Darcy's letter. Finally, she makes the choice to stop viewing the film. The projectionist disappears, "so I leaned out my own hand," she tells us, "to switch off the machine" (635). Still asleep, she begins "to read the words off a page" she has written. And this moment begins the end of her inability to write a satisfying novel, the outcome of which is, at least in one way, *The Golden Notebook*.

So the climax of the inscripted woman's story occurs as an imaginary film. With this film, we have a story that shows as well as tells. At the same time we have the ability to attend to the story in the same ways that are peculiar to alphabetic story. Anna as projectionist can slow down or speed up, stop and restart later. She even views the story in complete privacy. This is because she only imagines the film, but cinema does make a truly private showing—literally no other human being need be present—of story possible for the first time. Moreover, though the technology was not so widespread when Lessing wrote this novel, cinema also made possible for the first time the private creation of an actual story that shows. In some way, filmic story has saved Anna. She is portrayed as having to pass through the filmed version of her "story" in order to be able to write that story. Even though the film strikes her as quite conventional, and even though she must admit, as with her written stories, that it has been conformed to her memory, it still manages to "cure" her. Given the specific ways in which Lessing has invoked film in this specific novel, the only difference between filmic and alphabetic story is the ability to make visible to the (private) eye. Of course this film is, if anything, even more solipsistic than Anna's alphabetic sense of story. With writing, there is at least a "public-ation" of her verbal words into an entirely different kind of representation. The written text can at least possibly be seen by others. With this internal film, there is no difference between the faces in her memory and the faces in the representation—that is, no actors playing parts. Still, the internal imagination of the filmed version of her story is required to cure her.

Lessing's novel seems, then, to bring a conclusion to the trajectory we have seen unfolding as story gets more and more thoroughly conformed to the technology of writing. The built-in array of effects that have been present since the novel emerged—privacy, self-objectification, arbitrariness, individual responsibility—have come to a truly radical solipsism. The necessary, remaining sign of positivity is that it takes a novel to show how the novel has come to this impasse. Even so, the appearance of film seems a kind of just-in-time deliverance out of the entire realm of written story.

CHAPTER EIGHT

The Alphabetic Story
of *Atonement*

＊I

IAN MCEWAN'S *Atonement* opens with an epigraph from chapter 24 of
Jane Austen's *Northanger Abbey*, a novel that serves historically in the
English tradition in much the same way that *Don Quixote* serves in the
tradition of the novel in general. In Austen's novel the young heroine,
Catherine Morland, brings herself close to social disaster because she
begins to look at the real world as if it were a version of the gothic novels she is so fond of reading. Specifically, she begins to imagine that Henry
Tilney's father has faked his wife's death and now keeps her locked away
in a secret room in the old Northanger Abbey. The epigraph is taken from
the moment when Henry perceives how Catherine is thinking about his
father. He calls her back to her senses with a straightforward appeal to
everyday reality, both natural (her sense perceptions of the world around
her) and cultural (laws, social and literary intercourse, newspapers, and
the like). Now, this is a case of the realistic novel establishing itself as a
rejection of the gothic novel. But as I argue in the opening chapter, what
is more specifically being rejected is a literate person falling under the
spell of oralistic written fiction. The implied meaning for the novel as a
genre is that, like Henry and unlike gothic romance, the right kind of fiction will appeal to the everyday senses and everyday social life.

Following after these great predecessors, *Atonement* has much to do
with the "chasm that separates the world of the living from that of fictional invention" (Finney, 69), but it will significantly revise the historical pattern that we can trace beginning with *Don Quixote*. *Don Quixote*,
Northanger Abbey, and *Madame Bovary* are novels about literate characters who become so enchanted by oralistic written stories that they lose
their sense of the everyday real. With these novels, we also have a kind

of evolution over time. As the novel becomes more alphabetic, the remaining oralistic elements to be excluded become less and less fantastic. The epigraph places *Atonement* in this line of novels, but McEwan complicates the model in a most interesting way. On the one hand, his main character, Briony Tallis, will at least to a degree be thinking of herself and the world in terms of oralistic fiction when she commits the "crime" that brings about this novel's catastrophe. But on the other, she is more important for being a writer than she is for being a reader. McEwan's novel is, among other things, the story of how a young girl becomes a novelist, and so it is rather overtly metafictional. The author himself has said that he feels "that every sentence contains a ghostly commentary on its own processes" (McEwan 2002, 59). Further, as Pilar Hidalgo and Earl Ingersoll have noted in some detail, the novel is quite densely allusive to other novels. Taking all this together, we can see that *Atonement* is specifically "about" the nature of the novel, or what I am here calling alphabetic fiction. Indeed, for our purposes Briony Tallis's story is exemplary; it deals directly with the ways in which our built-in oralistic sense of story gets conformed to the technology of writing.

Writing, we know, has to do with the materialization of speech. From the beginning, McEwan makes much of Briony's enthrallment simply with the material results and the physical activity of writing. As a girl she loves to "contemplate" a finished draft as an object (3). "The pages of a recently finished story seemed to vibrate in her hand with all the life they contained" (7). Later in the novel, after spending many hours for many days in a row churning out her first long fiction, "she could hardly remember a greater pleasure than at the end, when she squared off the completed pile of pages . . . and felt at the tips of her raw fingers the weight of her creation" (264). This brings us to a curious byproduct of story-writing. Writing usually entails doing something with your hands. The nature of the technology is such that it requires specific tools and materials as well as a unique hand-and-eye coordination. So writing is a kind of handicraft. Though we do not perform the activity in order to produce a finished object of the same kind as, say, a clay pot or carved wood, we nonetheless feel the similarity to such handicraft activities. As with much other craftwork, there is the long period of individual shaping and molding in the shop, so to speak; then, when the task is done, we have a material object (at least as long as the story is printed on paper) to be looked at, touched, "squared off" into its properly uniform appearance, moved around, stored away, and brought out again later. Unlike an orally communicated tale, this story lasts past its immediate telling. It is a good feeling to have a visible, handleable object to show at the end of the work.

The handicraft effect of writing comes out in other ways as well. At a crucial moment the young Briony imagines writing up a dramatic event she has just witnessed; imagines "hurrying . . . to her bedroom, to a clean block of lined paper and her marbled, Bakelite fountain pen. She could see the simple sentences . . . unfurling at the nib's end" (38). Briony experiences the basic pleasure of having mastered a craft-technology. Like a woodworker or potter, she gets satisfaction just in having the proper materials and tools, and she gets a kind of visceral pleasure in witnessing the object take on visible form as she produces it. Later, at a similar moment, "the urge to be writing was stronger than any notion she had of what she might write. What she wanted was to be lost to the unfolding of an irresistible idea, to see the black thread spooling out from the end of her scratchy silver nib and coiling into words" (108).

We have discussed certain negative effects of writing and privacy: the sense of maximum responsibility for both sides of the verbal communication, the sense of originality, and the sense of arbitrariness. Now we see the corollary positive effects. Humans commonly take pleasure in activities that require manual dexterity, sustained and focused concentration, and that result in the production of an object. We enjoy losing ourselves — getting "lost" — in such activities. Briony experiences this kind of pleasure when she goes alone to her bedroom and witnesses the "black thread" of her words "spooling out" before her onto the paper. Why does the usually negative word *lost* seem right for this, since it is a positively valued experience? Lost, and in a good way, from what? The term seems to take on its meaning in relation to a roughly normal state of mind that is not so narrowly focused, not so concentrated on some one activity, one that is social and open to input from the world at large. This use of *lost* implies that the opposite state is our regular self-mode, and we must feel that it is somehow dangerous to limit our attention to (lose ourselves to) the activity upon which we so narrowly focus. Presumably, on some basic level we have a worry about failing to be aware of some possible threat or about possibly failing to refind our regular selves. (The fear of this latter threat seems to be what motivated those novels about literate readers losing themselves to oralistic story.) But at the same time, assuming that we do not become permanently lost, we enjoy the willed concentration of attention. It seems to give us a sense of self-improvement, with the additional charge of having managed to improve ourselves in spite of the risk of losing ourselves. And if we have managed to lose ourselves productively this way, not just to any idea, but to an "irresistible idea," then our pleasure, like Briony's, is all the more intense.

Another aspect of the sheer visual pleasure in seeing one's materialized words is tied, as always, to the issue of showing and telling. With the typical speech communication, the presence of other human beings reciprocally and continually makes visible to the teller on the most basic level that he or she is: firstly, communicating at all, and secondly, communicating well or poorly. In any oral-story scenario this reciprocal showing is necessarily a response to the unique individuality (the showing aspect) of the teller, apart from the content of the given tale. The storywriter, working alone in silence, almost never has the benefit of this ongoing, reciprocal showing. Although this can be a negative effect, it, too, has its positive corollary; for the materialized words continually "coiling" onto the page make plain to the eye of the writer that she does have something of herself "to show," and handwriting would make this yet more personal and idiosyncratic. Even as an adult, Briony never loses her "childhood pleasure in seeing pages covered in her own handwriting. It almost didn't matter what she wrote" (263).

So Briony is presented as thoroughly caught up in the technology itself, in its physical aspects. But of course it only "almost" does not matter what she writes. In fact the content is all-important. In Part One of *Atonement* we are given her writing history from its beginning at age eleven till its first, precocious climax at age thirteen. The narrator tells us outright that over these two formative years Briony writes "her way through a whole history of literature, beginning with stories derived from European folktales, through drama with simple moral intent, to arrive at an impartial psychological realism" (38). Our understanding of writing and the technologizing of story gives us a unique perspective on this microhistory. As we shall see, the "story" of the emergence of this novelist, like the story of the emergence of the novel in general, is directly a function of the unavoidable conflicts between the pleasures and the anxieties of conforming story to writing.

✺II

Two years before the time of the novel's opening, Briony, as an eleven-year-old, has a passion for secrets. Her everyday life fails to give her a supply, so she turns to writing. Writing teaches her that "the imagination itself was a source of secrets" because once she begins to write, she cannot tell anyone that she has begun: "Pretending in words was too tentative, too vulnerable, too embarrassing to let anyone know. Even writing out the *she saids*, the *and thens*, made her wince, and she felt foolish, appearing to know about the emotions of an imaginary being. Self-exposure was inevitable the moment she described a character's weakness; the reader was bound to speculate that she was describing herself. What other authority could she have?" (6). Though we have a general phrase here ("pretending in words"), it is specifically written story that causes these problems. It is not that Briony has trouble coming up with some specific story but that the activity of telling in writing simply feels wrong. After all, children constantly create outlandish stories without feeling the least bit tentative or vulnerable, and the "she saids" and "and thens" cause no problems in oral storytelling. Why would the "she saids" and the "and thens" make her wince? Why the sense of vulnerability?

Briony is experiencing the kind of difficulties we often experience when we first substitute a technology for an otherwise "natural" ability. As a comparison, we may think of our first uses, even as adults, of binoculars or a microphone. At first, we may well find it embarrassing as we try to conform our everyday seeing and speaking abilities to such devices. But the technologizing of story into writing is rather more problematic than these, because language and story are so central to our identity. Her fear of *self*-exposure in describing others, especially negatively, and her felt lack of authority are distinctly specific to alphabetic story. In, again, an archetypal and also precocious way, young Briony experiences her own version of Shelley's concerns as a child writer, Eliot's authorial concerns in *Adam Bede*, Esther Summerson's anxieties in *Bleak House*, Bernard's senses of failure in *The Waves*, and Anna's sense of failure in *The Golden Notebook*. She seems to know intuitively that when story is conformed to writing, the responsibility for the content falls ultimately on the writer as a private individual. Since an individual can only offer her subjective perspective, then the writer must necessarily be putting herself on the page and therefore making herself vulnerable in ways that do not happen with the usual case of telling a story verbally.

And what of her sense of feeling foolish about knowing the emotions of imaginary beings? This perhaps captures the problem in the largest way. Most generally understood, story (as opposed to a report of the real) always involves imaginary beings, and there is no problem at all with the teller knowing about the emotions of those beings. In fact, what else is a story but just this: the hero's emotions—fear, anger, a broken heart—and the action? To Briony, writing renders foolish the most fundamental elements of story. But this can only be true if she is on some level more or less automatically taking writing to be the obvious and right way for story to go. The effect is akin to binoculars rendering foolish the everyday nature of untechnologized seeing. The difference is that we do not typically conflate everyday seeing with binocularized seeing. We do, however, conflate writing and speech, alphabetic story and story in general. As we have seen many times before along the way, Briony is doing just this.

Unlike young Mary Shelley, Briony does press ahead in spite of her sense of anxiety. *Atonement* opens, significantly, as she has left behind her folktale stories and turned to drama. The unsuccessful staging of this drama—*The Trials of Arabella*—will be the dramatic childhood backdrop for the adult drama that initiates the novel. Briony's play is a "crude melodrama" (Finney, 70). She has written it to celebrate both her older brother's return from the university (with a schoolmate, Paul Marshall) and the arrival of her three cousins—the fifteen-year-old Lola and nine-year-old twins, Jackson and Pierrot—for an extended stay. We must assume the play is not as oralistic as the folktales she had begun with two years earlier, but its proximity to oral story is nonetheless apparent. The theme, after Austen, is that "love which did not build a foundation on good sense [is] doomed" (3). But this theme is expressed through "the reckless passion of the heroine, Arabella, for a wicked count," her near death by cholera as she elopes with him, and her salvation by, and marriage to, an impoverished doctor who turns out to be a prince in disguise.

The fundamentally oralistic nature of Briony as a storyteller also shows up in the way she needs an immediate audience even though the piece is written. She takes the finished draft to the one person who may be every writer's ideal reader: her mother. Sitting with an arm around her as she reads, Briony closely studies "every trace of shifting emotion" as her mother obligingly gives an exaggerated and always-affirming array of facial and verbal responses (4). The family as a whole plays this part as well, encouraging her "to read her stories aloud" to them in the library. She reads histrionically and looks up to "gaze into one face after another, unapologetically demanding her family's total attention as she cast her narrative spell" (6). Both the unsophisticated little girl and her family just assume that her written stories will be read aloud. The idea of a story that is only to be read alone in silence seems never to occur at this primary storytelling level. Showing is taken for granted as integral to the telling, even of a written story.

In turning to playwriting, Briony has felt relieved "not to be writing out the *she saids*, or describing the weather or the onset of spring or her heroine's face" (7). From this, we can see again that no matter what pleasures she has derived from her earlier written stories, she has evidently been feeling the burden of having moved into story that can only tell; for it is only with such a story that she would have to write out these kinds of things. And yet there is one aspect of written story that pleases her from the beginning. She has a fondness for tidiness and "miniaturization," for the ability to create a "world that is just so" (4), a "world in five pages . . . that was more pleasing than [the] model farm" that sits in perfect order on her windowsill.

With this, we get in a naïve way the positive corollary to certain anxieties that come with alphabetic story and that Briony herself has already experienced. The lack of embodied response to written story produces an anxious sense of responsibility, originality, and uncertainty; Briony experiences just this when she worries about herself as the only authority for her written words. At the same time, it can produce the great (though from the oralistic point of view, selfish) luxury of, precisely, not having to worry about other responses affecting the story. The writer can experience a sense of possession that an oral storyteller cannot. Without the give and take of living respondents and the communal requirements of the already-told content, a story-writer can be a godlike creator. A thinking adult, such as George Eliot (and a fictional writer such as Bernard in *The Waves*), feels very strongly and consciously the charge of willful arbitrariness that comes with this. Briony feels this at times but seems to overcome it by turning to drama. A play, she thinks, is a "universe reduced to what was said in it," and that is "tidiness indeed" (7).

But a story such as drama, which is ultimately all showing, has its own drawbacks. As Raymond Williams puts it, "a dramatic text, unlike texts written for silent reading . . . presumes both an inherent multivocal form — the composition is distributed between different speaking voices — and certain governing physical relations, in the relational presence of actors in a playing space and in the further (and often complex) relational presence of these actors with an audience" (44). Her sense of the tidiness of her written text cannot survive its incarnation into the necessary "different speaking voices." The "rehearsals," she finds, "offended her sense of order. The self-contained world she had drawn with clear and perfect lines had been defaced with the scribble of other minds, other needs" (34). The expressions here are revealingly convoluted. Strictly speaking, the written text of a play does not "tell" a story, though she is thinking of it that way. To equate the text and the produced story would be like equating a blueprint and a finished house or the sketches of a sculpture with the sculpted figure itself. Briony of course knows the play will involve actors interacting in a stage space, and she accordingly thinks in terms of showing. But the showing she imagines is a frozen, painterly image rather than an actual embodied enactment. For her, the play is a "drawn" sketch that is as true ("clear and perfect lines") to her original, tidy story idea ("self-contained world") as a good sketch is to what it represents. Accordingly, she experiences the differences between her text as written telling and its production into showing as a defacing of her drawing. But then writing is still the problem, for she also thinks of her drawing as being defaced by the writings, not the drawings, of others; and, worse, defaced with a script ("scribbles") that takes no care to be as visually precise and clear, as tidy and orderly as proper script should be.

The experience of story that depends on showing drives her back to the realm of telling, in which she can preserve her sense of self-contained order, but at the same time she almost instinctively does not want to give up showing altogether. She realizes that she should have written a story for her brother, so that she could have "put it in his hands herself, and [watched] as he read it" (35). In other words, she wants both the privacy and tidiness of written story and the audience response of oral story. The play also causes her to miss the materially self-contained nature of written story: "The title lettering, the illustrated cover, the pages *bound* — in that word alone she felt the attraction of the neat, limited and controllable form she had left behind when she decided to write a play" (35, McEwan's italics). Though a play may be published as a text, it cannot be "bound" in the way of a story because its production necessarily involves others as more than audience. A story, she thinks, "was direct and simple, allowing nothing to come between herself and her reader . . . a story was a form of telepathy. By means of inking symbols onto a page, she was able to send thoughts and feelings from her mind to her reader's" (35).

We could not ask for a clearer invocation of the telepathic effect of writing. Going simply by the private experience of seeing her unspoken words coil onto the page and by the comparison to the normal experience of conversation, she assumes the external possibility of what is only possible within her own mind: the immediate "hearing" of the written words by another in the same way that she "hears" them as she writes. "Reading a sentence and understanding it were the same thing; . . . nothing lay between them. There was no gap during which the symbols were unraveled" (35). She has turned one hundred eighty narrative degrees, from a fantasy of the perfect story (the play) that only shows, to a fantasy of the perfect story that only tells. She senses a truth about the way writing is experienced as a kind of telepathy, but she does not really understand the illusory nature of the effect, which will always be jeopardized by that which makes it possible: the disembodied materiality of writing. To be sure, she is a very young girl, who cannot be expected to have a sophisticated understanding of such things. But then, just this, as with the young Mary Shelley, is what makes her case revealing. Even more revealing is the example she goes on to consider: "You saw the word *castle*, and it was there, seen from some distance, with woods in high summer spread before it, the air bluish and soft with smoke rising from the blacksmith's forge, and a cobbled road twisting away into the green shade" (35). However precocious she is about these issues, she still takes oralistic story content, from medieval romance, as the obvious content.

At the moment of thinking this, Briony is, significantly, in the upstairs nursery of the old house, looking out the window over the grounds. The view, as if to reinforce her thoughts, "could easily have accommodated, in the distance at least, a medieval castle." By chance, at this moment she sees below her an interaction between her college-age sister, Cecilia, and Robbie Turner, a college-age young man who has been her father's ward and who has grown up at the house. This is the day on which Cecilia and Robbie will realize that they are in love with each other. That realization will begin, though not promisingly, with an encounter that Briony watches from above. Cecilia and Robbie are by a large stone fountain. Cecilia has come to the fountain with a porcelain vase of flowers that need water. She goes to dip in the vase. Robbie insists on helping her. In the little contest between them a piece of the vase breaks off and sinks into the basin. Cecilia abruptly takes off her blouse and skirt, steps into the water, and ducks underneath to retrieve the pieces. She climbs back out, puts her clothes on again, and stalks off with the vase, leaving Robbie dumbstruck. As Briony observes this, she is still in the "castle" story mode. When she first sees the two, who have always related more or less as brother and sister, she immediately thinks: "A proposal of marriage" (36). This seems possible because she "herself had written a tale in which a humble woodcutter saved a princess from drowning and ended by marrying her." Robbie, being a ward and therefore relatively humble compared to her own family, would fit the bill, because such "leaps across boundaries were the stuff of daily romance."

But when Cecilia disrobes and steps into the water, Briony thinks that the "sequence was illogical—the drowning scene, followed by a rescue, should have preceded the marriage proposal." The logic of her romance plot violated, she decides she does "not understand, and that she must simply watch." Looking through "unambiguous sunlight," she has her first inkling that "for her now it could no longer be fairy-tale castles and princesses, but the strangeness of the here and now, of what passed between people, the ordinary people that she knew" (37). Though she still feels tempted "to be magical" in the story that she conjures around the scene, she knows that this "was not a fairy tale, this was the real, the adult world in which frogs did not address princesses, and the only messages were the ones that people sent." From all this, she goes on to sense that "she could write a scene like the one by the fountain and she could include a hidden observer like herself" (37). Briony has just experienced, on a micro-level, the macro-level historical emergence of alphabetic story. She has gone directly to the notion of privately created story told with an unidentifiable teller (the omniscient "hidden observer") and to the notion that the real, the ordinary, the here and now are the proper content for telling.

She goes further, imagining that she "could write the scene three times over, from three points of view," hers, Cecilia's, and Robbie's. With this idea she steps even more fully into the realm of alphabetic story. She is now imagining not just *a* hidden observer but effectively no centralized teller of any sort; and yet she is not imagining drama. She imagines a written prose fiction that does its best in this way (by eliminating all vestiges of a single, master teller) to be all showing, that is, a fiction that would split the difference between the two kinds of story she has recently rejected. Almost automatically she also imagines a new kind of content as well. She suddenly feels an excitement "in the prospect of freedom, of being delivered from the cumbrous struggle between good and bad, heroes and villains. None of these three was bad, nor were they particularly good. She need not judge. There did not have to be a moral. She need only *show* separate minds, as alive as her own, struggling with the idea that other minds were equally alive . . . only in a story could you enter these different minds and *show* how they had an equal value" (38, italics added).

This "prospect of freedom" must remind us of Eliot trying to get free of her imaginary, oralistic reader, and even more so of Woolf trying to get free of those tyrannical requirements in "Modern Fiction," though Briony is not so radical. As she begins to conform herself to alphabetic story, she feels that the basic requirements of oralistic story, such as unambiguously good and bad characters, are no longer simply the obvious ways of storytelling but are a burden. And she takes this even further. Earlier, she had worried about the self-exposure that would occur when she, as narrator, passed judgment on a character. The more alphabetic the story, the more it will move toward what, from the oralistic perspective, is description, and the more it will move toward describing the real. As I have already noted, a story that works to describe the real without making judgments will strive just to display its contents in words, unaffected by the sense of a specifiable human teller at all. Such a story tries to operate as a kind of written photograph. Rather like a photographer, then, the maximally alphabetic teller simply records the real, thus avoiding the problem of making moral judgments at all. Or so it can appear to a young girl who is just discovering all this. Though she will change later on, at this point she is thrilled with what she experiences as a kind of "freedom."

Furthermore, it is true that a playwright enters different minds and, through creating speech and action, shows how different minds have equal value. But Briony wants to do this kind of thing in story that can only tell. So freedom involves disembodying herself as thoroughly as possible, removing any sign of her individual self as the originator of the telling. When she thinks of entering the different minds and showing them as opposed to telling about them, she hypothesizes stream of consciousness, which, after dialogue or letters, is the maximal attempt by writing to show rather than to tell a story. The premise of stream of consciousness is that the reader is not in any way being told about thoughts but is being given the thoughts directly, though in written form. Briony, then, has just had the experience that takes her out of the writer's nursery. From her experience she has intuited the nature of the novel as a genre of story. But because of what will come later it matters to see that she is initiated directly into, not just the novel in general, but the maximally alphabetic novel, which works to cast aside all evidence of orality, all evidence of a teller, in the attempt to be, impossibly, purely a showing.

Later, after another chance experience involving sexuality—this time a misdirected erotic love note (obscene to the young girl) from Robbie to Cecilia—Briony immediately thinks of beginning to write. But now she encounters the dilemma of actually creating the new kind of narrative she has imagined. Sounding much like Lessing's Anna Wulf, she feels "trapped between the urge to write a simple diary account of her day's experiences and the ambition to make something greater of them that would be polished, self-contained and obscure" (109). Obviously, one way to tell the story of the real itself would simply be a diary description. Although she feels the pull of this extreme, she also feels the basic, foundational urge to distinguish story (something "polished" and "self-contained") from report. She also seems to intuit that the kind of story she envisions will, in relation to story in a general sense, necessarily be "obscure." She feels, without having been put to any serious test, already comfortable about the basics of realism: "Actions she thought she could describe well enough, and she had the hang of dialogue" (109). But then, like Woolf, she feels an inadequacy in the traditional forms of written telling. She wonders about "how to do feelings? All very well to write, *She felt sad*, or describe what a sad person might do, but what of sadness itself?" (109). This is another version of the dilemma that continually plagued Bernard in *The Waves* and that helped induce madness in Anna Wulf. Having committed herself to leaving behind all vestiges of oralistic story, Briony is now faced with the intractable problem of trying to show, when, strictly speaking, all she can do is tell. To repeat, the only "thing itself" that a written story can actually show is writing. All else must be "shown" through telling.

With these issues established in the novel, Briony's writing project, like the performance of her play, will be postponed for years because of the events that now unfold. For at the very moment of her initiation into the complexities of the most alphabetic form of story, she plays a key role in the false conviction of Robbie for the rape of her cousin Lola. In part because of Briony's misperceptions and girlish enthusiasms, Robbie is sent to prison, and the family more or less explodes into resentments and guilt. Briony's role in this catastrophe places her in the line of literate misreaders coming down from Don Quixote.

After seeing her sister and Robbie by the fountain, and after reading the erotic note, Briony by chance walks into the library as Cecilia and Robbie are making passionate but awkward first love in a darkened corner. The sequence of events and Briony's complete ignorance of the love these two have just discovered cause her to assume that Robbie is assaulting Cecilia. But Cecilia simply walks out, and nothing is said. Later that night, the twin cousins run away, and everyone goes out in search of them. Briony goes by herself. As she hunts over the grounds, she thinks of what she now believes of Robbie, and of how "[real] life . . . had sent her a villain in the form of an old family friend" (148). With her new understanding of story, this makes perfect sense because it was just what "no one would have expected, and of course villains were not announced with hisses or soliloquies, they did not come cloaked in black, with ugly expressions" (148). In alphabetic story, the common expectations of (oralistic) story will not apply; the lack of melodrama will be just the norm. But then, on seeing her mother through a drawing room window, Briony begins to think of how old her mother is, and that one day she would die. She fantasizes that there "would be a funeral in the village at which [Briony's] dignified reticence would hint at the vastness of her sorrow. As her friends came up to murmur their condolences they would feel awed by the scale of her tragedy. She saw herself standing alone in a great arena, within a towering coliseum, watched not only by all the people she knew but by all those she would ever know, the whole cast of her life, assembled to love her in her loss" (151). Despite the intuitive leap to the most alphabetic story, the thirteen-year-old romantic self-melodramatist remains.

When the catastrophe arrives, this uneasy combination of romance and novel will help it occur. Even though it is very dark and Briony is alone, she presses on with the search because the events of the day "had proved to her that she was not a child, and that she was now a figure in a richer story and had to prove herself worthy of it" (153). Her chance to prove herself comes when she discovers her cousin Lola in the dark just as the shadow of a man sneaks away without speaking. McEwan constructs the story so that Lola is, like her namesake, Lolita, sexually precocious. But at the same time she is the victim of assault by an older man, the university friend, Paul, who is visiting with Briony's brother. Later, Lola and Paul marry, and we are never entirely sure to what degree Lola was forced. In any event Briony, with her mistaken convictions about Robbie, prods Lola into agreeing that Robbie was the man. "The truth" of this "was in the symmetry" with which such violence would follow after the day's events (161). Even when Lola hesitates to agree, Briony pushes the conclusion that she feels must be necessary for this "richer story" in which she finds herself. Lola goes along and as a result Robbie is sent to jail. So Briony, like her predecessor Miss Morland, misreads the real because of her reading.

This returns us to McEwan's opening invocation of *Northanger Abbey*. Given the epigraph and the "crime" in *Atonement*, we might think that the climax of self-recognition on Briony's part would be the realization that she has helped send an innocent man to jail because of her conflation of the real with fiction. Although we infer that this moment must happen, we never see it, nor are we told about it. The self-recognition that we do see is of a different kind, and the epigraph directs us to its nature. McEwan makes a point of quoting the entire, fairly long passage in which Henry Tilney calls Catherine Morland back to her senses. Interestingly, McEwan chooses this passage, which concludes with Catherine running away in shame, rather than any number of passages in the chapter immediately following that express in detail the outcome of her self-recognition, which is the transformation toward which the entire novel has been moving. So the epigraph pushes us to have more of an awareness of Henry and his speech than it does of Catherine (though Catherine does matter). This conclusion is reinforced much later when we find that the old house in *Atonement* has been renamed Tilney's hotel (342).

Like Catherine, Briony is given a transforming call to her senses, though it comes in writing and is about writing. It, too, is lengthy and comes from a male, though not a love interest. She receives it five years after the events around the assault, when she is eighteen and serving, after Cecilia's example, as a hospital nurse during World War II. In the meantime Cecilia has become entirely estranged from the family, and Robbie has managed an early release from prison in exchange for going to the front. Briony takes on her extremely demanding position as a kind of penance for what she had done five years before. She does continue to write, in a private journal: "artistic manifestoes, trivial complaints, character sketches, and simple accounts of her day which increasingly shaded off into fantasy" (263). However modest this writing, she feels that it is "her true self, secretly hoarded, quietly accumulating" (263). After a time, she has an opportunity to use a typewriter on a break from her work, and she types out as a novella the scene she had witnessed from the nursery window.

She is proud and excited by this accomplishment. As she thinks over her first serious attempt at fiction, even more elaborate echoes of Woolf's "Modern Fiction" appear, along with allusions to the equally famous "Mr. Bennett and Mrs. Brown" essay. What impresses Briony about her first large project is the "pure geometry and the defining uncertainty which reflected, she thought, a modern sensibility. The age of clear answers was over. So was the age of characters and plots." Such trivialities are now "quaint devices that belonged to the nineteenth century" (265). The "concept of character was founded on errors that modern psychology had exposed." What matters for the modern writer is "thought, perception, sensations . . . the conscious mind as a river through time" (265). Lastly, to lock in these allusions, we find that she has "read Virginia Woolf's *The Waves* three times and thought that a great transformation was being worked in human nature itself, and that only fiction, a new kind of fiction, could capture the essence of the change. To enter a mind and *show* it at work, or being worked on, and to do this within a symmetrical design —this would be an artistic triumph" (265, italics added).

Any student of Virginia Woolf will recognize certain ideas here, not least the famous claim in "Mr. Bennett and Mrs. Brown" that, "on or about

December, 1910, human character changed" (Woolf 2000, 746). The idea of entering a mind and showing its operation as opposed to telling a reader what to make of that operation describes much of Woolf's most famous work, especially *Mrs. Dalloway* and *To the Lighthouse*. To take *The Waves* as a model, however, is to take what, as we have already seen, may be the most experimental and, perhaps more significantly, the most poetic of all Woolf's various experimental novels. *Atonement* will offer an opinion about all this soon, but for now we can see that Briony is jumping onto the train of fictional experimentation that had by 1940 become rather well established.

Briony sends her story off to a historically real editor: Cyril Connolly of the then front-line literary magazine *Horizon*. In return Connolly writes her a long and intriguing letter of rejection. Connolly praises some of the imagery that as readers we have already encountered in *Atonement*, and he appreciates the way she captures "a flow of thought" in the act of creating character. He goes on:

> Something unique and unexplained is caught. However, we wondered whether it owed a little too much to the techniques of Mrs. Woolf. The crystalline present moment is of course a worthy subject in itself, *especially for poetry*; it allows a writer to show his gifts, delve into mysteries of perception, present a stylized version of thought processes, permit the vagaries and unpredictability of *the private self* to be explored and so on. Who can doubt the value of this experimentation? However, such writing can become precious when there is no sense of forward movement. Put the other way round, *our attention* would have been held even more effectively had there been an underlying *pull of simple narrative*. . . . Your most sophisticated readers might be well up on the latest Bergsonian theories of consciousness, but I'm sure they retain *a child-like desire to be told a story*. . . . Simply put, you need the *backbone of a story*. (294–96, italics added)

With this letter of rejection, the Austen epigraph takes on its full weight. As Tilney called Catherine back from her enchantment with the gothic; so Connolly calls Briony back from her enchantment with a maximal version of alphabetic story. We have come to another representation of the dialectical turn we found with Bernard at the end of *The Waves* and with the hallucinatory film experience in *The Golden Notebook*, though

McEwan stages the turn overtly in relation to the history of story. Whereas the novel as a genre positively established itself by eliminating the fantastic content and incantatory forms of oralistic story, that process of elimination has continued, if these works by Woolf, Lessing, and McEwan are any testimony, on to a negative excess. The more fiction tries to become a function of its determining technology, the less it has to do with anything like what has been commonly taken as story since ancient times. Briony, we must assume, has written what amounts to a report of scene and emotion, trying with elaborately poetic language to present perception itself, emotion itself, to catch the "private moment," as Woolf's Bernard called it, or what Anna Wulf called "simply, the truth." The result, in Connolly's mind, is content that reads word for word like poetry but that otherwise wants to work as story. The italicized preludes in *The Waves* might well have seemed merely precious in this sense if they had been presented as simply a stand-alone "story."

To return again to the primary terms *showing* and *telling*, as I presented them in chapter 1: the more writing works to eliminate signs of a teller, the more it tries to show instead of tell. This leads to either one of two opposites: a putatively objective description that remains strictly exterior, as if there is no filtering, individual perceiver at all, but only a disembodied sensory apparatus, heavily dependent on the eye; or a strict concentration on the interiority of the "private self," because perception can occur only in individual minds, and therefore any objective description (telling that tries to show) will have to represent the real interior, including the unstorylike "vagaries and unpredictability of the private self." But a price is paid for either choice. Recall the kinds of character and plot that, in nonliterate settings, have always been required to catch and hold the attention of an audience. Though written story does not require monumental characters and supernatural events, it must still hold the reader's attention as story of some kind. Otherwise, as Bernard discovered in *The Waves*, why would anyone be interested at all?

Connolly assumes as an obvious truth that no story can do without "forward movement," which is the fundamental "pull of simple narrative." "Simple" in this context means, ultimately, oralistic, because oral narrative is the ultimate model in relation to which any other narrative form may be evaluated as more or less complex. From the literate perspective oral narrative seems, usually in a negative sense, simple; but when story leaves behind all its oral foundations, then that simplicity can be discovered anew, so to speak, as the sine qua non of any story at all. Similarly, oral story is often looked down upon by the (hyper)literate as childish, but once alphabetic story has gone to this extreme, the "child-like desire to be *told* a story" appears, also in a new light, as an indispensable element of any story whatsoever. And yet as we have seen before, even in the act of positing the oralistic as the indispensable ground of story in general, Connolly still invokes the alphabetic standards that look down upon the oralistic as "child-like." And of course "*told*" is just the word. Briony's writing tries (impossibly) to do without telling, but it cannot show in the way of drama; therefore, it has a "static quality" that is alien to story (295). Lastly, his figure, "the backbone of a story," firmly replaces story in the human organism. Her novella is like a human body without its central, built-in core of solidity and support. All of Connolly's comments recall Briony to a more or less universal conception of story, a conception that can be questioned, deconstructed, investigated, ridiculed, thrown out, postmodernized, and otherwise experimented upon but one that will not, for those reasons, somehow disappear or lose its foundational status.

If the parallel to *Northanger Abbey* is to carry through, there must be a significant, shaming self-recognition on Briony's part that will illuminate, retrospectively, some fundamental, unpleasant truth about herself. And there is. When she considers Connolly's criticisms, she realizes that, "without intending to," he had "delivered a significant personal indictment" (302). His challenge, again much like the unnamed reader imagined by Eliot in *Adam Bede*, puts her on trial for doing what she has done to story. And like Bernard, in fully technologizing story she has left embodiment entirely behind: "What she needed," she must agree, "was backbone." In his review-letter, Connolly asks specific questions and makes specific suggestions about character and event in order to help Briony toward a story. Several of these sound very familiar because we have read through them earlier in *Atonement*. He even suggests (or perhaps intuits?) what was not in the story he has read: that the little girl observer might somehow come disastrously between the young man and woman whom she observes. Of this suggestion Briony thinks: "Yes, indeed. And having done so, might she obscure the fact by concocting a slight, barely clever fiction and satisfy her vanity by sending it off to a magazine?" None of her elaborately unconventional work "could conceal her cowardice." "Did she really think she could hide behind some borrowed notions of modern writing, and drown her guilt in a stream—three streams!—of consciousness?" (302). This must remind us again of Anna Wulf, constantly concluding that the way she has written her experience is an evasion. But unlike Anna, Briony has not been taken to the dead-end desire for a representation that is not a representation. The specific story she has written, not story in general, turns out to be the problem.

As Tilney's call to her senses leads Catherine Morland to take responsibility for the "voluntary, self-created delusion" (Austen, 201) of seeing the world through the gothic novel, so Connolly's letter leads Briony to take responsibility for the willful, self-created delusion of seeing her own past, not through story in general, but through experimental, modernist fiction. The difference between Catherine and Briony is that Briony is a literate person who has been enchanted, not by oralistic, but by hyper-alphabetic story. And the effects have changed accordingly. Another comparison to George Eliot will show us how. Lost in the deceptive luxury of privacy and self-containment, Briony has failed, albeit unintentionally, to hold to what Eliot realized was the only anchor for technologized story: honesty and sincerity. Eliot worried only about the risk of insincerity as a violation of a social communication; her sense of the storytelling act had not yet moved so very far from a sense of speech communication, so she worried about communicating falsely or insincerely to others. As writing continues to privatize the otherwise social nature of story, the threat of dishonesty and insincerity becomes more privatized as well, leading ultimately to the *mise en abyme* solipsism of Anna Wulf. Though Briony has not been so entirely inscripted as Anna by writing, still, her only risk is to herself. If her own telling of her own crime is insincere in this way, how can she hope for atonement?

In classic self-recognition fashion Briony emerges from all this a changed person. She goes to visit her sister to propose a formal recantation of her earlier charges against Robbie. Unexpectedly, Robbie is with her sister when Briony calls. The meeting is awkward. Briony is not forgiven by either, but she agrees to write a formal statement of retraction and a separate letter to the family in order to clear things as best she can. But more importantly, as she is returning home after this meeting, she thinks that the statement and letter will be easy and quick. The true realization is that "she knew what was required of her. Not simply a letter, but a new draft, an atonement, and she was ready to begin" (330). She begins the revision of her modernist novella into the novel we have just completed, which, though thick with the fine-grained psychological insight that we associate with twentieth-century fiction, is nonetheless very much in the great storytelling tradition of the realistic novel as it was established in the eighteenth and nineteenth centuries.

III

The end of Briony's novel is, however, not the end of McEwan's novel. If we consider the end of her novel, it seems most satisfyingly conclusive in the traditional realistic mode: formally tidy and self-contained, to use Briony's own standards. The protagonist has, even if unintentionally, committed a wrong; she has endured suffering (in this case both emotionally and physically, as a wartime nurse) as a result; she has had a moment of self-recognition; and at the end she has become a morally stronger person who is about to take action toward an atonement. McEwan could certainly have stopped his novel at this point and had a truly fine accomplishment. Like works as various as *The Prelude* or *Invisible Man*, the story would explain how the main character came to the point of telling the story that has just been told, though Briony's story is not in the first person. Telling the story in such cases becomes a sort of public testimony to—a "public-ation" of, we might say—the very dramatic, but private, psychological change. Because Briony is a writer, it is writing itself, rather than any other kind of experience or action, that is the vehicle for the change. Accordingly, writing will be the means of showing that the change has happened.

Because McEwan has invoked so much allusive historical "literary memory" (Hidalgo, 87) in staging all this, Briony's micro-level self-recognition is, on the macro-level, a self-recognition of the novel as a genre and is therefore a climactic, revelatory moment in the history of story. The constant, conflicted pleasures and anxieties involved with conforming story to writing have led Briony to the solipsistic and static extreme of experimental form and back again, in such a way that the old elements of storytelling look new. With our awareness of the way writing affects story, we can say that Briony's novel is an atonement for having become lost in and enchanted by hypertechnologized story, just as those earlier characters (and Briony herself) became enchanted by oral-istic written story. In other words, as a child her enchantment with oral-istic romance led her to commit the unintended crime; and as an adult her enchantment with alphabetic experimentation almost causes her to miss the self-recognition and atonement for that crime. But precisely because *Atonement* has been "about" the technologization of story, to have ended with Briony's signed, dated, tidy, self-contained text would have been untrue to the story she has told. Though her story has returned, very powerfully, to Connolly's recommended "pull of simple narrative," the story is still written. Because of the nature of human storytelling in general and because of the nature of the technology of writing, her success will necessarily also be her failure.

In a real sense the last chapter, which takes place decades after the internal novel, is about just this. Briony is old and has been diagnosed with a degenerative disease. She has managed to live her life as a writer, and now a celebration in her honor is being convened in the "Tilney" house. She has never found a publisher for the novel about her "crime" because Lola and Paul Marshall, who married each other and became very wealthy and powerful, would certainly sue. Over the course of the chapter she thinks about that time in the past, the novel she wrote, and how it will only appear after she dies. Even though she did, as Connolly suggested, return to the pull of simple narrative; even though she has long been a famous and successful author (to the point that her books, like Austen's, are being studied in high school [345]); finally, even though she has made sure that her novel will not appear until she is dead; she still does not somehow escape the alphabetic effects she experienced as a little girl.

Her rather anxious "talk"—the last chapter is represented as spoken words in relation to the text of her novel—about her own composition reminds us again of many passages we have already encountered in our earlier novels. She is worried, still, about the nature of alphabetic authority. This bothers her on one level because she had hoped to atone for the "crime" (349) by writing her novel, and she does not feel that she has succeeded. In the great tradition of the Victorian novel, it turns out that, as Adam Bede says, "There's a sort of wrong that can never be made up for" (Eliot, 450). But her case differs from Eliot's in that she has chosen to incorporate both micro (the family history) and macro (World War II) historical actualities into her fiction.

If there is a built-in anxiety about the novelistic appeal to the real, we might expect that anxiety to be lessened by including public, historical actuality, namely, an already commonly known, real-world content. But this is not the case. As speech is the default mode of human linguistic communication, and as oral story is the default mode of human story, so memory is the default mode of human history. This means that for the nonliterate community the past consists entirely of the memories of its oldest living members and of "repeated and collectively authored oral repositories," such as its legends and myths (Foley 1986, 5). Such a notion of the past offers little to disagree with. In contrast, writing enables the establishment of historical "fact." But the essentially private, asocial nature of writing means that literate facts, like literate story, automatically carry an inherent individual perspective, which from the more communal orientation of orality shows up as arbitrariness. So, ironically, historical "fact" causes, rather than eliminates, uncertainty and disagreement. Thus, Briony feels the need to declare, as if on oath, that she has taken it as a "duty to disguise nothing." The "names, the places, the exact circumstances" are all "there as a matter of historical record."

Most revealingly, she describes her work as a "forensic memoir" (349), a written personal reminiscence presented as evidence in a court of law. From this we can see that, although she may have revised directly according to Connolly's "indictment," she has not lost the sense of being on trial. The phrase "forensic memoir" crystallizes the intractably conflicted nature of alphabetic story. A memoir is not about the real in general but about the writer's very own experience. Since the story is not a fabrication in the strict sense, surely the automatic charge of arbitrariness would not apply. And yet Briony feels an unavoidable anxiety in having aligned herself with historical actuality. Once story turns toward the real, the very idea of fictional story as a distinct category is sooner or later called into doubt. As we have already seen, ultimately, if it matters to be true to the real, then why fictionalize at all? Less drastically, how much of the real is enough? Briony says she loves the "pointillist approach to verisimilitude," by which she means the kind of studied historical detail that is only possible with (in some ways required by) written story. But when a retired World War II colonel corrects her on some minor errors in her writing on the war, she says, "If I really cared so much about facts, I should have written a different kind of book" (340), presumably a history. Also, though her novel makes an appeal to the factual real, a memoir is distinctly not bound to historical facts as are biography and history. The very desire to write such a form expresses a sense that story ought to be special, ought to be other than just a report of the biographical real. But such a story would not be allowable as evidence in court. A "forensic memoir" is in this sense an oxymoron. Still, it captures the way in which Briony feels on trial even in the writing of her own story.

And yet, at the same time that she has been giving her story under oath, so to speak, and has therefore worried about verisimilitude, she has also willingly allowed herself to luxuriate in the possibilities of originality. She tells us outright that she has made up a tidy ending in which Robbie and Cecilia are reunited. In reality, both were killed in the war. Her explanation for such a change makes plain that the forensic appeal to the real as objective report can be just as much a dead end as the overzealous experimentalism she left behind after Connolly's letter. In defending her departure from the facts, she asks, "How could [the historical fact of the two deaths] constitute an ending? What sense of hope or satisfaction could a reader draw from such an account? Who would want to believe that they never met again, never fulfilled their love? Who would want to believe that, except in the service of the bleakest realism?" (350). Plainly, Briony at this point has stopped worrying about experimenting with form as such. Now she is thinking primarily about content, and directly in relation to a notion of the common reader. For that reader, story and report are different things; story, unlike the real, must involve conflict that resolves into hope or some other satisfyingly positive outcome. In the history of story only the "bleakest realism" has tried to tell stories that feel no obligation to do this. With such a standard, she steps even further back to the novel before the experiments in naturalism and modernism that began in the last decades of the nineteenth century.

In spite of this after-the-ending confession, Briony cannot herself achieve the satisfaction that she has wanted for the common reader. There is, even for the writer who rejects the bleakest realism and the most experimental modernism, an insoluble problem. How, she asks, "can a novelist achieve atonement when, with her absolute power of deciding outcomes, she is also God? There is no one, no entity or higher form that she can appeal to, or be reconciled with, or that can forgive her" (350–51). These comments reverberate far beyond the immediacy of her own attempt to atone for the specific wrong she committed as a girl. She speaks for herself in particular, of course, but also for novelists in general. To voice these opinions only makes sense in relation to some other, very basic storytelling that must be contrary to the situation of the novelist. That storytelling must ultimately be oral story in oral culture or, at the least, story that has not been conformed to writing. As we have seen, the paradigmatic oral teller, far from being a creator-god, always tells the already known and therefore experiences no problem with the basic believability of the story. But oral story is essentially communal and public, while alphabetic story is essentially individual and private. So Briony is expressing the same anxiety about being believed that she experienced as a girl.

In this passage, however, she moves to ideas we have not seen before quite so overtly: the need for reconciliation and forgiveness. Why should this be? Why should she feel guilty about writing *her* story as she sees fit, especially given her commitments to honesty, sincerity, and the well-being of the common reader? She must feel guilty about producing a particular kind of story. This kind of story carries an automatic sense of having violated some other unspecified, but evidently right, kind of story. The teller of that other kind of story would not be in the role of individual creator-god. That teller, who would have to be the conveyor of a community's stock of already-known tales, would not have these anxieties. She must want to be reconciled with this kind of storytelling, forgiven for having violated a form so fundamental that it need not even be named. This seems simply to be story in the most general sense, which is what the novel as a genre both violates and, in the act of violation, renews.

CHAPTER NINE

After Alphabetic Story

Citizen Kane

⁂ I

ALONG THE COURSE of this consideration of the novel, I have had occasion to mention another technologized form of storytelling: film. Indeed, to explain the novel in terms of its primary communications technology and in terms of oral story seems necessarily to imply clear and powerful implications about motion pictures, the most important of which is that, if the novel is a world-historical event in the history of story, the next such event, cinema, has already begun. As a conclusion to the present project, then, let us briefly consider film in the terms we have been using. Obviously, to tackle film in general would require a separate book. Looking closely at one example may provide a model for what might be done going forward from this beginning.

My sample case will be what is perhaps *the* most respected and discussed film in the relatively short history of motion pictures: Orson Welles's *Citizen Kane*. I choose this film because it is, like the novels already discussed, distinctively "about" writing and story. But before turning to the film itself, let me restate and further develop some preliminary ideas. I began this discussion of the novel by making the case that if we take the human body as a basis, then, literally speaking, "to show" means to make visible to the eye and "to tell" means to convey by words. Therefore, no written story can be a case of showing because, cognitively, we cannot see the story, and fiction film is usually an event of story-showing rather than storytelling. I have not yet explained, however, that to show a story must literally mean to show diachrony, since all story requires diachrony.

Diachrony means "across time." But to think again in a foundational way, that is, in terms of human cognition, time itself (whatever that might be) is never shown. Time is not directly apprehensible by our senses. Rather, we must be shown what humans can actually see: sequential change in state or space, which inescapably involves some form of visible motion (or, to use the term from which cinema is derived, *kinesis*). As George Lakoff and Mark Johnson have argued (137–70), we linguistic creatures generalize metaphorically from the experience of visual perception of change to a concept of temporality. With respect to kinds of story, our default kind, oral story, does involve a visible change of state, but only in the limited way possible for a performing teller. Otherwise, there are only two kinds of narrative that can literally show story: stage (or staged) performance and film. With these two genres, we should properly speak of story-showing/telling rather than just storytelling. But any stage performance essentially involves material performers before a flesh-and-blood audience, and this (among others, cf. Munsterberg, 401–7; Carroll, 66–70; Bazin 1967, 76–124) separates it entirely from film (including a film of a play) as a kind of representation. In the history of story, fiction film holds a unique place as the narrative form with the capacity to show story as a representation. Gerald Mast has observed that film is a "perfect synthesis of Aristotle's dramatic and narrative 'modes'" (18). This statement is even more strictly true in relation to my particular definitions of showing and telling.

Because fiction film is this kind of narrative, it follows that diegetic writing (writing internal to the story) will always necessarily be working in a special way both to show and to tell. I do not want to overstate this. The form (e.g., font type and size and color) of literally any example of writing will always be a kind of showing. But in the usual case of a written story, we look at the writing only as a means to apprehend the content. We do not attend to the visual appearance of the writing itself, unless, in an attempt to simulate showing, a text uses special fonts. But with any diegetic writing in a film, the script itself is an image in a visual narrative. As Gregory Currie writes, it functions "pictorially" (8), and therefore its visual form will be significant along with, and also apart from, its content. This becomes clear when we consider the other major uses of writing in filmic storytelling: the written intertitles that were common in silent film. These written words, typically being extradiegetic, have only one function: to tell what cannot be adequately shown by the visual images alone. The more complex the story, the more necessary the intertitles. With this example in mind, we can see that fiction film only truly takes on its unique role in the history of story once there is audio, because until then, even though "showing" is intrinsic to motion pictures, the story still regularly depended on writing to communicate its content. I will bring in some other, already-visited ideas as we go forward, but for now, we turn to *Citizen Kane*.

✳II

Citizen Kane is commonly considered the finest American film ever made. Whether or not this be true, it is almost certainly the most critically discussed. For example, in numerous essay-length studies the film has been considered in terms of Freudian and Lacanian psychoanalytic theory (Beja, Brinkley and Speidel, Mulvey), Aristotelian dramatic theory (Maxfield), evolutionary psychology (Billy, Schwartz), its use of audio (Altman, Thomas), its use of visual space (Jaffe), and its relationship to *The Great Gatsby* (Carringer 1975; Mass). Film criticism luminaries such as Pauline Kael and Laura Mulvey and André Bazin (1978) have considered *Kane* at length. There have been at least two essay collections dedicated to *Kane* (Naremore 2004; Gottesman). It is a safe bet that in the index of nearly any scholarly book on film, especially American film, *Kane* will have at least a handful of entries, if not an entire chapter. In nearly any college textbook on film, *Kane* will always be a prominent example used to illustrate all manner of terms and ideas. If a text's greatness may be inferred by how rich a field it continuously provides for serious critical attention, then *Kane* is unquestionably great.

And yet in all these studies, a distinctly prominent visual and thematic element of the film—writing—has received very little discussion. This is primarily for the same reason that the novel has not heretofore been seriously considered in terms of writing. Print is always taken as the primary, really the only, technology. As with the novel, print is unquestionably important, but much is lost by ignoring the larger category: writing. Since *Citizen Kane* has to do with newspaper journalism, it is hardly surprising to see images of written words onscreen, but such images abound, from beginning to end. Though the onscreen title of this film is a case of extradiegetic writing, nonetheless we must begin with it because there are a number of direct visual returns to its form later in the film. The title is shown in neon white letters on a black background. The letters are rather strikingly unornate and even by writing standards are decontextualized, not relatable to any particular other kind of lettering, but they are plainly mechanically produced, as opposed to being any kind of handwriting. There is no audio, no motion. This might as well be a photograph. The image fades to black. When it fades in again, we are quickly in the realm of the moving image. We also see our first image of diegetic writing. The camera looks at a No Trespassing sign, which, except that it is smudged with grime, would be a clear inversion of the title—mechanically produced black letters on a white background. Once we know the whole of Charles Kane's story, we know that this first image of writing is already a visual figure of the great reversals, always linked to writing, that will spoil Kane's wealth and success. The camera moves up over a gate's metal wire and iron bars until we stop with a low angle of a large, black letter *K* in ornate wrought iron. The *K*, which appears again in various forms throughout the film, becomes the title character's logo. The camera looks literally through the fence and takes us, by means of a series of dissolves, to the climactic extreme close-up of the unknown lips voicing the one famous, and at this point incomprehensible, word: *rosebud.*

In a film with many unusual shots, none is more unusual than the speaking of "rosebud." The image of the lips has at least three key qualities. First, the extreme close-up isolates the single bodily source of speech, apart from the rest of the body, that normally helps determine verbal meaning. The only way to get any closer to the physical production of the word would be to film the speaking somehow from inside the mouth. Second, the word is cut off from any other human presence. We have no other side of the verbal communicative act, no face to show us how the word should, or even might, be received. Third, though we have a material world context that necessarily gives us some information—wealth, prohibited access, a bedroom, etc.—nothing in that context has any decipherable relationship to the bud of a rose. Paradoxically, the sheer physicality of the act of verbalization gets compounded by its detachment from the usual elements of a speech-act. Here at the beginning, then, we have a maximal image of the bodily action of speaking.

After a fade to black, the film's second sequence begins. With it, things have changed in such a way that the purely cinematic nature of what we have just been shown in the opening sequence is all the more pronounced, because we are abruptly in a very different format. We have switched from fiction film to newsreel. Because the newsreel sets off the plot of the movie as a whole, I will look at it in some detail. We first see a still shot of a painting of flags and banners whose meaning is declaimed by a newscaster's voice as "news on the march." Then, redundantly, we see "NEWS on the MARCH" in white letters over the painting. Next appears an obituary announcing the death of "Xanadu's Landlord," which replays the visual form of the title, though this time the content of the neon white letters seems taken from a newspaper. This fades to a series of still shots and seconds-long action shots that introduce us to daytime views of the mansion we had seen only darkly at the outset. Unlike the images of the opening sequence, all these images come with verbal or written explanation. In other words, in spite of the act of showing, this is not really cinematic story-showing; fully cinematic story-showing, as opposed to silent film or film of news/information, does not need an extradiegetic voice or written words to tell the viewer the meaning of what he or she sees. The newsreel, then, is distinctly not a case of filmic story-showing.

News on the March is an almost encyclopedic mixture of the technological means of telling a man's story at this time in history: picture magazine, photography, painting, newspaper, radio news, and film. Its subject is Charles Foster Kane, but it comes at the actual man in an oddly oblique manner. After a sequence about the building of Xanadu, there is a fade to black and then back up to more neon lettering announcing the great man's funeral. Over footage of the service, the announcer tells us the one bit of information that the written words and the moving images have not divulged: the name of the deceased is Charles Foster Kane. Then, finally, we see the face of the title character. We first see Kane in what appears to be a freestanding photograph, until the camera pulls back to reveal a front page newspaper headline announcing Kane's death, followed by a series of other front page headlines over other photos of Kane. So the first actual visual image of the title character is distinctly nonfilmic; it is dependent on the written headlines to tell us the meaning of what we see.

We do not see an actual moving image of Kane himself until halfway through the newsreel, when we are shown footage of Kane in front of a microphone reading a written statement to a well-dressed crowd in an elaborate lobby. But this scene is immediately preceded by two other scenes of men speaking. First, we see and hear Mr. Thatcher, Kane's original guardian, reading a statement to a congressional committee in which he calls Kane a Communist. Thatcher is being questioned about his history with Charles Kane. He responds verbally until asked about the event in which young Kane attacked him with a sled. With this, he abruptly declares that he will read from a prepared statement and say nothing more. Faced with this apparently emotional memory—the other men in the room begin to laugh at him—he suddenly refuses to speak in his everyday voice and invokes the power of writing over speech. The statement is simply the written version of his own words and is only one sentence long. Why not just say it? Or, why not just hand it out to be read and say nothing more? Writing saves him from speech. As Socrates noted with disapproval long ago, written words "seem to talk to you as though they were intelligent, but if you ask them anything about what they say . . . they go on telling you just the same thing forever" (Hamilton and Cairns, 521). Thatcher is pointedly using the written statement to put a stop to questions and, more generally, to subordinate the unpredictable, flesh-and-blood qualities of speech to the constraints of writing. With this action, the film makes a point right at the beginning about the power of writing. The visual image works to support this as well. When he is being asked about the sled incident, Thatcher appears in a long shot, squeezed in at the lower right of the screen, simply one face among the crowd. When he turns to read, the shot cuts to eye level, medium. Now he is shown flanked just behind on either side by the torsos, not the faces, of black-suited men, one of whom rather ominously has his hand stuffed in his coat pocket. The image is of a mob boss flanked by armed bodyguards.

Immediately following the scene with Thatcher, we see and hear his political and social opposite, a nameless speaker at a workers' rally accusing Kane of being a fascist. This man's speech is obviously impromptu, inelegant, and halting but also histrionic, passionate, and sincere. He stands alone on stage, clearly lacking the institutional power that surrounds Thatcher. And yet the mise en scène ensures that he not appear simply powerless. The shot is from a low angle and so in the most conventional sense tends visually to augment the presence of the man. Interestingly, we do not see a microphone, the actual mechanism that would transform speech into electrical signals. Rather, we are shown only four huge horns, the "speakers" that render the signals back again into speech. Placed dramatically in the open sky above the man and trumpeting his words to the four points of the compass, they are an almost too-blatant metaphor for the raw power of spoken language. In one sense this man has a kind of power: informal, direct, emotional, kinetic. It is directly opposed to the previous image of Thatcher, in which writing was linked with institutional power. These two images establish early on an implicit struggle between the written and the spoken word, and this struggle will be essential to Kane's life story.

The two segments of newsreel prepare us for what would seem to be a climactic moment: actual film footage of Kane telling us his opinion of himself. But just when we appear to have arrived at the cinematic "actuality," we see silent film of Kane reading a statement before the microphone, then the neon letters appear again to tell us what he was saying: "I am, have been, and will be only one thing—an American." The officious voice-over announcer this time never vocalizes the written words. What are the implications of this arrival at the first motion picture of Kane? After the two previous scenes, this one clearly goes back to silent-film technology and therefore confers an aura of nostalgia around Kane. I will return to this later; more important now is that just previously the viewer has been given speech conjoined with writing, and then speech simply on its own. We might expect this third image to be some kind of synthesis of those two extremes. But the visual image of speech is conjoined with the written statement, and yet there is no audible speech at all. This time, though a microphone is plainly visible, there is no sense of the voice being recovered from its transformation into electrical signals by any "speakers," mechanical or otherwise. The suggestion is that Kane is like Thatcher in the sense of being linked to, even dependent upon, writing; after all, why would anyone have to read such a simple statement? But the lack of audible voice places Kane in an uncertain category, apart from either Thatcher or the worker. It is hard to find any kind of synthesis in this, so what do we have? Where is Kane in relation to the opposition, even antagonism between writing and orality? The rest of the film offers us, among other things, an answer to this question.

Toward the end of the newsreel the viewer does finally get a clip of an interview with Kane, in regular film footage and with audio. In moving from still photography with newspaper headlines to silent film with intertitles, and finally to the "talkie," the short newsreel biopic seems to flaunt its own technological comprehensiveness, making sure that we see how easily it incorporates other, competing means of mass communication. But, except for the "talkie" footage, writing has been indispensable to all the various means of getting Kane's story told. Besides the examples already considered, we also see different kinds of posters with writing; more newspaper headlines; more neon intertitles; and finally, on the side of a building, a public electronic news bulletin that announces Kane's death to the city in horizontally scrolling letters of light. So the stress on writing in the opening sequence and the *News on the March* sequence installs writing as, at least, a visual motif in the film. But it will become clear that *motif* is not really a strong enough term.

From the newsreel we abruptly switch to the newsroom scene. This scene, as Robert Carringer notes, "could easily be mistaken for something out of a newspaper comedy of [Frank] Capra or [Ben] Hecht or [Howard] Hawks" (1976, 189). It is very much after the traditional movie images of newspaper reporters in a smoky pressroom, haggling over the big story. Right away there is an implied similarity between newsreel and newspaper, and just this similarity will become the problem that sets off the plot of *Citizen Kane*. Mr. Rawlston, the newsreel producer, tells the main reporter, Thompson, that we have seen a "good short," but "what it needs is an end. All we saw on that screen was that Charles Foster Kane is dead. I know that. I read the papers." And yet death is as solid an ending to an individual life as we can ever have. So how can this ending be unsatisfactory? The key problem lies in the failure of the newsreel to provide something that a newspaper cannot provide. Shortly, Rawlston will bring up Kane's "dying words," and one of the shadowy voices in the room will ask: "What were they?" Thompson, chagrined, replies: "You don't read the papers," which draws an embarrassed laugh from the other newsmen. Further, the sense of communicative inadequacy will be reinforced twice later in the film when the waiter at the El Rancho and then Jed Leland both inadvertently taunt Thompson by mentioning that of course they know of "rosebud" from the papers. Taking all this together, it becomes clear that the plot to come depends on a conflict between two kinds of communications technologies. And yet we have plainly seen in the newsreel itself how cinematic news overtakes and surpasses the newspaper as a means of communicating information. The simple fact is that film can include images of newspapers and all previous means of written or photographic informational narrative, but newspapers cannot include film. Still, in Rawlston's mind the newsreel has failed to distinguish itself from the most successful contemporaneous print medium.

Rawlston complains that "it's not enough *to tell* us what a man did. You've got *to tell* us who he was" (italics added). What most matters is outdoing the newspaper at its own game: telling. The primary aim of both newspaper and newsreel is to tell. But the newspaper is almost entirely direct telling. Able to include only the minimum possible showing—the illustration or photograph—newspapers cannot show a story. The newsreel would seem to be straightforwardly superior to the newspaper because the newsreel is most definitely a showing, although it does require the indispensable help of direct telling by voice or writing. With respect to the "who he was" problem, this newsreel has made a point of revealing personal and emotional elements in Kane's story, not just what he did. It has included as much of loves, hatreds, and emotions as it has of anything like hard news. However, Rawlston is dissatisfied. Very much in the tradition of films about newspapers, he "stops the presses," postponing the newsreel's release in order to squeeze in the one remaining sensational scoop. The question of Kane's true identity remains, and that can only be answered by commissioning Thompson to find the meaning of Kane's "dying words."

Now, "dying words" is a cliché, so standard that it gets used even when, as in Kane's case, everyone knows there was only one such word. But considered in light of writing and orality, the everyday phrase invokes a specific set of qualities, some perhaps rather mythic. A person's last words are taken to be uniquely important, spoken when the body has become so weak that the physical act of speech may be the only motor function remaining under conscious control. Therefore, no tool or technology or artifice—no writing—of any kind can come between the thought and its verbal expression. The knowledge looms that soon the voice too will be gone. The very last energy of life gets devoted to these words. In *Citizen Kane* the magnified lips make the sheer orality of this all the more prominent. Here is a plot based on the struggle for superiority between two modern communications technologies—one based in print, the other in film—and, significantly, the outcome of that struggle will depend on communicating to the world the meaning of that most singular example of speech: a man's dying words. Given the extreme close-up of the lips that spoke the dying word, it as if Thompson must find the secret of orality itself. But the spoken word, unlike writing (and before the invention of audio recording), vanishes as soon as it has been uttered. So Thompson has two basic means of getting at the secret. He must read writings from the past or seek out the memories of the remaining witnesses to the past.

Thompson begins his search for the secret of the mysterious word. The camera pans up to reveal what will, in being repeated twice more during the film, become the written logo for Kane's second wife, Susan—the neon sign above the El Rancho night club. The camera passes through the words of this sign as it did the No Trespassing and the K logo of Kane's gate, but to no avail, because Susan establishes her own "no trespassing" sign by refusing to talk. Still, this establishes a visual motif of passing through written words in order to get at the one oral word that most matters. Next, Thompson visits the Thatcher Memorial Library, which houses a man whose only remains are his written words. The exaggerated security, the high marble-columned walls, and the museum-like lighting figure these documents as fabulously rare and valuable. Once in the inner sanctum the guard, Jennings, brings forth the bound volume, cradled as if it were a fragile, priceless treasure; then, after he delicately places it on the table, he continues to gaze on it, as a parent would on a sleeping child. Light falls across the library table from a high skylight, as if the room were in a cathedral, and the volume itself catches the light uniquely so that it seems to glow from within. This, Thompson may read. But the comically stern librarian repeats what Thompson has already been told by the museum directors: "Under no circumstances are direct quotations from his manuscript to be used by you." Though he is a reporter, he cannot bring pen and paper with him, cannot copy anything from the text.

It turns out that Thatcher is now, even (or especially) after his death, threatened by the very technology that earlier had protected him. In fact, this reveals the double nature of all writing. On the one hand, his writing preserves his words so that in a way he can "speak" apart from his body —in this case, from the grave. On the other hand, he can no longer read along with his words or otherwise "authorize" them. Other people can take them and (again as Socrates worried long ago) place them into altogether other contexts, thereby warping their meanings in unpredictable ways. The restriction on quotation is in a way the exact opposite of the scene with Thatcher during the congressional hearing. There, his power manifested itself when he controlled his speech by limiting it to writing.

Now his estate controls his writing by rendering it effectively into the form of speech. Without written quotes, it will be as if Thompson has only listened to someone talk. He will have to recall as best he can what was actually "said." Even the relatively loose precision of journalistic writing is denied him. The power of writing over speech is clearly at issue, and as before, Thatcher is the master of that power.

Thompson is finally left alone with the text. In a repetition of the camera movement through Xanadu's fence and the neon El Rancho sign, the camera looks over his shoulder and down at the page. After scanning the first line of script, we look, by means of a dissolve, through Thatcher's handwritten words directly into a flashback scene from Kane's boyhood. Before turning to that scene, what can be said about this now well-established visual motif of "looking through" writing? In a film that makes so much of writing, this has an intriguing effect. Writing takes on its peculiar powers by solidifying, by materializing the otherwise ephemeral nature of speech. But in *Citizen Kane* the camera, with its ability to look through writing, in a way renders that materiality itself ephemeral. Figuratively, film is taking on a certain kind of power over writing. Recognizing this is important for our understanding of the film as a whole.

For now, what matters is that the past into which we look shows the event of Mrs. Kane literally signing her son over to Thatcher. This entire scene revolves around a written contract, which in its turn depends on a previous written document: a deed in which the Colorado lode was signed over only to Mrs. Kane, not to her husband. Reading, signing, talking about, and handling of documents is the main action in this famous long take. The signing of this document begins the identity of the man who will later be important enough for a newsreel story. In a sense the boy is "born" into an entirely new identity as a function of a handwritten contract that effectively deprives him of his own speaking voice. At the end of this scene, the boy, who obviously does not want to leave his home, simply falls silent. All he can do is "look" his resistance to Thatcher.

The flashback continues on through the young adult Kane's confrontation with Thatcher over the *Inquirer*'s Spanish war campaigns, and then we return to our position as Thompson's eyes sliding over Thatcher's handwriting. When we reach the date 1929, we once again look through the handwriting to a scene of legal writing. This time a typewritten legal document emerges through the dissolve to take up the entire middle of the screen. It is being read by Mr. Bernstein, and it turns the *Inquirer* back over to Thatcher. Having ensured that we see the form of this document, the camera then makes sure we witness first Thatcher and then Kane actually writing in their signatures. So it turns out that the story of citizen Charles Kane involves an initial loss of his own speaking voice as well as a later loss of what becomes his written "voice," the *Inquirer*. That first moving image of Kane in the newsreel now begins to take on more significance. Ultimately, Kane does not have the power of either Thatcher or the speaker at the workers' rally. If there is a conflict between writing and orality, he is caught right in that conflict's murky center.

It is hardly surprising that these two legal documents would be important in Thatcher's written record of his encounters with Kane. But in both scenes the strong focus, not just on the content but also on the actual writing itself (Kane works with the pen for nearly twenty-five seconds as he signs away his newspaper), pushes forward the film's general attention to writing in an important way. Clearly, most people in modern society are aware of the significance of writing with respect to, for instance, legal documents. We all know that signing our names commits us to a document's contents in a fundamentally different way than simply giving our word. But still, because of the sheer ubiquity of writing in any modern culture, the nature of writing as a technology tends to be obscured by the content of any given example of writing. The writing in a contract appears to be only a kind of final recording of the actual information, qualifications, and specifications that precede the writing of the document. The writing on a birth certificate appears to be simply the verification of an already-established event. The writing on a marriage certificate appears to be only the ratification of an already-made commitment. In each case, the writing does communicate pre-existing content, but what gets lost is the fact that only with writing do any of the examples I have given become possible in the first place.

Strictly speaking, writing does not just communicate this kind of content; rather, it enables, forms, and ultimately, requires this kind of content. In a modern literate culture in substantial ways neither a birth nor a marriage, not to mention a business agreement between parties, is quite real without the authentication of a written certificate. Though writing has many positive effects in human life, nonetheless a certain purely bodily sense of self-sufficiency gets lost when authentication becomes so broadly dependent on writing. In making the signing of these two specific contracts so visually and narratively prominent—the first one literally ending the idyll of Kane's boyhood life, the second one making irrevocable the defeat of all his dreams as a young newspaperman—the film gives us a monumental image of a man who has in a sense lived by the pen and died by the pen.

Of all the possible enterprises available to the twenty-one-year-old Charles, he chooses the newspaper. And he will, at least at first, come at the newspaper in a thoroughly idealistic, reformist way, committed to helping those "who have no one to look after their interests." Having been ripped out of the family union as a helpless child by the written contract, he seems to turn to the newspaper as a way of "writing" (we might say) that originary wrong. And at least early on in his trust-busting days, he succeeds.

Yet, although as a newspaper publisher Kane is associated with print, the film also makes a strong point of associating him with handwriting. In my consideration of *Bleak House*, I discussed the particular nature of handwriting. In terms of writing as a technology handwriting is, on both the large historical level as well as the level of each individual human learner, always the original move out of orality. Also, in terms of a continuum from the maximal bodily individuality of speech to the maximal mechanical uniformity of print, handwriting may be as close to a middle ground between the two as we can expect to find. Handwriting necessarily bears visible signs of a specific individual hand and thus, especially after the invention of mechanical print, carries a kind of authenticity unavailable to any kind of type. *Citizen Kane* makes much of this.

For instance, Kane establishes his coming of age through a handwritten note to Thatcher in which he announces that he will take over the *Inquirer*. Later, he announces his marriage to his first wife by hand-delivering a handwritten notice (just after which we see Kane's workers, including Jed and Bernstein, looking through the enormous letters on the façade of the *Inquirer* building, as if, unlike him at this point, they have been fully subsumed by Kane's own magnification of the print medium).

But most importantly, handwriting is featured when Kane, by writing his declaration of principles, establishes himself as a new kind of newspaperman. The unlikely blocking (the positioning of bodies on the screen) in this scene stresses, again, not just the content but also the activity of writing, for Kane is shown from a frontal and then a rear shot standing up and writing on a sheet of paper held flat against a window. (In the shooting script Kane was to be seated on the bed, which would have significantly downplayed the act of writing [Kael, 170].) Kane feels a commitment to provide the news honestly and to champion citizens' rights. He distinctly does not want to operate just another newspaper, which will publish, as he says, only "pictures and print." Rather, he wants to make the newspaper as important to the city as the gas by which it illuminates the darkness. He seems to feel that the newspaper as it currently exists fails to get at what most matters, just as Rawlston will come to feel the inadequacy of the newsreel in relation to the kind of newspaper that Kane is at this moment creating. And again, just like Rawlston, Kane stops the presses in order to get this last, most important item—his declaration of principles—in. This scene, then, directly associates his youthful idealism with handwriting, even though he is turning to newspaper print as a medium. For this moment in time Kane is achieving some kind of middle ground between his lost childhood voice and his eventual assimilation to print. This point is made visually when we see his declaration on the newspaper's front page. The statement is in print, but validated with his handwritten signature.

Jed, impressed, wants to keep the handwritten note. He calls the two-sentence statement a "historical document," like, he says, the Declaration of Independence or the Constitution, on the one hand, or like a child's first report card, on the other. And this statement, as the act of declaring his independence from the already-established norms of the medium, does constitute Kane as a new kind of publisher. Committing his declaration to writing gives material solidity to his words, and so he will in a way be bound by his statements as a nation is bound by its written self-establishing documents. A child's first report card is the material proof of first participation in the educational system. In literate cultures, where so much of life comes to require written documentation, the actual attendance at school must be certified by written documentation in order to take on its full legitimacy. The first report card is also rather monumental in life because, for most of us, it is the first official written documentation for something we have done as human beings apart from parents and family. It authenticates the first move into a truly social, and literate, arena. Kane's handwritten declaration, even more strongly than the newspaper itself, is figured as the material proof that he is now a news-paperman; and given his life story to this point, it also certifies and memo-rializes his first full step into the adult social, business, and political world.

The difference between the report card and the declaration, though, is that Kane gives himself his own written certification. In this and other ways the film makes clear that there are two sides to what he is doing. Rather portentously, he turns off the lamp just as he claims that the paper needs to be like the gas in the light. His face is in shadow as he stares down at his writing, but at the same time he looks almost worshipful and reads his own words aloud in a theatrically solemn tone, very much as if read-ing from a hallowed historical document. The moment is an ironic replay of the manner in which the guard at Thatcher's library looked upon Thatcher's memoir. Once again the camera features the signing of a sig-nature, with Kane, Bernstein, Jed, and the viewer all looking on. Through both this kind of visual image and Kane's idealism about the newspaper, writing accrues a near-sacred glorification.

But where Jed tends to see the positive side of putting the declaration into writing, Mr. Bernstein sees the downside. "You don't wanta make any promises, Mr. Kane, you don't wanta keep," he says, by which he means that once the spirit of the young Kane's promise is inscribed in the letter of writing, it will act, as Jed had said, much like a constitution. It takes on the power to command what he will be legitimately able to say and do in the future. In other words, Kane is signing what he himself looks upon as a handwritten contract that will shortly appear in print on the front page, complete with a facsimile of his signature. At this point Kane is idealistic and thus unworried by Bernstein's warning. Both liter-ally and figuratively, he begins the project of "writing" the wrong he expe-rienced as a boy.

I have mentioned the sense of nostalgia that comes with the first mov-ing image of Kane in the newsreel, the silent film of him reading a writ-ten statement. Nostalgia shows up around Kane in other ways as well. Even before the meaning of "rosebud" is revealed, the way Kane thinks of the newspaper as a public service makes it clear that he is choosing this profession with a perhaps unconscious sense of nostalgia for the time before he had been victimized by writing. Added to this is a key element of Kane's later life. For Kane is associated not only with print and hand-writing but also, very conspicuously, with orality. All the characters speak, of course, but that is hardly evidence for a distinct and significant association with orality. But once Kane has established himself as a successful newspaper publisher, he turns to politics, and at this time in history that meant a turn to political oratory. We see and hear only one of Kane's campaign speeches, but it is a spectacular example. He goes on at length, orating spontaneously in the most classic premicrophone manner—flamboyantly bombastic, verbally and histrionically dramatic, easily filling a large auditorium with the strength of his voice. As Kane and his declaration of principles connected him back to the image of Thatcher in the newsreel, so this speech in both its form and its content returns to the image of the worker in the newsreel.

Furthermore, the speech places Kane directly in the grand tradition of American political oratory while directly associating his move into politics with his lost boyhood in Colorado. Earlier, when his mother is signing him over to Thatcher, the young boy is outside in the snow, calling out slogans that allude to Andrew Jackson's famous second inaugural speech: "The union forever! You can't lick Andy Jackson," he shouts. Jackson, who is still known as the first true "people's president," was himself a famous orator in a golden age of political oratory (along with the likes of Daniel Webster, John Calhoun, and Henry Clay), and he dealt at length in his famous second inaugural address with the states' rights issue as a serious threat to the union. The adult Kane, both as a crusading newspaper publisher and a populist candidate for office, follows directly in Jackson's tradition. Given the way the story has dealt with writing as a technological power, it is as if Kane, having succeeded through the newspaper in "writing" the wrong that was originally done to him as a boy, is now able to regain the voice that was lost to him in the past. Writing and orality evidently need not be antagonistic forces in human affairs. At this point, he seems to be a positive synthesis of the opposed images from the newsreel: Thatcher and writing on the one hand, the worker and orality, on the other.

And yet even by the time of *Citizen Kane*, the grand Jacksonian oratory had become all but a relic of the political past. Fiery passion and theatrical skill will, once there are microphones (not to mention television), come to look like the ranting and raving of a lunatic. On both the individual level of Kane's life and the national historical level, the film at once celebrates and creates a sense of nostalgia for this golden age of the voice.

Because of this historical allusion, the nostalgia built into that first moving image of Kane in the newsreel accompanies even his great moment of triumph; and in any case, speech once again cannot withstand the power of writing. No matter how great Kane is as an orator, his words cannot overcome the printed headline: "Candidate Kane Caught in Love Nest with 'Singer.'"

The one word in quotes, *singer,* in a real sense sets the conflict that will power the second half of Kane's life. This is especially ironic because Kane's mistress, Susan, is not a "singer" when the headline appears. All she has done is perform in private for her lover, Kane. Indeed, the *Chronicle* headline creates and destroys her (and Kane) as a "singer" at the same time. We see that quoted word three different times: twice—in the newsreel, and then again the morning after Kane refuses to give in to Gettys—in the form of newspaper headlines; and the third time as another version of the decontextualized neon lettering of the film's title: "Kane Marries 'Singer.'" But this time the lettering is black on white instead of white on black, so that once again the form, the visual appearance itself, embodies the reversal in Kane's fortunes. Further, Jed Leland will specifically mention the "singer" problem in his interview with Thompson. According to Leland, Kane was "going to take the quotes off the 'singer,'" and to this end set out to make Susan an opera star. So in a parallel to the film's stress on not just the content but also the action of handwriting, there is now a stress on not just the content but also the form of this printed word. Once again writing is figured as playing a key role in reversing the direction of Kane's life. As has been noted before, Kane, the individual, becomes emblematic of certain historical "turn-of-the-century types" in all this (Naremore 1978, 83). Ironically, the kind of writing that he himself has made a historically new force in public affairs—the newspaper—is what now turns round to crush his political ambitions.

Citizen Kane pushes this complex of orality and writing even further when Kane commits to making Susan, and himself, an opera star. "We're going to be a great opera star," he declares to the press on his wedding day. Clearly, he experiences the quotes around "singer" as quotes around himself. He has displaced his failed oratory onto her singing voice. Since opera is the definitive highbrow form of musical theater, and since it has always depended on the sheer expressive power of the voice unamplified by microphones, we now have a figure of the voice as artistic power to parallel Kane's oratorical voice as political power. With this, the implied search for the lost past continues, but it fails again. In a moment of yet more powerful irony, which builds upon the written form of the *Chronicle*'s "singer" headline, we are shown an extreme close-up of typewriter keys violently striking in the letters to "weak" as Kane himself writes out Jed's unfavorable review of Susan's performance. The magnification of stamping in the word figuratively magnifies the reversal of the power that writing has had in, and over, Kane's life. It is the visual counterpart in writing to the magnified lips in the opening sequence, and it dramatically removes Kane from his former association with the relative authenticity of handwriting. Now, the undoing of Kane's attempt to "write" his past through the newspaper comes full circle, for it is his own *Inquirer* that will print the self-condemning review.

After this failure there cannot be a return even to the second golden age of his life, the now-lost time when, as a young, principled newspaperman, he worked successfully to "write" the wrongs committed by news-distorting special interests. We are pointedly shown the false headlines through which Kane tries to create Susan's success. He himself becomes the self-serving special interest. The material sign of the loss of this second golden age appears when Jed returns Kane's original, handwritten declaration of principles. More than any of the bold, mass-circulated headlines, these words in his own hand make plain how his present is in contradiction with his past. Finally, in spite of all his efforts, Susan tries to kill herself, and Kane must admit defeat. The most thoroughly public of men takes his wife and retreats behind the No Trespassing sign at Xanadu.

That first silent motion picture image of Kane in the newsreel now takes on its full meaning. No matter that at various times in his life he has been elaborately successful in the realms of both oratory and print; no matter that he has been shown figuratively as both the extreme close-up of speaking lips and as the extreme close-up of stamping type. In the end he is left with neither the individual authenticity of the speaker at the workers' rally nor the institutional power of Thatcher. Furthermore, he cannot achieve a workable synthesis of these polar opposites. The story of Charles Kane, then, is about a man split irreparably between writing and orality.

But this is only the end of Charles Kane's story, not the end of *Citizen*

Kane. The latter ends with a counterpart to Kane's failure to remove the quotes from around "singer": Thompson's failure to remove the quotes that implicitly surround "rosebud." For until its meaning is discovered, "rosebud" remains only a contextless piece of spoken language and cannot be accurately written as a meaningful freestanding word. I have already alluded to "dying words." *Citizen Kane* offers a special case of dying words because "rosebud" remains an enigma until the end of the film. It must be conclusive, and yet no one except Kane knows what it means. The result, as the newsreel producer sees, is that some crucial, secret story must exist within Kane's very public life, which makes the meaning of "rosebud" all the more intriguing. If Thompson can tell that story, the newsreel will have outdone the newspaper; it will, so Rawlston believes, have told the world "who" Kane really was.

Taking all this in the context of the film as a whole, we find a stark contrast to the representation of orality that we have already considered. Earlier, political oratory and opera were eclipsed simply by the power of the one written word in a newspaper headline: *singer*. But with *rosebud* it turns out that an inviolable oral core of identity remains. No newspaper can even discover the meaning of, much less somehow overcome, this dying word. Evidently, no newsreel can get at that meaning, either. After all his searching, Thompson wearily tries to cover his failure by concluding: "I don't think any word can explain a man's life." The newsreel never succeeds in distinguishing itself from the newspaper. Further, taking Rawlston's earlier stress on "telling," along with the way that showing, telling, and writing have become central to the conflict between newsreel and newspaper, then *Citizen Kane* implies that "telling" *in general* cannot by itself communicate *the story* of innermost identity. That story must be both shown and told. The newspaper cannot do this because it depends on writing and because, lacking motion pictures, it cannot show story. The newsreel fails because, though it shows story, it depends on written or vocal explanation to do its telling. The struggle between newspaper and newsreel was, from the start, doomed to have no winner. (This was of course prepared for early on by the figurative equations of the two, beginning with the screening room scene after the newsreel.)

Getting at identity on the most intimate level of "dying words" requires story, not information, which always privileges telling over showing. Only fiction film, because it has the power to look through writing and to subsume informational film, can show/tell the story of the definitive oral core of identity. This notion is visually and thematically wrapped up by the fact that no one in the film learns what the dying word *rosebud* means. Finally, at the very end we are shown that the secret dying word exists not only as lost speech but also as lost writing: the brand label on the young boy's sled. Writing is in a visual sense once more equated with the ephemerality of speech. We look through "Rosebud" as it disappears into flames. With the viewer's privileged looks at both the one first spoken word and the one last written word, we have the final proof of what only film can do. As a storytelling art it subsumes both the oralistic and the alphabetic. In a curious way, this is another version of the event of generic change that we have found with *Don Quixote*, *Northanger Abbey*, and *Madame Bovary*. As, for instance, the gothic novel was to *Northanger Abbey* and the novel, so the newspaper and newsreel are to *Citizen Kane* and fiction film. Just this has been the "story" of *Citizen Kane*.

⟨⟩III

I began this study by anchoring speech and story in the human biological organism and by explaining writing as an invented technology. This groundwork established a set of roughly universal effects and qualities in relation to which I could make claims about both the novel as a genre as well as about specific elements of specific novels, and even about film. In examining my selection of novels in English from the eighteenth through the early twenty-first century, I have charted a significant sequence of change as the possibilities of the technology were carried to an extreme. Another way to consider this history is in terms of my earlier analogy with the automobile and the modern city. The invention and implementation of the automobile has unquestionably been one of the most powerful determinants of the modern American city. As the automobile has changed the nature of large groups of humans living in close proximity, so writing has changed the nature of story.

It is always unwise to push analogies too far, but this one provides one further useful parallel to the novel. At some point, reached at various times, depending on the individual case, cities become overconformed, so to speak, to the automobile. The technology that had much to do with enabling—or, more strongly, determining—the modern city in the first place becomes a curse. Too much traffic, too much money devoted to this one element of life, too much of the land sacrificed to roads and other artificial surfaces, too much pollution, not enough parking; all too many of us know all this firsthand. From the evidence of, especially, *The Waves*, *The Golden Notebook*, and *Atonement*, it appears that the conformation of story to writing may have gone as far as it can go, at least with respect to formal experiment. And then *Citizen Kane* seems to be, brashly enough, making the case that cinema supersedes any kind of story that depends on writing.

All this may sound like another entry in the list of "death of the novel" prognostications—but not so. The sense of intimate communion between written story and reader, so peculiar to the novel, guarantees an apparently endless audience, and the originality, responsibility, and self-skepticism that are built into alphabetic story guarantee an apparently endless creativity. Given the nature of modern literate, and especially hyperliterate, culture, I suspect that the novel will always be with us.

NOTES

Chapter One: To Begin

1. Derrida discusses writing in various ways in a number of his important works: *Of Grammatology* (Baltimore: Johns Hopkins University Press, 1976); *Speech and Phenomena and Other Essays on Husserl's Theory of Signs* (Evanston, IL: Northwestern University Press, 1973); *Writing and Difference* (Chicago: University of Chicago Press, 1978); *Dissemination* (Chicago: University of Chicago Press, 1981); *Margins of Philosophy* (Chicago: University of Chicago Press, 1982); and *Limited Inc* (Evanston, IL: Northwestern University Press, 1988).

2. For Greek literature, see, e.g., Bakker; Havelock 1963, 1982, 1986; and Foley 1990, 1991. For medieval literature, see, e.g., Amodio; Bynum; Chaytor; Niles 1999; and Stock 1983.

3. At this point the consideration of writing as a technology in relation to orality has become quite substantial. Among others, see Chartier 1989, 2002; Clanchy 1993; Eisenstein 1979; Goody 1968, 1977, 1986, 1987, 2000; Havelock 1982, 1986; McLuhan 1962; Olson 1994; Ong 1967, 1977, 1982; Stock 1983; Gates 1986, 1987, 1988; Appiah 1992; Chafe 1994.

4. We can trace this effect readily enough on the macro-level of cultural history. Developmental psychology shows it happening, as well, on the micro-level of the individual becoming literate; see, e.g., Tochinsky 2003.

5. Cf. also Eric Havelock: "It is only as language is written down that it becomes possible to think about it. The acoustic medium, being incapable of visualization, did not achieve recognition as a phenomenon wholly separable from the person who used it. But in the alphabetized document the medium became objectified. There it was, reproduced perfectly in the alphabet, not a partial image but the whole of it, no longer just a function of 'me' the speaker but a document with an independent existence" (1986, 112). The "perfectly" is a serious overstatement.

6. This conflict has so far been most thoroughly explored in early ambivalences about print; cf. Kiefer, Eisenstein, and Kernan.

7. There is quite revealing evidence of the tendency to conflate speech and writing in scholarly work on the novel. The otherwise convincing ideas of, for instance, Mary Louise Pratt (1977) and Richard Ohmann (1972) on speech-act

theory and the novel fail in certain key ways from the outset because of a lack of attention to this fact. The same holds at times in the work of Mikhail Bakhtin (1986). In more psychologically oriented writings the problem also arises. Most of the claims that Richard Gerrig's book *Experiencing Narrative Worlds* (1993) makes about narrative in general should, strictly speaking, be restricted to written narrative. Finally, Jerome Bruner provides a particularly striking example of how conflating writing and speech can be problematic. In his very fine book *Acts of Meaning*, he claims that "the existence of story as a form is a perpetual guarantee that human kind will 'go meta' on received versions of reality. May that not be why dictators must take such draconian measures against a culture's novelists?" (1990, 55). Bruner makes a global statement about story inducing a "meta" perspective into human life, but, interestingly, he then specifies novelists as his example. The fact is that the kind of "meta" he intends is specific to literate cultures. Oral story apart from writing does not induce a mind or culture to "go meta." This is only true of written narrative.

8. See also McLuhan 1962; Altmann, 178; Martin, 36.

9. This too has a basis in our neurology. David Morris explains that beyond "the left-hemispheric cerebral activity in areas typical of speech, alphabetic readers also require activity in the visual cortex. English-speakers appear to have separate systems within the brain for aural understanding of language and for silent visual understanding" (541).

10. The literature on this understanding of narrative in human consciousness, which is primarily psychological, is by now very extensive. For a sampling, see Bruner 1986, 1990; Calvin 1990; Polkinghorne 1988; Sarbin 1986. Dennett (1991) and Damasio (1994) argue for narrative structures on the physiological level as well. Mark Turner (1996) may be the best-known literary scholar to take up the significance of the psychological research.

11. See also Havelock: "The true 'thought' or content of oral epos is traditional, to be found in the formulaic and stanzaic patterns of the text, not in the conscious intentions of the singer-composer" (1982, 156); and Amodio: "Just as meaning in traditional poetry inheres in the structures that constitute its expressive economy, so, too, does an oral poem's authority lie chiefly in the tectonics of the tradition itself rather than in the person of the poet" (14).

12. In the history of story, there have certainly been representations of everyday life, but they are, until the emergence of the novel, nearly always comic. This fact alone supports the taken-for-granted sense of the fantastic and the heroic as the obvious content for story that matters. Before the novel, the everyday either did not count as content or had always to be rendered into the special case of comedy.

13. Richard Green makes this same point about preliterate forms of contract. When there is no writing by which to "remember" a formal agreement, rituals,

ceremonies, and witnesses are systematically employed as ways "to make the contract an unforgettable event" (42).

14. Cf. also Ong: "Originality consists not in the introduction of new materials but in fitting the traditional materials effectively into each individual, unique situation and/or audience" (1982, 60).

15. I use the term *hyperliterate* when I need to distinguish between a broadly average degree of everyday literacy and the kind of literacy associated with, at least, college-educated people.

16. Oral story, including ancient epic, connects in this way as much or more with poetry than it does with what literate culture typically thinks of as story (Havelock 1982, 113–19). Tightly aligned with music, chant, and the speaking voice, poetry has been until modernity the pre-eminent form of oral literature (Niles 1999, 9). Human cognitive faculties—as established in, for instance, psychological studies (Chafe)—have also helped to determine the formal elements of this literary form. The original written stories were all transcriptions of chanted, versified tales.

17. On the idea of this continuum, see also Amodio, chap. 1.

Chapter Two: Writing, Reading, and Disembodiment in Pride and Prejudice

1. I say "not required" because that is the actual state of affairs. From the alphabetic perspective it can too easily seem that what an alphabetic reading reveals about the text is somehow necessary, that the text is not authentically read unless it is close-read. But this is an untenable alphabetic value judgment, whose opposite is the oralistic position that close-reading murders the text in order to dissect it. There are experimental texts—certain modernist and postmodernist texts—that must be reread in order to achieve any valuable comprehension at all; and there are texts that offer little new comprehension (though they may still satisfy) even with many rereadings. And then there are texts like Austen's that satisfy, it appears, all manner of readers.

2. It should be noted that throughout this work I use *speech-act* to refer only to oral acts of speech. In my terms, a speech-act can be represented in writing, but a speech-act as such consists of spoken language.

3. I say most forms of storytelling because with the advent of film, we finally have a story form that can possibly show such states and such interactions. If these states register outwardly, the eyes are most often the primary means of expression. Only film can show faces in such ways as to make these extremely subtle expressions visible to the viewer's eye. Before film, only written story could tackle these intimate kinds of human interiority.

4. In doing this the analyst would be examining not the play, but the description of the play. Any given enactment of the play might present the scene quite

differently, depending on director and actors and audience involvement. In effect, to analyze a scene from a play this way is more akin to analyzing a scene from a film, which, once released, does not change. Analyzing the text rather than a given performance of a play is always positing a particular instantiation of the work in the process of analyzing it. Still, because of the stronger affiliation of a theatrical performance to its written text, drama enables close-reading analysis in a way that a screenplay typically does not. Film marks a major evolution in the history of storytelling, in part, because of the work's relation to its written source. We may generalize that every enactment of a play requires the same written source, even though each enactment is different. Obviously, this is only true of the initial event of producing a film. Because of the nature of technological representation, a screenplay does not describe the story of a film in quite the same way as does the text of a play. With the advent of in-home projection technology, viewers can now analyze film in the way that we can analyze written texts. We can freeze an image, rewind and rewatch, use slow motion, etc. We can treat the film as a kind of object. Such viewing was always possible in principle, of course, but now it is much easier.

5. Strictly speaking, the maximal alphabetic reading would necessarily involve a written response to the text because only a written response would involve something like the same level of cognitive work done by the writer. To explore this any further, however, would take us too far from the project at hand.

Chapter Three: The Monstrous Writing of Frankenstein

1. For my purposes, it makes no serious difference that the preface, as Shelley later records (229), was actually written by her husband, Percy. Its position before the story is a historical fact, it does make a defense of the story that follows, and its contents are revealing, regardless of their author.

2. In recent years a new entry into the arena of writing—email—makes this point even more forcefully. With email, many (more and more) people tend to send quick messages in writing that, before, they would more likely have delivered by phone or might not have taken the trouble to communicate at all, even by phone. So they choose writing instead of speech. In the history of writing, email in its normative technological form is uniquely in between telephoning and writing a letter. For the first time, anyone with the proper machinery and skills (and they have become quite common now) can communicate relatively easily, from the home or office or any computer that is connected to the relevant communications web. Previous quick-writing message systems, such as the telegraph, could never become common because they lacked this ease of use. The message is dispatched so rapidly—sometimes instantaneously—that it operates at or near the speed of vocal exchange. The kinds of messages that are sent this way tend

to be very brief, a sentence or two. But just here in describing the messages as brief, I have invoked an alphabetic standard; the messages are only "brief" when compared to the usual length of written texts of whatever kind. In fact, by conversational standards they are not brief. They are very much like the usual chunks of speech we use all the time. Because the content is typically more or less casual, even spelling and grammar and typos can be ignored. Text messaging takes this dumping of the usual alphabetic rules even further. Cognitively, then, this kind of writing comes closest to the amount of work involved in regular conversation. Its success makes clear why people would otherwise not write when they can speak. Indeed, email has now taken over the personal letter as the writing that is truly most like speech.

3. The concept of a human theory of mind has been well established in psychological studies. The best introduction to theory of mind for literary scholars is Lisa Zunshine's *Why We Read Fiction*.

4. I am indirectly assuming a relationship between oral story forms in general and a child's imagination. This runs the risk of falling into the idea that oral story is childish, that childishness is primitive, simple, inferior, etc., and that "good" literature has matured beyond those childish and primitive forms. But this negative value judgment is not a necessary one, and is another example of an alphabetic standard being taken for granted as the universally right standard. Why, if we can find a continual similarity between the more or less spontaneous imaginative creations of children and certain historically reoccurring popular adult stories, would we automatically lump these creations into a negative category of childish rather than a positive category of commonly human? This does not mean that no value judgments can be made, that we can never label a given story childish within a specific context of values; it means only that we must be careful about alphabetic standards operating as universal standards.

5. Another inconsistency in the story occurs here because we later learn that Safie's Christian Arab mother had "taught her daughter to aspire to the higher powers of intellect" and that she had become "accustomed to grand ideas" (119).

6. In claiming an anxiety that seems built into writing and in showing how that anxiety manifests itself, not fully consciously, in alphabetic story, I am aware of the similarities between my position and poststructruralist positions about the anxiety built into language in general. But one reason for carrying forward my project is that I have become convinced that the poststructuralist generalization is not sound. Speech in general is not an anxious activity. Humans use it most of the time with remarkable ease and remarkable success. If we do not dogmatically rule out any concept of the natural; if we can take it that elements of human existence that are determined by our genetic predispositions are natural, are evolutionarily determined functions of the nonhuman nature of the planet earth;

then language in general is natural. Like so much else in human life, it can produce anxiety in special situations. As I have shown, however, because writing is an invented technology for reproducing speech, it is automatically anxious as a linguistic activity and is always experienced in the way that only a special case of spoken language is experienced.

Chapter Four: Letters and Spirits in Bleak House

1. Mrs. Pardiggle is another example of this in religion, and she is even more directly tied to literacy. She reads aloud to the brickmaker's illiterate family from the "good book" as if she is a constable who is taking "the whole family into custody." She makes reading a "mechanical way of taking possession of" those who cannot read (82).

2. We can possibly see a large-scale historical parallel between law and religion here. Jesus saw himself as revolutionizing the old Mosaic Law by reinvesting it with spirit. The original Chancery had much the same relation to old secular law. Whether the parallel keeps going, and the New Testament, as the written institutionalization of "Jesus," went on to become the new, spiritless letter in its turn, I leave my readers to decide.

3. Two other examples of learning to write directly oppose Krook's self-education. Caddy explains to Esther that if Prince Turveydrop were "not so anxious about his spelling, and took less pains to make it clear, he would do better" as a writer. As it is, he put "so many unnecessary letters into short words, that they sometimes quite lost their English appearance" (149). But Caddy, who as her mother's amanuensis is an accomplished writer, does not try to fix her fiancé. She says that it is better to be "amiable than learned," and in any case she can "write letters enough for both" of them (149). The other case of teaching writing presents Esther as teacher and Charley as a child student. Charley, Esther reports, seems "to have no natural power over a pen." In her hand the pen seems to "become perversely animated, and to go wrong and crooked" as if with a will of its own (325), but Esther simply encourages Charley to keep practicing.

4. See, e.g., Belsey, 80; J. Hillis Miller, 13; Lucas, 211; Serlen.

Chapter Five: The De-Composition of Writing in A Passage to India

1. The song is alluded to directly or indirectly at least seventeen times, on 85, 93, 114, 124, 146, 150, 151, 166, 198, 217, 266, 273, 298, 299, 326, and 358.

2. Echo is mentioned or alluded to on 43, 54, 104, 126, 155, 162, 163, 185, 211, 214, 215, 221, 222, 228, 233, 236, 265, 307, and 325.

Abbott, H. Porter. *Diary Fiction: Writing as Action.* Ithaca, NY: Cornell University Press, 1984.

Altman, Janet Gurkin. *Epistolarity: Approaches to a Form.* Columbus: Ohio State University Press, 1982.

Altman, Rick. "Deep-Focus Sound: *Citizen Kane* and the Radio Aesthetic." *Quarterly Review of Film and Video* 15 (1994): 1–33.

Altmann, Gerry T. M. *The Ascent of Babel: An Exploration of Language, Mind, and Understanding.* Oxford: Oxford University Press, 1997.

Amodio, Mark C. *Writing the Oral Tradition.* Notre Dame, IN: University of Notre Dame Press, 2004.

Appiah, Anthony. *In My Father's House: Africa in the Philosophy of Culture.* Oxford: Oxford University Press, 1992.

Armstrong, Paul B. "Reading India: E. M. Forster and the Politics of Interpretation." *Twentieth-Century Literature: A Scholarly and Critical Journal* 38.4 (1992): 365–85.

Austen, Jane. *Northanger Abbey.* Edited by Anne Ehrenpreis. New York: Penguin Books, 1985.

———. *Pride and Prejudice: A Norton Critical Edition.* 3rd ed. Edited by Donald Gray. New York: W. W. Norton, 2001.

Bakhtin, Mikhail. *The Dialogic Imagination: Four Essays.* Edited by Michael Holquist. Translated by Caryl Emerson and Michael Holquist. Austin: University of Texas Press, 1981.

———. *Speech Genres and Other Late Essays.* Edited by Caryl Emerson and Michael Holquist. Translated by Vern W. McGee. Austin: University of Texas Press, 1986.

Bakker, Egbert J. *Poetry in Speech: Orality and Homeric Discourse.* Ithaca, NY: Cornell University Press, 1997.

Barchas, Janine. *Graphic Design, Print Culture, and the Eighteenth Century Novel.* Cambridge: Cambridge University Press, 2003.

Barratt, Robert. "Marabar: The Caves of Deconstruction." *Journal of Narrative Technique* 23.2 (1993): 127–35.

Bazin, André. *What Is Cinema? Volume 1.* Translated by Hugh Gray. Berkeley: University of California Press, 1967.

———. *Orson Welles: A Critical View.* Translated by Jonathan Rosenbaum. New York: Harper & Row, 1978.

Beja, Morris. "Where You Can't Get at Him: Orson Wells and the Attempt to Escape from Father." *Literature Film Quarterly* 13.1 (1985): 2–9.

Belsey, Catherine. *Critical Practice.* London: Methuen, 1980.

Bender, John B. *Imagining the Penitentiary: Fiction and the Architecture of Mind in Eighteenth-Century England.* Chicago: University of Chicago Press, 1987.

Benjamin, Walter. *Illuminations.* Edited by Hannah Arendt. Translated by Harry Zohn. New York: Schocken Books, 1968.

Bigelow, Gordon. "Market Indicators: Banking and Domesticity in Dickens's *Bleak House.*" *ELH* 67.2 (2000): 589–615.

Billy, Ted. "Montage à trois: The Extrinsic Self in *Heart of Darkness, The Great Gatsby,* and *Citizen Kane.*" *Journal of Evolutionary Psychology* 14.1–2 (1993): 41–50.

Bonaparte, Felicia. "Conjecturing Possibilities: Reading and Misreading Texts in Jane Austen's *Pride and Prejudice.*" *Studies in the Novel* 37.2 (2005): 141–61.

Booth, Wayne. *The Rhetoric of Fiction.* 2nd ed. Chicago: University of Chicago Press, 1983 (1961).

Bradbury, Malcolm. "Two Passages to India: Forster as Victorian and Modern." In *Aspects of E. M. Forster,* edited by Oliver Stallybrass, 123–42. London: Edward Arnold, 1969.

Brantlinger, Patrick. *The Reading Lesson: The Threat of Mass Literacy in Nineteenth-Century British Fiction.* Bloomington: Indiana University Press, 1998.

Brinkley, Robert, and Sara Speidel. "Narrative Mimicry: *Citizen Kane* and the Function of the Gaze." *New Orleans Review* 14.2 (1987): 72–84.

Bronson, Bertrand. *Facets of the Enlightenment: Studies in English Literature and Its Contexts.* Berkeley: University of California Press, 1968.

Brooks, Peter. *Reading for the Plot.* New York: Vintage, 1985.

Bruner, Jerome. *Actual Minds, Possible Worlds.* Cambridge, MA: Harvard University Press, 1986.

———. *Acts of Meaning.* Cambridge, MA: Harvard University Press, 1990.

Bugg, John. "'Master of Their Language': Education and Exile in Mary Shelley's *Frankenstein.*" *Huntington Library Quarterly: Studies in English and American History and Literature* 68.4 (2005): 655–66.

Buzard, James. "Anywhere's Nowhere": *Bleak House* as Autoethnography. *Yale Journal of Criticism* 12.1 (1999): 7–39.

Bynum, David E. *The Daemon in the Wood: A Study of Oral Narrative Patterns.* Cambridge, MA: Harvard University Press, 1978.

Calvin, W. H. *The Cerebral Symphony: Seashore Reflections on the Structure of Consciousness.* New York: Bantam Books, 1990.

Cantor, Paul. *Creature and Creator: Myth-making and English Romanticism.* Cambridge: Cambridge University Press, 1984.

Carringer, Robert. "*Citizen Kane, The Great Gatsby* and Some Conventions of American Narrative." *Critical Inquiry* 2.2 (1975): 307–26.

———. "'Rosebud, Dead or Alive': Narrative and Symbolic Structure in *Citizen Kane.*" *PMLA* 91.2 (1976): 185–93.

Carroll, Noel. *Theorizing the Moving Image.* Cambridge: Cambridge University Press, 1996.

Chafe, Wallace. *Discourse, Consciousness, and Time: The Flow and Displacement of Conscious Experience in Speaking and Writing.* Chicago: University of Chicago Press, 1994.

Chartier, Roger. *A History of Private Life.* Vol. 3, *Passions of the Renaissance.* Translated by Arthur Goldhammer. Cambridge, MA: Belknap Press of Harvard University Press, 1989.

———. *The Order of Books.* Stanford: Stanford University Press, 1994.

———. "The Practical Impact of Writing." In *The Book History Reader*, edited by David Finkelstein and Alistair McCleery, 118–42. London: Routledge, 2002.

Chaytor, H. J. *From Script to Print: An Introduction to Medieval Vernacular Literature.* Cambridge: W. Heffer, 1950.

Citizen Kane. Directed by Orson Welles. RKO Radio Pictures, 1941. DVD, Warner Bros. Home Video, 2001.

Clanchy, M. T. *From Memory to Written Record: England, 1066–1307.* 2nd ed. Oxford: Blackwell, 1993.

Colmer, John. "Promise and Withdrawal in *A Passage to India.*" In *E. M. Forster: A Human Exploration; Centenary Essays*, edited by G. K. Das and John Beer, 117–28. New York: New York University Press, 1979.

Cook, Elizabeth Heckendorn. *Epistolary Bodies: Gender and Genre in the Eighteenth-Century Republic of Letters.* Stanford: Stanford University Press, 1996.

Currie, Gregory. *Image and Mind: Film, Philosophy, and Cognitive Science.* Cambridge: Cambridge University Press, 1995.

Damasio, Antonio. *Descartes' Error.* New York: Avon, 1994.

Davis, Lennard. *Factual Fictions: The Origins of the English Novel.* New York: Columbia University Press, 1983.

Day, Robert Adams. *Told in Letters: Epistolary Fiction before Richardson.* Ann Arbor: University of Michigan Press, 1966.

D'Cruz, Doreen. "Emptying and Filling along the Existential Coil in *A Passage to India.*" *Studies in the Novel* 18.2 (1986): 193–205.

Defoe, Daniel. *Robinson Crusoe: A Norton Critical Edition*. 2nd ed. Edited by Michael Shinagel. New York: W. W. Norton. 1994.

Dennett, Daniel. *Consciousness Explained*. Boston: Little, Brown, 1991.

Devine, Jodi. "Letters and Their Role in Revealing Class and Personal Identity in *Pride and Prejudice*." *Persuasions* 27 (2005): 99–111.

Dickens, Charles. *Bleak House*. Edited by Morton Dauwen Zabel. Boston: Houghton Mifflin, 1956.

Dissanayake, Ellen. *Homo Aestheticus: Where Art Comes from and Why*. Seattle: University of Washington Press, 1995.

Dolin, Kieran. *Fiction and the Law: Legal Discourse in Victorian and Modernist Literature*. Cambridge: Cambridge University Press, 1999.

Dowling, David. "*A Passage to India* through 'The Spaces between the Words.'" *Journal of Narrative Technique* 15.3 (1985): 256–66.

Eisenstein, Elizabeth. *The Printing Press as an Agent of Change: Communications and Cultural Transformations in Early Modern Europe*. Cambridge: Cambridge University Press, 1979.

Eliot, George. *Adam Bede*. Edited by John Paterson. New York: Houghton Mifflin, 1968.

Favret, Mary. "A Woman Writes the Fiction of Science: The Body in *Frankenstein*." *Genders* 14 (1992): 50–65.

———. *Romantic Correspondence: Women, Politics, and the Fiction of Letters*. Cambridge: Cambridge University Press, 1993.

Finney, Brian. "Briony's Stand Against Oblivion: The Making of Fiction in Ian McEwan's *Atonement*." *Journal of Modern Literature* 27.3 (2004): 68–82.

Flaubert, Gustave. *Madame Bovary: A Story of Provincial Life*. Translated by Alan Russell. Baltimore: Penguin Books, 1968.

Foley, John Miles, ed. *Oral Tradition in Literature: Interpretation in Context*. Columbia: University of Missouri Press, 1986.

———. *Traditional Oral Epic: The "Odyssey," "Beowulf," and Serbo-Croatian Return Song*. Berkeley: University of California Press, 1990.

———. *Immanent Art: From Structure to Meaning in Traditional Oral Epic*. Bloomington: Indiana University Press, 1991.

Forster, E. M. *A Passage to India*. New York: Harcourt Brace Jovanovich, 1984.

Fouroli, Carolyn. "Doris Lessing's 'Game': Referential Language and Fictional Form." *Twentieth Century Literature: A Scholarly and Critical Journal* 27.2 (1981): 146–65.

Franken, Lynn. "Poor Terrestrial Justice: Bakhtin and Criminal Trial in the Novel." *Comparative Literature* 49.2 (1997): 113–27.

Frantz, Sarah. "'If I loved you less, I might be able to talk about it more': Direct Dialogue and Education in the Proposal Scenes." In *The Talk in Jane Austen*, edited by Bruce Stovel and Lynn Weinlos Gregg, 167–82. Edmonton: University of Alberta Press, 2002.

Gates, Henry Louis. *Figures in Black: Words, Signs, and the "Racial" Self.* Oxford: Oxford University Press. 1987.

———. *The Signifying Monkey: A Theory of African-American Literary Criticism.* Oxford: Oxford University Press, 1988.

———, ed. *"Race," Writing, and Difference.* Chicago: University of Chicago Press, 1986.

Gerrig, Richard. *Experiencing Narrative Worlds: On the Psychological Activities of Reading.* New Haven: Yale University Press, 1993.

Gilbert, Sandra, and Susan Gubar. *The Madwoman in the Attic: The Woman Writer and the Nineteenth-Century Literary Imagination.* New Haven: Yale University Press, 1979.

Gladfelder, Hal. *Criminality and Narrative in Eighteenth-Century England: Beyond the Law.* Baltimore: Johns Hopkins University Press, 2001.

Goody, Jack. *The Domestication of the Savage Mind.* Cambridge: Cambridge University Press, 1977.

———. *The Logic of Writing and the Organization of Society.* Cambridge: Cambridge University Press, 1986.

———. *The Interface between the Written and the Oral.* Cambridge: Cambridge University Press, 1987.

———. *The Power of the Written Tradition.* Washington, DC: Smithsonian Institution Press, 2000.

———, and Ian Watt. "The Consequences of Literacy." In *Literacy in Traditional Societies*, edited by Jack Goody, 27–68. Cambridge: Cambridge University Press, 1968.

Gottesman, Ronald, ed. *Focus on* Citizen Kane. Englewood Cliffs, NJ: Prentice-Hall, 1971.

Green, Richard Firth. *A Crisis of Truth: Literature and Law in Ricardian England.* Philadelphia: University of Pennsylvania Press, 1999.

Greene, Gayle. "Feminist Fiction and the Uses of Memory." *Signs* 16.2 (1991): 290–321.

Grossman, Jonathan. *The Art of Alibi: English Law Courts and the Novel.* Baltimore: Johns Hopkins University Press, 2002.

Hack, Daniel. "'Sublimation Strange': Allegory and Authority in *Bleak House.*" *ELH* 66.1 (1999): 129–56.

Hamilton, Edith, and Huntington Cairns, eds. *Plato: The Collected Dialogues.* Princeton: Princeton University Press, 1961.

Harper, Howard. *Between Language and Silence: The Novels of Virginia Woolf.* Baton Rouge: Louisiana State University Press, 1982.

Havelock, Eric. *Preface to Plato.* Cambridge, MA: Belknap Press of Harvard University Press, 1963.

———. *The Literate Revolution in Greece and Its Cultural Consequences.* Princeton: Princeton University Press, 1982.

———. *The Muse Learns to Write: Reflections on Orality and Literacy from Antiquity to the Present.* New Haven: Yale University Press, 1986.

Henstra, Sarah. "Nuclear Cassandra: Prophecy in Doris Lessing's *The Golden Notebook.*" *Papers on Language and Literature: A Journal for Scholars and Critics of Language and Literature* 43.1 (2007): 3–23.

Herman, David, ed. *Narrative Theory and the Cognitive Sciences.* Stanford: Center for the Study of Language and Information Publications, 2003.

Hidalgo, Pilar. "Memory and Storytelling in Ian McEwan's *Atonement.*" *Critique* 46.2 (2005): 82–91.

Hite, Molly. "Doris Lessing's *The Golden Notebook* and *Four-Gated City*: Ideology, Coherence, and Possibility." *Twentieth Century Literature: A Scholarly and Critical Journal* 34.1 (1988): 16–29.

Ingersoll, Earl G. "Intertextuality in L. P. Hartley's *The Go-Between* and Ian McEwan's *Atonement.*" *Forum for Modern Language Studies* 40.3 (2004): 241–58.

Jaffe, Ira. "Film as the Narration of Space: *Citizen Kane.*" *Literature/Film Quarterly* 7.2 (1979): 99–111.

Johnson, Samuel. "From *A Dictionary of the English Language.*" In *Johnson on the English Language.* Vol. 18, *The Yale Edition of the Works of Samuel Johnson,* edited by Gwin Kolb and Robert Demaria Jr., 63–115. New Haven: Yale University Press, 2005.

Kael, Pauline. *The Citizen Kane Book: Raising Kane.* Boston: Little, Brown, 1971.

Kellogg, Ronald. *The Psychology Of Writing,* Oxford: Oxford University Press, 1994.

Kelly, Gary. "Reading Aloud in *Mansfield Park.*" *Nineteenth-Century Fiction* 37.1 (1982): 29–49.

———. "The Art of Reading in *Pride and Prejudice.*" *English Studies in Canada* 10.2 (1984): 156–71.

Kernan, Alvin. *Printing Technology, Letters and Samuel Johnson.* Princeton: Princeton University Press, 1987.

Kiefer, Frederick. *Writing on the Renaissance Stage: Written Words, Printed Pages, Metaphoric Books.* Newark: University of Delaware Press, 1996.

King, Jeanette. *Doris Lessing,* London: Edward Arnold, 1989.

Krouse, Tonya. "Freedom as Effacement in *The Golden Notebook*: Theorizing Pleasure, Subjectivity, and Authority." *Journal of Modern Literature* 29.3 (2006): 39–56.

Lakoff, George, and Mark Johnson. *Philosophy in the Flesh.* New York: Basic Books, 1999.

Lamb, John. "Mary Shelley's *Frankenstein* and Milton's Monstrous Myth." *Nineteenth-Century Literature* 47.3 (1992): 303–19.

Lessing, Doris. *The Golden Notebook.* New York: Ballantyne Books, 1962.

Levin, Harry. *The Gates of Horn: A Study of Five French Realists.* New York: Oxford University Press, 1963.

Levine, George. *The Realistic Imagination: English Fiction from Frankenstein to Lady Chatterley.* Chicago: University of Chicago Press, 1981.

Levi-Strauss, Claude. *Tristes Tropiques.* Translated by John and Doreen Weightman. New York: Penguin Books, 1992.

Lipking, Lawrence. "*Frankenstein,* the True Story; or, Rousseau Judges Jean-Jacques." In *Frankenstein: A Norton Critical Edition,* edited by J. Paul Hunter, 313–31. New York: W. W. Norton, 1996.

Lord, Albert. *The Singer of Tales.* New York: Atheneum Press, 1971.

Lougy, Robert. "Filth, Liminality, and Abjection in Charles Dickens's *Bleak House.*" *ELH* 69.2 (2002): 473–500.

Lucas, John. *The Melancholy Man.* London: Methuen, 1970.

Luria, A. R. *Cognitive Development.* Edited by Michael Cole. Translated by Martin Lopez-Morillas and Lynn Solotaroff. Cambridge: Harvard University Press, 1976.

Marder, Elissa. "The Mother Tongue in *Phedre* and *Frankenstein.*" *Yale French Studies* 76 (1989): 59–77.

Marshall, David. *The Surprising Effects of Sympathy: Marivaux, Diderot, Rousseau, and Mary Shelley.* Chicago: University of Chicago Press, 1988.

Martin, Henri-Jean. *The History and Power of Writing.* Translated by Lydia Cochrane. Chicago: University of Chicago Press, 1994.

Mass, Roslyn. "A Linking of Legends: *The Great Gatsby* and *Citizen Kane.*" *Literature Film Quarterly* 2.3 (1974): 207–16.

Mast, Gerald. *Film/Cinema/Movie: A Theory of Experience.* New York: Harper & Row, 1977.

Maxfield, James. "'A Man Like Ourselves': *Citizen Kane* as an Aristotelian Tragedy." *Literature Film Quarterly* 14.3 (1986): 195–203.

McEwan, Ian. *Atonement.* New York: Anchor Books, 2001.

———. Interview by Adam Begley. *Paris Review* 162 (2002): 59.

McKeon, Michael. *The Origins of the English Novel, 1600–1740.* Baltimore: Johns Hopkins University Press, 1987.

McLane, Maureen Noelle. "Literate Species: Populations, 'Humanities,' and *Frankenstein.*" *ELH* 63.4 (1996): 959–88.

McLuhan, Marshall. *The Gutenberg Galaxy: The Making of Typographic Man.* Toronto: University of Toronto Press, 1962.

McWhir, Anne. "Teaching the Monster to Read: Mary Shelley, Education, and *Frankenstein.*" In *The Educational Legacy of Romanticism,* edited by John Willinsky, 73–92. Waterloo, ON: Wilfrid Laurier University Press, 1990.

Miller, D. A. *The Novel and the Police.* Berkeley: University of California Press, 1989.

Miller, J. Hillis. "Introduction." In *Bleak House,* edited by Norman Page, 11–34. Harmondsworth, UK: Penguin Books, 1971.

Moers, Ellen. *Literary Women.* New York: Anchor Press, 1977.

Morris, David B. "Reading Is Always Biocultural." *New Literary History* 37.3 (2006): 539–61.

Mulvey, Laura. *Citizen Kane.* London: BFI Publishing, 1992.

Munsterberg, Hugo. "The Means of the Photoplay." In *Film Theory and Criticism: Introductory Readings.* 5th ed. Edited by Leo Braudy and Marshall Cohen, 401–7. Oxford: Oxford University Press, 1999.

Naremore, James. *The Magic World of Orson Welles.* New York: Oxford University Press, 1978.

———. *Orson Welles's* Citizen Kane. New York: Oxford University Press, 2004.

Newey, Katherine. "'What Think You of Books?': Reading in *Pride and Prejudice.*" *Sydney Studies in English* 21 (1995–96): 81–94.

Newman, Beth. "Narratives of Seduction and the Seductions of Narrative: The Frame Structure of *Frankenstein.*" *ELH* 53.1 (1986): 141–63.

Niles, John. *Homo Narrans: The Poetics and Anthropology of Oral Literature.* Philadelphia: University of Pennsylvania Press, 1999.

Ohmann, Richard. "Speech, Literature, and the Space Between." *New Literary History* 4 (1972): 47–63.

Olson, David. *The World on Paper: The Conceptual and Cognitive Implications of Writing and Reading.* Cambridge: Cambridge University Press, 1994.

Ong, Walter. *The Presence of the Word: Some Prolegomena for Cultural and Religious History.* New Haven: Yale University Press, 1967.

———. *Rhetoric, Romance, and Technology: Studies in the Interaction of Expression and Culture.* Ithaca, NY: Cornell University Press, 1971.

———. *Interfaces of the Word: Studies in the Evolution of Consciousness and Culture.* Ithaca, NY: Cornell University Press, 1977.

———. *Orality and Literacy: The Technologizing of the Word.* London: Methuen, 1982.

———. "Writing Is a Technology That Restructures Thought." In *The Written Word: Literacy in Transition,* edited by Gerd Baumann, 23–50. Oxford: Clarendon Press, 1986.

Orange, Michael. "Language and Silence in *A Passage to India.*" In *E. M. Forster: A Human Exploration; Centenary Essays,* edited by G. K. Das and John Beer, 142–60. Oxford: Clarendon Press, 1986.

O'Rourke, James. "'Nothing More Unnatural': Mary Shelley's Revision of Rousseau." *ELH* 56.3 (1989): 543–69.

Page, Norman. *The Language of Jane Austen.* Oxford: Basil Blackwell, 1972.

Parry, Benita. "Materiality and Mystification in *A Passage to India*." *Novel: A Forum on Fiction* 31.2 (1998): 174–94.

Parry, Milman. *The Making of Homeric Verse: The Collected Writings of Milman Parry*. Edited by Adam Parry. Oxford: Oxford University Press, 1971.

Patterson, Charles. "Hazlitt's Criticism in Retrospect." *Studies in English Literature, 1500–1900* 21.4 (1981): 647–63.

Polkinghorne, Donald. *Narrative Knowing and the Human Sciences*. Albany: State University of New York Press, 1988.

Posner, Richard A. *Law and Literature*. Rev. ed. Cambridge, MA: Harvard University Press, 1998.

Pratt, Mary Louise. *Toward a Speech Act Theory of Literary Discourse*. Bloomington: Indiana University Press, 1977.

Ragussis, Michael. "The Ghostly Signs of *Bleak House*." *Nineteenth Century Fiction* 34 (1979): 253–80.

Richardson, Alan. "From *Emile* to *Frankenstein*: The Education of Monsters." *European Romantic Review* 1.2 (1991): 147–62.

———. *British Romanticism and the Science of the Mind*. Cambridge: Cambridge University Press, 2001.

Rieger, James. "Dr. Polidori and the Genesis of *Frankenstein*." *Studies in English Literature, 1500–1900* 3.4 (1963): 461–72.

Sarbin, Theodore. *Narrative Psychology: The Storied Nature of Human Conduct*. New York: Praeger, 1986.

Schneider, Gary. *The Culture of Epistolarity: Vernacular Letters and Letter Writing in Early Modern England, 1500–1700*. Newark: University of Delaware Press, 2005.

Scholes, Robert. *The Nature of Narrative*. London: Oxford University Press, 1968 (1966).

Schramm, Jan-Melissa. *Testimony and Advocacy in Victorian Law, Literature, and Theology*. Cambridge: Cambridge University Press, 2000.

Schwartz, Richard A. "*Citizen Kane*: The Neurotic's Tragedy." *Journal of Evolutionary Psychology* 13.3–4 (1992): 274–80.

Serlen, Ellen. "The Two Worlds of *Bleak House*." *ELH* 43.3 (1976): 551–66.

Sharp, Michelle. "If It Be a Monster Birth: Reading and Literary Property in Mary Shelley's *Frankenstein*." *South Atlantic Review* 66.4 (2001): 70–93.

Shelley, Mary. *Frankenstein; or, The Modern Prometheus: The 1818 Text*. Edited by James Rieger. Chicago: University of Chicago Press, 1982.

Spacks, Patricia Meyer. "The Privacy of the Novel." *Novel: A Forum on Fiction* 31.3 (1998): 304–16.

Steiner, Emily, and Candace Barrington. *The Law and Literature: Legal Practice and Literary Production in Medieval England*. Ithaca, NY: Cornell University Press, 2002.

Sterne, Laurence. *Tristram Shandy: A Norton Critical Edition.* Edited by Howard Anderson. New York: W. W. Norton, 1980.

Stewart, Garrett. *Dear Reader: The Conscripted Audience in Nineteenth-Century British Fiction.* Baltimore: Johns Hopkins University Press, 1996.

Stock, Brian. *The Implications of Literacy: Written Language and Models of Interpretation in the Eleventh and Twelfth Centuries.* Princeton: Princeton University Press, 1983.

Thomas, François. "*Citizen Kane*: The Sound Track." In Naremore, *Orson Welles's* "Citizen Kane," 161–83.

Tinsley, Molly. "Muddle et cetera: Syntax in *A Passage to India.*" *Journal of Narrative Technique* 9.2 (1979): 191–98.

Tochinksy, Liliana. *The Cradle of Culture and What Children Know about Writing and Numbers before Being Taught.* Mahwah, NJ: Lawrence Erlbaum Associates, 2003.

Turner, Mark. *The Literary Mind.* New York: Oxford University Press, 1996.

Vanden Bossche, Chris. "Class Discourse and Popular Agency in *Bleak House.*" *Victorian Studies* 47.1 (2004): 7–31.

Vygotsky, L. S. *Thought and Language.* Edited and translated by Eugenia Hanfmann and Gertrude Vakar. Cambridge: MIT Press, 1962.

Watt, Ian. *The Rise of the Novel: Studies in Defoe, Richardson, and Fielding.* Harmondsworth, UK: Penguin Books, 1966.

Welsh, Alexander. *Strong Representations: Narrative and Circumstantial Evidence in England.* Baltimore: Johns Hopkins University Press, 1992.

Williams, Raymond. *Writing in Society.* London: Verso Editions, 1984.

Wiltshire, John. *Jane Austen and the Body: The "Picture of Health."* Cambridge: Cambridge University Press, 2006.

Woolf, Virginia. *"Jacob's Room" and "The Waves."* New York: Harcourt, Brace & World, 1959.

———. *The Common Reader: First Series.* Edited by Andrew McNeillie. New York: Harcourt, Brace, Jovanovich, 1984.

———. "Mr. Bennett and Mrs. Brown." In *Theory of the Novel: A Historical Approach,* edited by Michael McKeon, 745–58. Baltimore: Johns Hopkins University Press, 2000.

Young, Kay. "Word-Work, Word-Play, and the Making of Intimacy in *Pride and Prejudice.*" In *The Talk in Jane Austen,* edited by Bruce Stovel and Lynn Weinlos Gregg, 57–70. Edmonton: University of Alberta Press, 2002.

Zunshine, Lisa. *Why We Read Fiction: Theory of Mind and the Novel.* Columbus: Ohio State University Press, 2006.

Atonement (McEwan), 64, 168–91;
Briony as a hyperliterate character
enchanted by alphabetic story, 182–
87; Briony as a literate character
enchanted by oralistic story, 180–81;
Briony's revelation about alphabetic
story, 176–80; the macrohistory of
the novel in, 187–91, 212; young
Briony's conflicted sense of alphabetic
and oralistic story in, 172–77; and
writing as handicraft, 169–71
Austen, Jane, 38–56 passim, 173, 185–
86; *Northanger Abbey*, 32–34, 64,
168, 181, 183, 186–87, 211. See also
Pride and Prejudice

Bakhtin, Mikhail, 214n7
Bakker, Egbert, 18, 63
Barchas, Janine, 21
Barratt, Robert, 103
Barrington, Candace, 81
Barthes, Roland, 2
Bazin, Andre, 193
Beja, Morris, 194
Bender, John, 80
Benjamin, Walter, 14
Bigelow, George, 84
Billy, Ted, 194
biography, 138–41
Bleak House (Dickens), 79–102; fig-
ures of illiteracy in, 87–94; hand-
writing and the plot of, 81–83; the
law and the letter/spirit dichotomy
in, 87–88; oralistic and alphabetic
conflict of Esther's story in, 94–102,
106, 172
Bonaparte, Felicia, 38
Booth, Wayne, 35
Bradbury, Malcolm, 103
Brantlinger, Patrick, 32, 66
Brinkley, Robert, 194
Bronson, Bertrand, 19, 23
Brooks, Peter, 65, 125
Bruner, Jerome, 214n7
Bugg, John, 66
Burke, Edmund, 24
Buzard, James, 96
Bynum, David, 13–14, 15, 16

Calvin, William, 214n10
Cantor, Paul, 66
Carringer, Robert, 194, 199
Carrol, Noel, 193
Cervantes Saavedra, Miguel de, 32; *Don
Quixote*, 32–34, 64, 168, 211
Chafe, Wallace, 3
Chancery court, 85
Chartier, Roger, 4
Chaucer, Geoffrey, 23, 25
Chaytor, H. J., 14
children and oralistic story, 217n4
Citizen Kane (Welles), 192–211; close-
up of Kane's lips in, 195; dying words
in, 200; fiction film's relationship to
oralistic and alphabetic story in, 210–
11; handwriting in, 204–6; newsreel
vs. newspaper in, 199–200; orality
in, 206–9; Thatcher and the power
of writing in, 197; workers' rally
speaker and power of speech in,
197–98; writing vs. orality in the
newsreel sequence of, 196–99;
written contracts in, 202–4
Clanchy, M. T., 4, 11
Colmer, John, 103
Cook, Elizabeth H., 19, 22
courtroom testimony: and alphabetic
writing, 31; and *Atonement* as a
"forensic memoir," 189–91; effect in
Pride and Prejudice, 53; in *A Passage
to India*, 116, 118–20; as speech most
like writing, 30. See also alphabetic
story and the law
Currie, Gregory, 193

Damasio, Antonio, 214n10
Davis, Lennard, 37, 80
Day, Robert, 22, 133–34
D'cruz, Doreen, 103, 104, 113
Defoe, Daniel, 23, 78; *Robinson Crusoe*,
77–78
Dennet, Daniel, 214n10
Derrida, Jacques, 2, 213n1
Devine, Jodi, 38
diachrony, 192–93
Dickens, Charles, 79–102 passim, 106,
160. See also *Bleak House*

diegetic writing in film, 193, 195
Dissanayake, Ellen, 3
Dolin, Kieran, 80
Don Quixote (Cervantes), 32–34, 64, 168, 211
Dowling, David, 103

echo, in *A Passage to India*: effects on Adela Quested, 116–20; effects on Fielding, 120–22; effects on Mrs. Moore, 112–16
Eisenstein, Elizabeth, 4
Eliot, George, 137, 145–46, 160, 161, 172, 174, 185, 186; *Adam Bede*, 26–32, 129, 188
email, 216n2
epistolary novel, 22, 34–35

Fantasmagoriana, 58
Favret, Mary, 65
Fielding, Henry, 25; *Tom Jones*, 25, 95
film: in *Citizen Kane*, 192–211; in *The Golden Notebook*, 158–60, 164–67
Finney, Brian, 168
first-person narration, 23–25, 95
Flaubert, Gustave, 33; *Madame Bovary*, 32–34, 168, 211
Foley, John M., 189
Forster, E. M., 103–22 passim. See also *A Passage to India*
Franken, Lynn, 118
Frankenstein (Shelley), 57–78; conflicted oralistic and alphabetic genesis of, 58–65; conflicted oralistic and alphabetic genesis of the creature in, 66–69; the creature as alphabetic monster in, 69–77; as a post-novel folktale, 77–78
Frantz, Sarah, 40
Fuoroli, Carolyn, 163

Gates, Henry Louis, 9
Gerrig, Richard, 214n7
Gilbert, Sandra, 66
Gladfelder, Hal, 80
Golden Notebook, The (Lessing), 144–67; alphabetic history and memory in, 146–48; alphabetic self-

objectification in, 149–64; Anna's conflation of writing and memory in, 156; Anna's idea of the novel in, 149–55; Anna's Marxist esthetic in, 153–55; Anna's turn to film in, 158–60, 164–67; the character Anna in, 172, 179, 180, 183, 186, 212; dead end of alphabetic story in, 163
Goody, Jack, 1, 2, 4, 10, 15, 146
Gothic novel, 19
Gottesman, Ronald, 194
Green, Richard Firth, 4, 81, 214–15n13
Greene, Gayle, 145
Gronniosaw, James Albert Ukawsaw, 8–9, 70, 86, 88, 91
Grossman, Johnathan, 69, 80
Gubar, Susan, 66

Hack, Daniel, 94
handwriting: in *Bleak House*, 81–83; in *Citizen Kane*, 204–6; in *The Waves*, 133–35
Harper, Howard, 126
Havelock, Eric, 11, 14, 16, 112, 213n5
Henstra, Sarah, 144
Herman, David, 11
Hidalgo, Pilar, 169, 187
Hite, Molly, 144
holy writ, 115–16
hyperliteracy, defined, 16, 18, 24, 63, 105, 106, 118, 122, 130, 185, 212, 215n15

Ingersoll, Earl G., 169

Jackson, Andrew, 207
Jaffe, Ira, 194
John 8:11, 1–2, 36; in *Bleak House*, 84, 86
Johnson, Mark, 193
Johnson, Samuel, 5–8, 24, 86, 88, 107

Kael, Pauline, 194
Kellogg, Ronald, 11
Kelly, Gary, 38, 39, 54
Kernan, Alvin, 213n6
Kiefer, Frederick, 213n6
King, Jeanette, 145
Krouse, Tonya, 145